WHO ARE THE SCOTS?
and
THE SCOTTISH NATION

Edited by
GORDON MENZIES

EDINBURGH UNIVERSITY PRESS

© Gordon Menzies and contributors, 2002

Edinburgh University Press Ltd
22 George Square, Edinburgh

Typeset in Minion
by Pioneer Associates, Perthshire, and
printed and bound in Finland by
WS Bookwell

A CIP record for this book is available from the British Library

ISBN 1 902930 39 8 (hardback)
ISBN 1 902930 38 X (paperback)

The right of the contributors
to be identified as authors of this work
has been asserted in accordance with
the Copyright, Designs and Patents Act 1988.

CONTENTS

The Scottish Nation

LIST OF FIGURES

LIST OF PLATES

PREFACE

T. C. Smout

There is unlimited enthusiasm for all aspects of Scottish history today. Any good bookshop has a section devoted to the subject, covering a bewildering variety of topics, from the latest study of the enigma of Pictish carvings to the experiences of the Canadian Timber Corps in the Highlands during the Second World War. In this great flowering of scholarship the unwary and the newcomer can lose their way, and perhaps be deceived by the balance of modern writing into thinking that all that has really mattered in Scottish history has taken place since the parliamentary union of 1707.

This collection starts from a different perspective, and takes the story up to 1707, when the Scots nation, as formally constituted, was displaced to become part of a united British state. It was, of course, written three decades ago and views of the past change and are deepened by new research. For this reason, this new edition is accompanied by a new additional reading list to enable the reader who wants to take any aspect further to discover the latest views. But the original chapters, all by different specialists in their respective fields, have not been rewritten. Together, they still present a view of our past in a very accessible form.

In at least one respect, the viewpoint taken in the edition of 1971 was very much in advance of its time, in uniting archaeology with history and thus stretching our story very much further back than was usual. This depth of focus is still too often lacking. Scottish history does not start to be relevant to people living now only with the Union of 1707 or the Industrial Revolution. It does not begin with the Covenanters and John Knox, or with Bannockburn, central though the Reformation and the Wars of Independence may be to Scotland's modern identity, sense of character and enduring tensions. It does not even begin with Malcolm Canmore and Queen Margaret, or even with the Picts, though each of these epochs helped to pile the building blocks that make us what we are. The story of the people of Scotland, strictly speaking, began with the Mesolithic, perhaps 9,000 years ago, and connects us with the world of the hunter-gatherer living in a land of forest and bogs, like an untamed Siberia. When the highly distinguished archaeologist Stuart Piggott wrote the opening paragraphs of *Who are the Scots?* in 1971 he pointed out that our arrival in this land was our starting point.

This edition perforce takes a later starting point, because archaeological research on the earliest period has changed so fundamentally that to reproduce the two chapters on the earliest period would have been seriously misleading. Of course history always moves on, but the later chapters have been allowed to stand as an introduction to Scottish history from the Romans onward, with no revision of the text but with revised lists of further reading to enable readers to catch up on the latest scholarship.

The authors carry forward the story: about the many peoples who came to live in northern Britain and their melding, about the early monarchy and its success despite enemies external and internal; about the Stewart dynasty, the religious strife of the sixteenth and seventeenth centuries and the political shifts and strife that edged Scotland towards the Union of 1707. It is a tale told in as scholarly a way as the authors could contrive, but still with something of the pace and excitement of the original TV presentation of 1971 that held half a million entranced on a Monday evening.

As one of the original contributors I am delighted to see the books republished as one volume by Edinburgh University Press. The books were not the last word – no history, however learned, ever can be that. But the chapters remain, if you like, a first word, an entry point for those to whom the history of Scotland remains important. To answer the questions 'who are the Scots?' and 'what was the character of the Scottish nation?' is to explore something very important about where we have come from: and if we do not know where we have come from, how can we tell where we are going?

FOREWORD

Gordon Menzies

BOTH *Who are the Scots?* and *The Scottish Nation* were television series that I produced for BBC Scotland some thirty years ago. Television by its very nature tends to be ephemeral and in spite of the brilliant presentation of the late Ian Grimble television programmes are overtaken by new tastes and different styles. Not so the accompanying books, which have stood the test of time and still adorn many bookshelves. A few of the writers have passed on but most are still contributing to Scotland's history and archaeology.

When I look back at the Foreword I wrote for *Who are the Scots?* in 1971 some of the sentiments are uncannily relevant: 'There is an increasing interest in the past, an awareness of a distinctively Scottish heritage and culture and, perhaps, a deeply-felt need for some kind of identity in the wider world of today'. *Who are the Scots?* was a trail-blazing series thirty years ago, achieving as it did some half a million viewers at 11.15 p.m. on BBC Scotland on Monday evenings. It examined our origins, it looked at where we came from and, ultimately, it questioned who we think we are.

The original chapters in *Who are the Scots?*, with the exception of the first two, stand up surprisingly well. The first two were concerned with prehistory but there have been many developments in archaeology in the past thirty years. More sophisticated radio-carbon dating, the growth of aerial photography and the increase in rescue excavations have radically changed perspectives on prehistory. Written history begins with the Romans. The biography of Agricola, the Roman governor of Britain from AD 78–84, written by Tacitus, refers to a tribe of Caledonians living north of the Forth–Clyde isthmus.

Many different peoples and groupings were to be found in Scotland in the millennium following the Roman invasions. Some must have been the indigenous population of prehistory, perhaps the Picts amongst them. But who are the Scots? Are they to be found among those enigmatic Picts, or the Gaels of Dalriada, or among their contemporaries, the British tribes who survived the Roman occupation, the Angles of Northumbria and, latterly, the vigorous Norsemen who began to colonise the north and west around AD 800? Who, then, was a Scot in that turbulent ninth century? And, later still, in the eleventh and twelfth centuries, yet another ingredient was thrown into the melting-pot of the emerging nation – the Anglo-Normans, whose ultimate contributions were stability and organised government.

Perhaps some of the regional differences of present-day Scotland find their roots in our history. Could it be that the distinctive character of the folk of the north-east has something to do with the fact that Aberdeenshire, Kincardineshire and Angus was pre-eminently the area of the Picts? Obviously that somewhat mysterious quality associated with the Gaelic-speaking islander reflects the earlier Christian culture of the Scots of Dalriada. And, perhaps, the hard-headed Lowlander, that canny Scot of history, owes much to the influence of the Angles and the Normans.

Many new people came to Scotland in the first 6,000 years but change must have been painfully slow and changes must have been even more painfully achieved. There were invasions, conquests, perhaps exterminations, more often assimilations. But certainly by the time of Wallace and Bruce a recognisable entity called Scotland was in being. And that is where *Who are the Scots?* metamorphoses into *The Scottish Nation.* As Geoffrey Barrow indicates in his 'Wars of Independence' (Chapter 9), and subsequent chapters echo, the relationship with England is the key factor in the birth, growth and, perhaps, the decline of the Scottish nation.

From Edward I through the centuries and on to the unions of crown and parliament, Anglo-Scottish relations are ever significant in the life of the Scottish nation. To the English, Scotland was a recalcitrant northern neighbour, a perennial thistle in their flesh. English efforts to bring the Scots into their political orbit did more to fan the flame of Scottish patriotism than anything else.

Yet Scotland is more than one nation. Highlands have always been different from Lowlands. Any aspirations that the Celtic peoples of the north and west had of extending their sway to the

xi

rest of Scotland were dimmed by the intrusions of the Anglo-Norman feudal nobility in the twelfth and thirteenth centuries. It took another four centuries and many thousands of lives before they were finally brought under royal control. But Gaelic culture survived and continued to flourish alongside that of the alien Scots of the Lowland areas. Meanwhile the newer Scottish culture, akin to English in some respects yet so different in others, was also developing until it flowered in the late fifteenth and early sixteenth centuries. In any roll of honour for the Scottish nation Henryson, Dunbar and Gavin Douglas deserve a place alongside Wallace, Bruce, James VI and Montrose.

We have not changed or altered any of the words or views written some thirty years ago. The writers know that subsequent research might modify opinion and that is reflected in the additions we have made in the section on books for 'Further reading'. Although technically the Scottish nation came to an end in 1707, posterity inherited a social, cultural and religious heritage that is still part of our national life. And it is heartening that at the beginning of a new millennium the terms 'Scotland' and 'Scots' still have their own distinctive national meaning.

Many people contributed to the preparation of this volume some thirty years ago and I remember with gratitude all those in universities, museums and the BBC itself who so generously provided help, guidance and advice. I particularly remember the valuable suggestions of the late Kenneth Jackson, Professor of Celtic Studies at the University of Edinburgh, and the late Gordon Donaldson, Professor of Scottish History at the University of Edinburgh. Scottish history has come a long way in the past thirty years. I am very impressed that Edinburgh University Press had the vision and the confidence to reproduce this combined volume. Hopefully, it will encourage an even greater interest in our past, especially in our schools.

ACKNOWLEDGEMENTS

Grateful acknowledgement is made to the following copyright holders for permission to reproduce material in this book. Every effort has been made to trace copyright holders but if any have inadvertently been overlooked, the publishers will be pleased to make the necessary arrangements at the first opportunity.

Thanks to Historic Scotland for supplying the following photographs: Ring of Brodgar, Orkney, Broch of Mousa, Shetland, Pictish stones at Glamis manse and Aberlemno churchyard, Dumbarton Rock, Iona Abbey (and St Martin's Cross), Ruthwell Cross, Dumfriesshire, Kildalton Cross, Islay, Anglian panel (detail) from Jedburgh Abbey, Norman church, Leuchars, Fife, Dirleton Castle, East Lothian, Caerlaverock Castle, Dumfriesshire, Lochindorb Castle, Morayshire, Elgin Cathedral, Morayshire, Tomb of the Wolf of Badenoch in Dunkeld Cathedral, Angel figures playing musical instruments, Rosslyn Chapel, Midlothian, North-west tower, Holyrood Palace, Lochleven Castle, Kinross-shire, Hermitage Castle, Roxburghshire, Linlithgow Palace, West Lothian, Crichton Castle, Midlothian, Earl Patrick's Palace, Kirkwall, Orkney and Part of Norse settlement, Jarlshof, Shetland; The Trustees for the National Museums of Scotland for the Celtic bronze trumpet, Deskford, Banffshire (the Deskford Carnyx is part of the collections of Banff Museum and has been on loan to the National Museums of Scotland since 1947), Monymusk reliquary, Viking hoard, Skaill, Orkney, Bute mazer (Private Scottish Collection, on loan to The National Museums of Scotland), James III – early portrait coin, The great *Michael*, The Fetternear banner, Late seventeenth-century silverware, The Riding of Parliament, 1685 (detail); Hunterian Museum and Art Gallery, University of Glasgow for the Roman distance-slab, Hutcheson Hill, Glasgow; Médiathèque Municipale d'Arras for Sir Bernard Stewart, Lord d'Aubigny; The Scottish

National Portrait Gallery for The Second Earl of Arran attributed to Arnold Bronckhorst: In the collection of Lennoxlove House (photography by Antonia Reeve), James IV with a Hawk by Daniel Mytens: In a private Scottish collection (photography by Antonia Reeve), The Execution of Charles I by unknown artist: In the collection of Lord Dalmeny (reproduced by permission of Lord Dalmeny) (photography by Antonia Reeve), The first Duke of Lauderdale by Sir Peter Lely, The first Marquis of Montrose attributed to Willem van Honthorst, The first Marquis of Argyll by David Scougall, James VI as a child by Arnold Bronckorst, George Buchanan attributed to Arnold Bronckorst, John Knox after Adrian Vanson and Mary, Queen of Scots (unknown artist); Blair Castle Collection, Perthshire for James V and Mary of Guise; Crown Copyright/MOD for the Mote of Urr, Kirkcudbrightshire and Threave Castle, Kirkcudbrightshire both reproduced with the permission of the Controller of Her Majesty's Stationery Office; The National Trust for Scotland for Chapel Royal in Falkland Palace, Fife; The Royal Commission on the Ancient and Historical Monuments of Scotland for Crathes Castle, Kincardineshire and Sir William Bruce's Kinross House, Kinross-shire; The Trustees of the National Library of Scotland for Andrew Myllar's printing device and Slezer's prospect of Perth, 1693; Ashmolean Museum Oxford for The Battle of Dunbar (from a contemporary plan).

Who are the Scots?

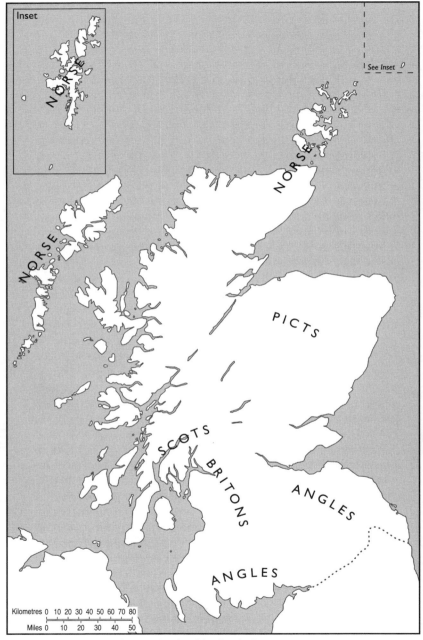

Figure 1 Scotland in the ninth century AD

CHAPTER 1

THE ROMAN FRONTIER

Anne S. Robertson

A TTEMPTS by the Romans to find a satisfactory frontier for the Roman province of Britannia spanned almost two centuries in time, and created a varying series of relationships between the Romans and the inhabitants of what is now called Scotland. Written records of these relationships all come from Roman sources, but even through 'the Roman version' there gleams part at least of 'the other side of the story'. Still more of that story can be pieced together from archaeological evidence, for example from Roman military structures, and contemporary native sites in North Britain, and from finds of Roman material on non-Roman sites.

The earliest Roman search for a frontier in North Britain was the work of Gnaeus Julius Agricola, governor of Britannia from AD 78–84 in the Flavian period (that period, AD 69–96, during the reign of the three emperors whose family name was Flavius). Agricola's search for a frontier influenced all subsequent Roman activity in North Britain, and his search is also the most fully documented. The biography of Agricola written by his son-in-law, the historian Tacitus, about AD 98, preserves a long account of Roman campaigns in North Britain between AD 80 and 84.

In AD 80 Agricola's army advanced from the Tyne–Solway isthmus through the territories of 'new tribes', until he reached the Taus estuary, which it is generally agreed must have been the Tay. The 'new tribes' were not named by Tacitus himself, but the Lowland tribes at least can be identified from the early second-century AD geographer Ptolemy (and his late first-century sources), as the Votadini of Northumberland, Berwickshire and East Lothian, the Selgovae of the Central Lowlands and the Damnonii of Ayrshire, the Clyde Valley and part of Stirlingshire. To the territory of the Votadini Ptolemy assigned three place-names. One of them was Curia, a tribal hosting-place, which may have been the great oppidum of the Votadini on Traprain Law, East Lothian. To the Selgovae Ptolemy gave four place-names, three unlocated and the fourth Trimontium, the triple peak of the Eildon Hill, on the north side of which stood another great oppidum. The lands of the Damnonii included Vindogara on Irvine Bay.

Tribal oppida were gathering-places and market-towns to which came farmers, homesteaders, villagers and small townsfolk to exchange their produce for manufactured goods, and to hear the latest news. In and from the tribal oppida news of the Roman advance would spread like wildfire. In such tribal oppida, if anywhere, resistance to the Roman invader could have been organised and leaders have been found. Yet Tacitus states that 'the enemy', terror-stricken, did not dare to harry the Roman army as it swept northwards. There was even time for the building of forts, as distinct from the temporary camps constructed in the initial stages of the campaign. Such forts would lie along Agricola's main lines of advance so as to secure communications with the legionary fortresses at York and Chester, whence came the Ninth Legion and the Second Adiutrix and the Twentieth Legions, which, together with auxiliary, light-armed units, made up the invasion army. The distribution of such forts shows that Agricola used the two main natural routes from the south, the eastern route by way of the Tweed to the Forth, and the western route up Annandale to Upper Clydesdale, and thence north-eastwards to the Forth.

The most important Agricolan site in south Scotland was the great fort at Newstead on the Tweed, named Trimontium after triple-peaked Eildon Hill whose great oppidum it confronted. The tribal oppidum has not yet been excavated, but it has not so far yielded any chance Roman finds of the late first century AD. It may either have been evacuated by the Romans, or have been abandoned by refugees fleeing before the Roman advance. A Roman signal tower placed at the west end of Eildon Hill may date to the Flavian period. In sharp contrast the Votadinian oppidum on Traprain Law continued in native occupation. Evidently its folk had succeeded in coming to some kind of terms with the Romans which enabled them to acquire late first-century glass vessels and pottery.

From the Forth–Clyde isthmus to the Tay there was one single natural route, that imposed by the configuration of the country.

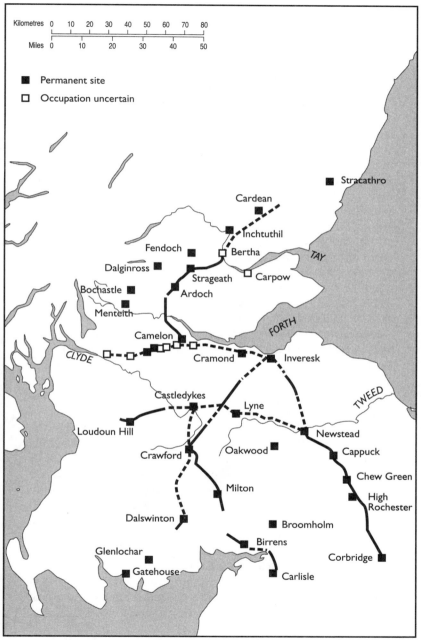

Figure 2 North Britain in the Flavian period

Temporary camps lie along this route, on which in time there were also built permanent forts. The tribes through whose territory the Forth–Tay route must have passed were the Venicones and Vacomagi of Ptolemy. The territory of the Venicones included Fife. The Vacomagi lived further north in Strathmore and beyond.

In the next year Agricola's army made no further advance beyond the Tay, but took measures to secure the territories overrun, by road-building, fort-construction and the complete pacification of the Lowlands. Those North Britons who came to terms with the Roman invader, like the folk of Traprain, could be left in peace, but irreconcilable elements would be exterminated or become homeless exiles. Where the intractable exiles fled to for refuge is indicated both by Tacitus' narrative and by the location of Flavian forts on and to the north of the Forth–Clyde isthmus. 'The estuaries of Forth and Clyde,' said Tacitus, 'carried far inland by the tides of opposite seas, are separated by but a narrow strip of land which at this time was strengthened by garrisons (or small forts?), and the whole tract of nearer country was held, the enemy being removed as it were into another island.' Several sites on the Forth–Clyde isthmus, which were later occupied by forts on the Antonine Wall, have revealed evidence for earlier occupation, probably of the Flavian period. At Bar Hill and Croy Hill, two of the highest sites on the isthmus, remains of small early forts, each with an annexe, have been located. At four or five other isthmus sites Flavian pottery and glassware have been found.

There was of course no Flavian frontier barrier on the Forth–Clyde isthmus. Agricola, as Tacitus indicates, recognised the merit of the isthmus as a frontier but disdained it so far as he was concerned. His frontier was to be the far northern sea, and his aim was the complete conquest of Caledonia, a name used by Tacitus to cover the whole Highland region. Within it the tribe Caledonii occupied territory extending from the Tay Valley to the Great Glen.

North of the Forth–Clyde isthmus there was 'as it were another island'. The pattern of Roman forts north of the isthmus demonstrates that hostile elements were to be forced back into their own mountains west of the Roman route from Forth to Tay, and to be kept there by forts blocking the exits to mountain passes, of which four are now known – at Menteith, Bochastle near Callander,

Dalginross and Fendoch. Behind this cordon of Roman forts the North Britons watched and waited and prepared their final resistance against the invader. The Romans too kept watch, from their forts, and probably from a line of small wooden signal towers on the Gask ridge between Strageath and Perth.

In the next year, AD 82, Agricola, according to Tacitus, 'subdued tribes hitherto unknown in several successful battles, having crossed over (somewhere) in the leading ship, and having placed troops in that part of Britain which looks towards Ireland'. Of the tribes hitherto unknown one must have been the Novantae of Galloway and lands west of the Nith, in whose territory Ptolemy named two sites, one being Rerigonium on Loch Ryan. The other new tribe may have been the Damnonii. It may have been in this year rather than in AD 80 that Agricola's army laid out the western route from Carlisle to the Upper Clyde Valley and thence to the Forth, and the cross-road from Newstead on the Tweed via Castledykes on the Clyde towards Loudoun Hill in Ayrshire. Evidently the west end of the cross-road was making for a port on the Ayrshire coast, possibly near Ardrossan. No remains of a Flavian port or fort on the Ayrshire coast have yet been found, but Flavian pottery from a native dwelling-site at Glenhead, near Ardrossan, was probably acquired from a nearby Roman site, possibly on the north side of Irvine Bay (the Vindogara of Ptolemy).

Some of the Damnonii lived in crannogs or lake-dwellings. One of these at least, at Hyndford near Lanark, has its occupation dated to this period by the presence of Roman glassware and pottery, all of Flavian types. If this was acquired peacefully through trade with the nearby Roman fort at Castledykes it may suggest that some of the Clyde Valley folk at least went over to the Roman side without a struggle. The Novantae on the other hand probably gave more trouble. In their territory Flavian forts cluster close.

The scene of Agricola's crossing may have been the Solway, and the part of Britain looking towards Ireland would include south-west Scotland and the Cumberland coast. The 'crossing' was not a crossing to Ireland. The only Roman discoveries in Ireland are of moveable finds, usually coins and a little pottery, which had been taken over the Irish Sea by way of trade.

It may be that in AD 82 Agricola's fleet sailed among the western isles, for the second-century geographer Ptolemy knew the names of several west-coast tribes: the Epidii ('horse-folk') of Kintyre, the Cerones ('folk of the rough lands') further north, the Carnonacae ('folk of the cairns or rocky hills') of Wester Ross, the Caereni of north-west Sutherland, and the Cornavii ('folk of the promontory') of Caithness. The initial campaigns of Agricola had aroused the 'Caledonian confederacy' which included also the Taezali of the extreme north-east, the Decantae ('noble-folk') of Easter Ross, the Lugi ('raven-folk') of Sutherland, and the Smertae, between the Lugi and Caereni. Some of these folk at least had been threatening the Roman line from the Forth to the Tay.

In AD 83 therefore Agricola enveloped the area north of the Forth, and made considerable use of his fleet. His land army advanced in three columns, according to Tacitus, and the enemy struck by concentrating a night attack on the Ninth Legion as being the weakest. An inscription proves that in this year a detachment from this legion was taking part in the operations of the Emperor Domitian against the Chatti across the Upper Rhine. Evidently the fact that the Ninth Legion was not at full strength was no secret to the North Britons! Agricola's advanced campaigning base would by now have been at Inchtuthil, where a great legionary fortress may already have been a-building. An advance in three columns on a broad front would suit Strathmore, five miles wide, with the flanks of the advancing force along the foothills of the Perthshire Grampians and the Sidlaws.

In his final campaign, in AD 84, Agricola sent his fleet ahead on a series of harassing forays, with the aim of forcing the enemy to make a stand in a pitched battle. His army, which now included some Britons (from the south), used the same line of advance as in AD 83, from Inchtuthil through Strathmore and Kincardine into Aberdeenshire, until his way was barred by a Caledonian army drawn up on the slopes of Mons Graupius. The battle was fought somewhere near an entrenched position, that is a Roman camp, and Tacitus seems to imply that it was the furthest point north reached by Agricola. The final Roman advance then may be supposed to have led from Aberdeenshire towards Inverness, by way of Keith commanding the Pass of Grange, between the Grampians and the Knock Hill group, which opens on the lower Spey and the lowlands about Elgin and Nairn. Near Keith it may be the 'Caledonians' were waiting with a line of retreat through Dufftown into the Highlands.

According to Tacitus 'the strength of all the tribes' amounting to 30,000 men had been summoned. Native structures north of the Forth proved by Roman material found in them to have been in use during the late first century AD include a homestead, a dun, a stack-fort and a broch. From dwellings such as these there flocked in a large army, among whose leaders the most outstanding was Calgacus ('the swordsman'). The speech which Tacitus puts into the mouth of Calgacus represents an intellectual Roman interpretation of the 'Caledonian' view of the Roman invasion. 'They make a desert place and call it peace' is only one of its memorable phrases. Tacitus also gave Agricola a speech justifying the Roman policy of conquest. Mons Graupius marked yet another Roman victory. The losses according to Tacitus were 10,000 of the 'enemy' and 360 Romans.

After the battle Agricola led his troops down into the territory of the Boresti, probably in the lowlands of the Moray Firth. He then ordered his fleet to sail round Britain, thus proving it to be an island. In the course of the voyage the fleet subdued the Orkney Islands and saw Thule (the Shetlands). His army made a land journey to quarters in the south. In AD 84–5 Agricola's governorship of Britain came to an end.

Meanwhile the native survivors of Mons Graupius had melted away again into the Highlands. Agricola's plan, however, for the consolidation of the conquest remained in operation. Its aim was to isolate the Highlands by blocking exits from the passes, and to establish a major striking force in a legionary fortress at Inchtuthil with a screen of auxiliary forts to the north of it, of which two are known, at Cardean and Stracathro. The road system and forts from Tay to Forth, and forts on the two main routes through south Scotland and on the cross-road continued in use, with other forts on spur-roads at Oakwood and Broomholm. The small posts on the Forth–Clyde isthmus may have had a shorter life.

The Agricolan plan for North Britain justifies the Tacitean phrase – *Britannia perdomita* ('Britain thoroughly conquered'). But *et statim amissa* ('and immediately given up') followed. The plan had to be abandoned because shattering Roman defeats on the Danube required the withdrawal of one of the four legions stationed in Britain, perhaps as early as AD 86. As a result, the legionary fortress at Inchtuthil was given up, before building had been completed and soon after the date of its six latest coins, all newly minted bronze Asses of AD 86. This also involved the evacuation of auxiliary forts to the north, and possibly, of all the Flavian forts in North Britain except for the great fort at Newstead on the Tweed. This fort seems to have been held longer than the rest, perhaps until about AD 100.

For the decades following Agricola's governorship in North Britain there is an almost complete lack of literary evidence. Archaeological evidence from the native side suggests, however, that the withdrawal of Roman garrisons encouraged a freer movement of native peoples. This resulted, for example, in the building of brochs far from the broch province, for example at Hurly Hawkin, Angus, and at Torwoodlee, Selkirkshire. At both these sites, the broch had been built within or over an earlier native fort, and both sites yielded Flavian pottery.

It is probable too that these decades marked an influx of new settlers into south-west Scotland. The hill-fort on Birrenswark Hill, Dumfriesshire, may have been constructed at this time. Some of the folk of south-west Scotland even threatened the peace of the Roman province of Britannia, which now received its first continuous frontier barrier, Hadrian's Wall, running from the Tyne to the Solway, with outlying forts in the west at Birrens, Netherby and Bewcastle. So fierce and unrelenting was the pressure of the south-western folk on Hadrian's Wall that less than twenty years after it was built the Emperor Antoninus Pius had to move the frontier northwards to the Forth–Clyde isthmus, the old east–west line which Agricola had strengthened with small forts sixty years earlier.

The land between the Tyne–Solway and the Forth–Clyde isthmus was contained and added to the Roman Empire. The only literary evidence is one sentence by a late third-century writer, Capitolinus, *Vita Antonini Pii*, 'For he [i.e. the Emperor Antoninus Pius] conquered the Britons through Lollius Urbicus the governor [i.e. of Britain] and after driving back the barbarians, built another wall, this time of turf.' Bronze coins of Antoninus Pius commemorate the victory won in North Britain. They have on the reverse side the figure of Britannia subdued, in the guise of a female figure seated

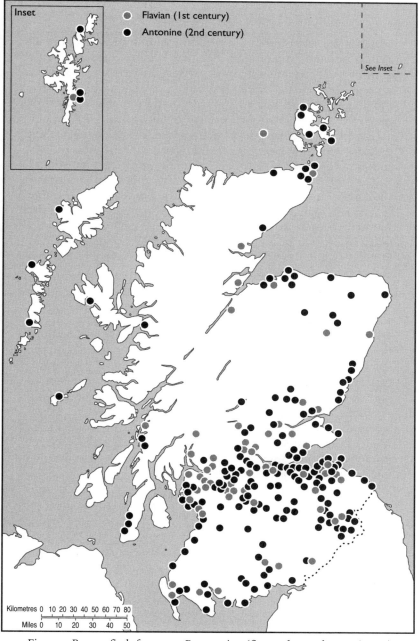

Figure 3 Roman finds from non-Roman sites (first and second centuries AD)

Inset

Flavian (1st century)
Antonine (2nd century)

See Inset

Kilometres 0 10 20 30 40 50 60 70 80
Miles 0 10 20 30 40 50

left, with her head leaning on her right hand in the conventional attitude of mourning or subjection, and her left arm resting on a great spiked shield. These coins, minted in late AD 142, or early AD 143, determine the date of Lollius Urbicus' campaigns in North Britain and also provide an approximate date for the building of the Antonine Wall which followed swiftly thereafter.

The army of Lollius Urbicus doubtless moved northwards along the same two main natural routes into Scotland which Agricola had laid out sixty years before – one route by way of the Tweed and Lauderdale to the Forth, and the other by Annandale and Upper Clydesdale. Lower Clydesdale, however, featured in the Antonine system, although not apparently in the Flavian road system. In the Antonine period, forts were in time built not only at Castledykes near Lanark, but also at Bothwellhaugh near Hamilton. A road linked these forts and must have continued north towards the west end of the Forth–Clyde isthmus.

The troublesome North Britons were once again pushed back into their own mountains, and a penetrative road, guarded by forts, was driven far into Perthshire. The irreconcilable elements in south-west Scotland in particular were kept in check by a network of roads, forts and fortlets, probably linked with a harbour on the Solway. The cross-road from Newstead via Lyne and Castledykes past Loudoun Hill indicates that there was once more a Roman port on the Ayrshire coast, probably on Irvine Bay. The breaking up of disaffected elements in south Scotland may have led to the deportation of some irreconcilables to the Roman frontier on the Rhine, where units of Britons have recorded their presence on inscriptions of Antonine date. It may have been now that the hill-fort on Birrenswark Hill was evacuated. It may even be that the lonely little Roman fort of Raeburnfoot, Eskdalemuir, with its very large compound, and apparently short life, belonged to an early Antonine phase when prisoners were being rounded up and placed in 'concentration camps'.

The Antonine Wall itself was built from Bridgeness on the Forth to Old Kilpatrick on the Clyde, a distance of about 37 miles. For most of its length it clung to the southern slopes of the isthmus valley with a clear view across the valley to the threatening hills on the north. The Wall was constructed of turves, as the Roman writer

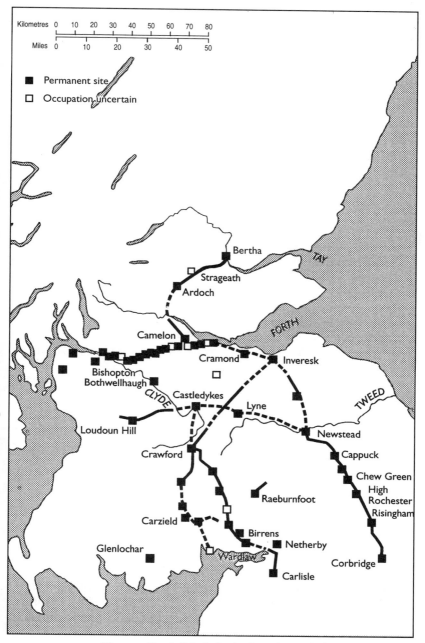

Figure 4 North Britain in the Antonine period

said, underpinned by a stone base, not less than fourteen feet wide. To the north of the Wall there ran a Ditch, about forty feet wide and twelve feet deep. To the south of the Wall at an average distance of 40–50 yards, there ran a cambered road, the Military Way, 16–18 ft wide. The construction of the Antonine frontier was carried out by working squads from the Second, Sixth and Twentieth Legions. They were doubtless protected while at work by units of light-armed auxiliary troops and they may have had enforced assistance in the unskilled tasks of fetching and carrying by native North Britons.

There have been recovered from the line of the Antonine Wall eighteen 'distance slabs' set up by legionary working squads to commemorate the distance or length of the Wall which they had completed. Several of them represent conquered North Britons, kneeling with their hands tied behind them. The most remarkable of the known distance slabs was found as recently as 1969, on Hutcheson Hill, west of Castlehill, Bearsden. It records the completion of 3,000 ft of the Wall by a detachment of the Twentieth Legion. The inscription has been arranged within an architectural framework representing either a triumphal arch or the shrine of the standards. The central niche or panel encloses a female figure holding out a little wreath to a legionary eagle held by an aquilifer. The panels on either side contain kneeling captives.

On the line of the Antonine Wall forts were built very close together, at two-mile intervals. They were situated on ground which in Roman times afforded a very wide outlook to the north and usually in all directions. It seems virtually certain that the building of the Wall itself was begun from the east, and that some sites at least in the western sector had forts built on them before the Wall arrived. Evidently a watchful control had to be maintained over the restless resentful North Britons to the north of the west end of the Wall while its building was in progress.

Between at least three pairs of Antonine Wall forts there were built small interval-fortlets. One of these, between Falkirk and Rough Castle, stood at a check-point where a major Roman road passed through the frontier northwards in the direction of the forts at Camelon and Ardoch. At certain places on the line small turf signalling-platforms were attached to the rear of the Wall. Three pairs of such platforms are known, one pair to east and one pair to

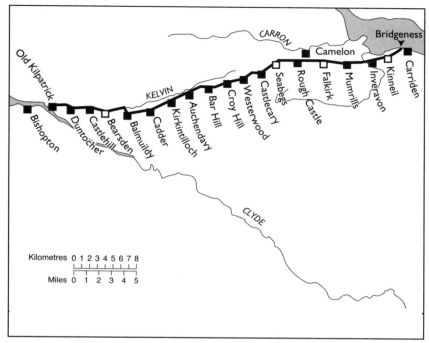

Figure 5 The Antonine Wall

west of the fort at Rough Castle, and another pair on the western slope of Croy Hill. At only two points had the Antonine Wall to be carried across rivers of any size – the Avon near its east end and the Kelvin near its west end. The Kelvin crossing was guarded by the great stone-walled fort of Balmuildy, which overlooked a wooden bridge on stone piers. The Avon crossing was watched by a small fort at Inveravon, on the east bank.

The Romans had also to guard against enemy landings on the south banks of the Forth and Clyde. The danger was lessened on the Forth by the existence of a Roman road running along its south bank from Inveresk through Cramond, where there was a harbour, to the east end of the Wall. Attempts by North Britons to land on the south bank of the Clyde were anticipated and provided against by a fort at Whitemoss, Bishopton, just over two miles as the crow flies from the west end of the Antonine Wall, and by at least two fortlets, on Lurg Moor, above Greenock, and at Outerwards, above Largs. These kept watch on the coasts of the Firth of Clyde.

A North Briton who made his way south through a gap in the hills on the north side of the isthmus, like the Blane Valley, and looked towards the southern scarp, would see, running east and west for mile after mile, the great barrier of the Wall itself, towering up with its wooden breastwork, to a height not far short of twenty feet, and the deep ravine of the Ditch in front. His eye would pick out the forts, close-set at intervals of about every two miles, between which patrols carried out their ceaseless vigil along the rampart-walk on top of the Wall. As his gaze strained hopefully, or despairingly, westwards beyond the west end of the Wall itself, there would come into view the Roman harbour below Old Kilpatrick, busy with Roman shipping, and the Roman stations along the south bank of the Clyde. Even a distant view of the great frontier would impress the native beholder with a sense of his own helplessness against the power and majesty of Rome.

Britons who lived in occupied territory seem to have accepted the situation, and even to have turned it to their material advantage. As long as the Romans held the Antonine Wall, there was a steady 'drift' of Roman coins and other objects to native sites – crannogs, caves, huts, souterrains, enclosed settlements and the great oppidum of Traprain Law, still preserving its *modus vivendi* with the Romans. The most valuable Roman goods (like gold and silver coins, bronze vessels and brooches) evidently remained in Roman-occupied territory in south Scotland, while a little of the more everyday material – glass bottles, beads, pottery – penetrated either by land or sea to the duns and brochs of the north and west. The latter may perhaps represent interchange between tribal peoples rather than direct contact between Roman and native. Contact between Roman and native took its most friendly form in the annexes attached to Roman forts on the Antonine Wall and in south Scotland. In time there grew up alongside these Antonine forts settlements of traders and civilians, some of them women and children. One settlement at least at Carriden at the east end of the Wall attained the status of a vicus, meaning a recognised village community.

The Antonine system in North Britain lasted for 40–50 years.

During that period, the Wall served as a base for military opera-tions, with a line of outpost forts running to the gate of the Scottish Highlands; It also formed a physical and psychological barrier separating the tribes north of the Forth–Clyde line from Roman-protected territory to the south.

At the beginning of the third century AD Hadrian's Wall was restored as the frontier of Britannia, and the Emperor Severus crossed to Britain to prepare for campaigns against the Cale-donians, one of the two strongest tribes in North Britain, the other being the Maeatae, according to the third-century writer Dio Cassius. Before the Caledonian campaigns, Severus 'bought peace from the Maeatae'. Early Severan coin hoards found in the eastern counties of Scotland north of the Forth may represent part of the purchase price.

Severus' campaigns against the Caledonians took place in AD 209–11. His army may have been transported by sea from South Shields at the mouth of the Tyne to the fort and harbour of Cramond on the Forth, and to Carpow on the Tay, where a legionary base was constructed. According to Dio Cassius, Severus reached the extremity of the island (probably the Moray Firth), following much the same routes as Agricola, as suggested by the series of large temporary camps in the north-east. He forced the Caledonians to come to terms, but trouble broke out again with both Caledonians and Maeatae. In AD 211, Severus died at York, and his son Caracalla quickly concluded the Caledonian campaigns and returned to Rome. Hadrian's Wall remained the frontier of the Roman province for the next two centuries, with outpost forts at Netherby, Bewcastle, High Rochester and Risingham.

In the third century these forts accommodated not only infantry cohorts with cavalry contingents, but also units of irregulars who operated as long-range scouts, or *exploratores*, far to the north of Hadrian's Wall. In this century some of the souterrain folk of Angus, who may have been included among the Maeatae, moved into south Scotland. Some of them used Roman-carved stones in the construction of souterrains at Crichton (Midlothian), and near Newstead (Roxburghshire), and apparently even incorporated Roman tombstones into a souterrain at Shirva near the Antonine Wall. In this century too, several of the great hill-forts of south

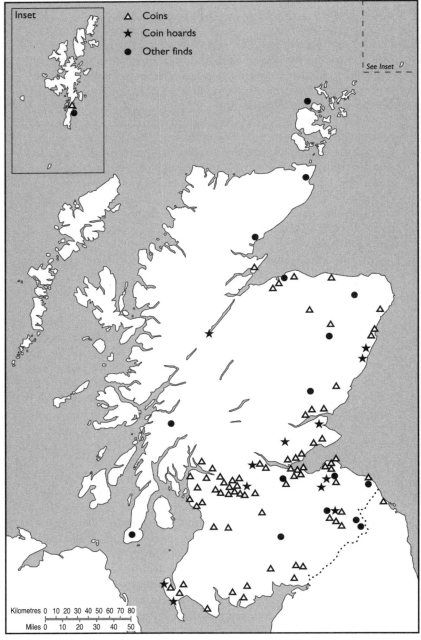

Inset

△ Coins
★ Coin hoards
● Other finds

See Inset

Kilometres 0 10 20 30 40 50 60 70 80
Miles 0 10 20 30 40 50

Figure 6 Roman finds from non-Roman sites (third and fourth centuries AD)

Scotland, formerly evacuated as a result of Roman invasions, had native villages built over their defences. Some of these villagers may have been among the *areani* (mentioned by Ammianus Marcellinus) or 'homesteaders' who seem to have replaced the exploratores as scouts in the fourth century AD, until there came the 'barbarica conspiratio' of AD 367, a barbarian plan for a concerted attack on Britain. The subsequent 'restoration' of Count Theodosius transformed the tribes of the forward areas north of Hadrian's Wall into foederati ('treaty states').

In the third and fourth centuries AD Roman coins and other objects continued to reach Traprain Law in a steady flow. To other North British sites they came intermittently, some of them at least as the result of forays into the Roman province of Britannia.

On this, the most north-westerly frontier of the Roman Empire, the Roman army left to later centuries a permanent legacy, both through its relationships with the native peoples – which ranged from conquest and deportation, to re-settlement, trade and even intermarriage – and through its system of roads and forts. The road system offered convenient routes to contemporary and to post-Roman travellers, and accelerated the movement and intermingling of peoples in the early centuries of the Christian era. The massive Roman forts remained a familiar feature of the post-Roman landscape, and provided shelter for folk otherwise homeless. Almost every Roman fort-site in North Britain has produced medieval pottery left behind by such visitors. The Antonine Wall, in particular, stood century after century, serving as a boundary, a march or a trysting-place.

CHAPTER 2

THE PROBLEM OF
THE PICTS
Isabel Henderson

THE one thing that most people know about the Picts is that
together with the Scots they resisted the Romans so successfully
that the Romans had to build Hadrian's Wall to keep them out of
the province of Britain. Fortunately, this is probably the best starting point for an account of the Picts. The first reference to a people
of this name living in North Britain is found in a panegyric poem
written by an anonymous Roman towards the end of the third
century AD, at the time when Constantius Chlorus had succeeded
in repairing the Wall after it had been overrun and destroyed by the
northern tribes. The name is found regularly thereafter in classical
and medieval writers.

Only a few years after this first reference another Roman writes
of 'the woods and marshes of the Caledones and other Picts' and
this suggests that the single tribe, the Caledones, was part of a
larger whole called 'Picts'. In the fourth century the Picts are said
to have been divided into two peoples. This may be an oversimplification, but again it is clear that 'Picts' is being used as a
collective name for the inhabitants of North Britain. Roman writers
also used 'Caledonians' as a collective name for these tribes, by
extension from the single tribe of that name. The Caledonii appear
on Ptolemy's map, occupying a large territory stretching from the
Beauly Firth to southern Perthshire. Ptolemy's information for
North Britain came from sources that belong to the first century
AD, and it includes the names of a dozen or so tribes who lived
north of the Forth–Clyde line – the southern boundary of the
historical kingdom of the Picts. None of these tribes is called Picti
and this suggests that the name only existed as a collective name.
It may, in fact, simply have been a Roman nickname, 'the painted

people' – a comment on their habit of painting and tattooing themselves. It could also be a translation of a very early British collective name, Pritani, which may mean 'the people of the designs', and which came to be used in the form Priteni to refer exclusively to the peoples north of the Forth. Priteni is a P-Celtic name, that is to say it belongs to the British dialect of Celtic. When this word was used by Q-Celtic speakers, those who spoke the Irish dialect of Celtic, it had to become Cruithni because Irish Celtic has no *p*. It is worth mentioning this because when reading about the Picts one may sometimes find them referred to as the Cruithni.

Who were these tribes whose names have been recorded by Ptolemy? What sort of lives did they live, what sort of houses and fortifications did they build? Previous chapters in this book will have explained how difficult it is to answer these questions. Archaeological studies in Scotland are at present engaged in coming to terms with the recent discovery, due to radiocarbon dating techniques, that the timber-framed forts (often called 'vitrified forts' because of the fusion of the stonework that occurred when the walls were burned) found in eastern Scotland belong, not as had been thought to around 100 BC, but to as early as the seventh century BC. This discovery has naturally seriously disturbed interpretations of what was happening in North Britain at the time of Ptolemy's tribes. The significance attached to the evolution and adoption of the broch-tower has also been affected, for being roughly contemporary with the vitrified forts as originally dated the builders of the two types of structure were inevitably thought to stand in some relation to each other. These matters concern deeply the probable make-up of what can be called the proto-Pictish culture.

Writers on the Picts have been at pains to emphasise the probability that the peoples lumped together by the Romans under the name 'Picts' had a mixed racial and cultural background, in order to stress, correctly, that there is no trace of the Picti having arrived at some point in time to settle in North Britain in the way that the Scots arrived in Argyll and the Anglo-Saxon peoples arrived in the south. For reasons that will be given later the concept of a mixed cultural background for the Picts must be sustained but it should be noted that archaeologists are at present feeling their way towards the definition of what may be a single proto-Pictish culture for at least a large part of the Pictish area, whatever its later superficial tribal and political fragmentation.

Even if, however, we confine ourselves to the period after the appearance of the collective name 'Picts', there is not, as yet, a great deal of help to be had from archaeology in defining the nature of the culture of the people who lived in the north from the fourth century. Only a few instances of surface dwellings beside the underground structures known as souterrains bring us within sight of the historical period. The material culture of the souterrain builders, who were flourishing in the second and third centuries, is disappointingly meagre, and it has not been possible to estimate their role in proto-Pictish affairs. There is in general a great dearth of settlement sites from the fourth century onwards so that the opportunity of moving from the series of sites known to belong to the historical period back into prehistory is not available. It is true that one type of fort that belongs to the Dark Age period has been identified, and some examples, as at Moncrieffe Hill (Perthshire), are found in the Pictish area, but finds from these sites too have so far been small and unilluminating.

It has been necessary to touch on these matters to explain why the nature of the often-asked question 'Who were the Picts?' is unsatisfactory. It should be rephrased as 'Who made up the Picts?', a form of question that underlines the fact that the Picts are composite and that a number of different answers is anticipated. At present we can point to the builders of the vitrified forts, whose ancient culture may have persisted right down to the historical period, the builders of the brochs and wheelhouses, themselves originally a mixed culture of incoming Celts and indigenous natives, and the souterrain builders, who may simply represent a development of the old vitrified fort culture. There are also other strands of archaeological evidence for the arrival of small groups of settlers but they need not concern us here.

Finding links between the prehistoric and the historical period is a major problem in Pictish studies. One satisfactorily strong link is found in the language spoken by the inhabitants of the north. In his classic review of the evidence for Pictish language Professor Kenneth Jackson was able to analyse names from classical writers and from early medieval sources contemporary with the historical Picts. The evidence from both periods was found to be consistent, and it is further confirmed by the modern place-names found in the Pictish area.

Professor Jackson shows that there were Celtic speakers in the Orkneys in the first century BC and possibly from as early as the fourth. There are many Celtic names in Ptolemy's map, which, as we have seen, is relevant for the end of the first century AD. A significant number of these names are P-Celtic, while none of them can be positively said to be Q-Celtic. The P-Celtic, however, is not absolutely identical with the Celtic spoken by the Britons but may perhaps have affinities with Gaulish. Celtic speakers may therefore have arrived in the north either directly from Gaul or from southern England during the last few centuries BC when the Celts there would have spoken a language akin to that of Gaul. By the turn of the Christian era this early Celtic in southern England was overlaid by the Brittonic speech of the later phase of Celtic arrivals. The archaeological background of the broch builders suggests that they would have spoken Brittonic but the later evidence and the place-names show that this Gallo-Brittonic Celtic prevailed in the historical period. It used to be speculated, for a number of good reasons, that the vitrified fort builders provided a suitable archaeological context for the Gallo-Brittonic speakers but the backdating of the forts rules this out and an archaeological setting has yet to be found for them.

Professor Jackson not only found evidence for Gallo-Brittonic speakers but also for a population that spoke a non-Celtic, indeed non-Indo-European, language. This he concludes must have been the language spoken by the indigenous tribes. The indications of this are clearly seen in Ptolemy's map where the names of the four chief tribes who occupy the main Pictish area, the Caledonii, Vacomagi, Taezali and Venicones are by no means clearly Celtic. Traces of this non-Celtic language are found in the historical part of the list of the kings of the Picts, and the Pictish Ogam inscriptions are written in it entirely.

The linguistic make-up of Britain north of the Forth–Clyde line seems therefore, on the basis of the available evidence, to have been the same from at least the beginning of the Christian era, and the fact that two languages were apparently spoken in Pictland has to be taken into account at all periods. The answer then to another frequent question, 'Were the Picts Celtic?' is 'partially so'. And to the further question, 'What sort of Celtic did they speak?', the answer is that it was akin to British Celtic but not exactly like it, having sufficient associations with Gaulish to justify its being given the name Gallo-Brittonic. When these facts are appreciated it is not difficult to see why we should expect to find Pictish culture and society significantly different from that of their Celtic-speaking neighbours, the Scots of Dalriada and the Britons of Strathclyde.

The differences indeed must have been very considerable for the evidence does not suggest that the non-Indo-European speakers became a subject population living under the rule of the Celts. The fact that this aboriginal language survived at all implies that the pre-Celtic element was strong. The most striking confirmation of this is the fact that the incoming Celts adopted the indigenous custom of matrilinear succession. Matrilinearism is not found in other Celtic societies and it would seem that the newcomers failed to impose their own law of succession on a population that out-numbered them. Bede, writing in the first half of the eighth century, says that the Pictish custom of choosing their kings from the female royal lineage was well known in his day, and the evidence of the list of the Pictish kings taken in conjunction with the kings' obits in the Irish annals shows that the rule that a son should not succeed his father was strictly maintained.

The evidence for the Pictish law of inheritance through the female comes from historical sources but there is also perhaps some indirect evidence for it from an earlier period in the somewhat sensational accounts of Caledonian sexual practices found in classical writers. Dio Cassius, who wrote in the third century AD, records an interesting conversation on this matter between a Roman matron and the wife of a Caledonian chief. When the Roman lady expresses her surprise at the flagrant promiscuity of Caledonian women, the chief's wife replies with dignity that theirs is the better way, to give themselves openly to the best men, rather than as Roman women do, to let themselves be debauched in secret by the vilest. 'Such', writes Dio, 'was the retort of the Caledonian woman.' It is clear that the Caledonians had some kind of polyandrous society perhaps of the type where a woman has a legal husband but where her other sexual partners have a recognised and respectable status. Matrilinearism is frequently found with polyandry as an obvious solution to the difficulty of proving paternity. To the observers on the other side of the Wall these subtleties would have been lost and an impression given of untrammelled licence.

These same classical writers were also greatly fascinated by the way in which the northern tribes painted and tattooed themselves. The word 'Picti' itself may, as we have seen, be a reference to this habit. Many writers refer specifically to this custom, often in terms of tattooing rather than mere daubing with colour in the manner of Caesar's Britons. It is true that much of this evidence is second hand but there seems no reason to doubt that the Picts, quite far on into the Roman period, liked to decorate themselves in this way. It is impossible to tell when or where the habit originated. The Pritani of South Britain may themselves have got their 'designs' from an older population and the habit moved north with the Celts and hung on there. Alternatively the older population in the north may have had its own tattooing traditions. Why they did it is not clear either. The motives for tattooing are broadly magical: to keep off sickness and wounds, to indicate caste or rank, or, most common of all, simply to decorate. Isidore of Seville, writing soon after AD 600, writes that the Pictish aristocracy tattooed itself 'ad sui specimen', but whether this should be translated simply as 'in a manner appropriate to itself' or more particularly as 'according to the personal rank of the individual', as some scholars have thought, is a matter of opinion. Professor Charles Thomas has suggested that the tattoo designs referred to by classical writers are the same as the symbolic designs used by the Picts, mainly on stone monuments, throughout the historical period. If this were so then we should have another very impressive link between the proto-Pictish and Pictish period proper.

The Pictish historical period really begins with the coming of Christianity around 565. By this time the situation in the north was such as to allow the king whom Columba visited, Bridei, son of Maelcon, to control the Orkneys from his royal residence near Loch Ness. Roman pressure and, later, the failure to dislodge the Scottish settlement of Argyll in the fifth century must have stimulated a will to unite for the common good. According to Adomnan in his *Life of Columba*, written towards the end of the seventh century, Bridei controlled the Orkneys by holding hostages, and presumably this would be how he kept control over other districts as well. Bede called him a 'most powerful king' but it is not known how far south his kingdom extended. There is no evidence for any other Pictish king having been influential during his long reign, but in 584 he died fighting in a civil war in a district of southern Pictland and this may mean that the south wished to maintain a measure of independence.

Adomnan gives us a glimpse into Bridei's court, or at least a picture of what he thought was an appropriate setting for him. He gives Bridei a council, a priesthood, slaves (one of whom at least is Irish), messengers on horseback and a royal treasury. The chief priest is said to have been the *nutricius* of the king. This means 'foster-father' and it would seem, therefore, that the Picts practised the Celtic custom of 'fosterage', a system whereby the children of noble families were sent away from home to be brought up. In his journeying among the Picts Columba is said twice to have witnessed Picts being buried. This is interesting because so little is known about Pictish burial customs of any period. A Pictish household is described as comprising husband and wife, children and servants – an orderly and devoted group that comes as a surprise after the lurid reports in classical writers. One Pict is described as a 'captain of a cohort', a title that has yet to be satisfactorily explained. Certainly Bridei must have had an efficient army and fleet.

Even allowing for an element of anachronism, Adomnan's picture of Pictish society shows that by the sixth century the Picts had developed into a coherent people led by a typical Dark Age monarch who had all the resources of his foreign contemporaries. The Picts are referred to regularly in the written sources of these contemporaries and it should be stressed that there is never any suggestion in these sources that the Picts were regarded as a backward or in any way peculiar people. This contrasts strongly with the accounts given of them by classical writers, who clearly, perhaps largely through ignorance and lack of sympathy, found them very alien.

In the years that followed the introduction of Christianity the Pictish kingdom undoubtedly comprised all the districts north of the Forth–Clyde line and was ruled by one king based in southern Pictland. Like their neighbours the Scots and the Britons, the Picts suffered from Northumbrian aggression from the middle of the seventh century. Eventually the Scots and Britons had to acknowledge the English as their overlords and pay them some kind of tribute. The Picts fared worse, actually losing some of their territory in the south. This period of the occupation by the English cannot have been all loss for it brought the Picts into close contact with the Northumbrians politically and ecclesiastically at a period when they were in the midst of an intellectual and artistic flowering of a remarkable kind. In the end the Picts from the north won a great victory over the Northumbrians in 685 at Dunnichen (Nechtansmere) in Angus. By this victory the Picts regained the southern part of their kingdom and released the Scots and the Britons from their obligations to the English. In 685 there is no doubt that the Picts were politically the most important people in North Britain. At this time it has been suggested, with some probability, that the Picts redefined their frontier with the Scots, giving to the Scots, in exchange perhaps for Scottish settlements in Perthshire, all the land to the west of Druimalban. This was the boundary between the two peoples at the time when Adomnan was writing his *Life of Columba* very shortly after the victory of 685.

The political confidence gained at the end of the seventh century together with the prolonged contact with the Northumbrians may account for a major change in Pictish affairs taking place at the beginning of the following century on the initiative of the reigning king. Bede records that about 710 King Nechton sent messengers to Abbot Ceolfrith of Jarrow, in Northumbria, asking him to send convincing arguments for the adoption of Roman methods of calculating the date of Easter and other Roman customs in order that he might persuade his people to make these changes. He also asked for architects to be sent to build him a stone church which he promised to dedicate to St Peter. This was in effect a programme for the abandonment of the Irish Columban Church and the establishment of a truly national Pictish church. Iona with its veneration for St Columba was no longer to control the church in Pictland. In its stead was to be Nechton's stone church in the heart of the kingdom, dedicated to St Peter.

Ceolfrith sent a long letter, drafted for him by Bede, and also by the architects, whose work may perhaps be seen in the curious narrow door at the base of the tower of Restenneth Priory in Angus. Bede, like Adomnan before him for the sixth century, describes the Pictish king's court in the eighth century, when the letter arrived. The Picts have come a long way. The king is no longer surrounded by pagan priests, but by learned men hard at work translating the letter. Nechton is at the centre of it all giving orders that the new Easter Tables be transcribed throughout his kingdom, contrasting with the apparent lack of interest in Columba's doings shown by Bridei. It is not known whether Bridei even agreed to be baptised himself and he appears to have made no move to grant Columba a piece of land near the royal residence on which to build a monastery.

Nechton's initiative seems to have placed the Pictish church under direct royal authority. Towards the end of the ninth century it is recorded that the reigning Scottish king was the 'first to give liberty to the Scottish church, which was in servitude up to that time after the custom and fashion of the Picts'. Some kind of taxation imposed by the civil authorities is presumably implied by this interesting note.

For the rest of the century the Picts more than held their own politically. A leader, Oengus, son of Fergus, emerged, whose steady rise to power can be followed in entries in the Irish annals. In 741 he 'utterly destroyed' the Scots and had his ambitions stopped there we might all be living in Pictland today. But he wanted to master the Britons also, and when he failed to do so he lost Dalriada as well.

Since the origins of the Picts are obscure it is a pity that they disappear from the pages of history in a rather mysterious way. In the early medieval period kingdoms were always being lost and won, often as a result of a single victory, but that the Picts failed to recover their position when the Scots defeated them in the mid-ninth century requires explanation. There is in fact little doubt that this lies in the introduction of a new element in northern politics – the arrival of the Norse. Not very long after Oengus' death, Norse raiding had begun on the northern and western coasts. As time passed, both Picts and Scots were seriously weakened fighting against them, and the Scots' position on the west coast must soon have become intolerable. As soon, therefore, as they snatched a relatively minor victory over the Picts, who were by this time losing large tracts of territory in the far north, the Scots moved bodily into eastern Scotland, well away from the Norse encroachments. This was something quite different from the Northumbrian occupation of southern Pictland. The whole administration moved east, establishing itself perhaps at Forteviot, where, eventually, Kenneth mac Alpin, the first king of the new kingdom of Picts and Scots, died. Kenneth also transported the relics of Columba into Pictland and built a church at Dunkeld to hold them, which for a time became the chief church in the kingdom.

This is really a hypothetical solution to the way in which the Scots swamped the Picts, but it accounts for their political extinction for it would have exterminated the administration if not the population. It also accounts for the ease with which the Norse established their settlements on the west coast. A movement of the Scottish population into eastern Pictland at this period also fits well with a recent interpretation of the characteristic Pictish place-names that begin with the element *Pit-*. The second element in these names is always Irish and their formation has been dated to the period after the end of the Pictish kingdom when the two peoples were living side by side in peaceful co-existence, and Professor Jackson suggests that the incoming Irish overlords adopted the Pictish landholding system with its 'manors' (petta) intact.

After the end of the political kingdom the Picts drop out of the records with astonishing rapidity. As a political concept they ceased to exist. The only use that medieval chroniclers found for their written sources was to use the list of the Pictish kings to extend the antiquity of the Scottish line by tacking it on behind their own king-list.

It is a notorious fact that Pictish history has to be pieced together from Irish, English and British sources and the lack of surviving Pictish sources has inevitably raised doubts as to whether in fact they had any, apart from the king-list – the most primitive of all historical records. It is true that the hold maintained by the Columban church on Pictish monasteries may have inhibited the development of written Pictish learning, particularly since initially the Irish monks may have provided a strictly classical education in their monastic schools. It is also possible that the Pictish languages may never have become fully developed written languages. After the establishment of the Pictish church, however, things must have been very different. It seems very unlikely that Nechton was unappreciative of the value of the written record and that efforts would not have been made to write down native law codes and the like. A number of reasons for the lack of surviving sources can be offered but by far the most important one must be that as the Pictish language and Pictish institutions became obsolete there would be no reason to preserve or transcribe either their Latin or vernacular sources. That the Picts participated fully in the intellectual life of the time is shown most clearly in their monumental art. The evidence it provides is full and clear and Pictish art affords a unique opportunity to comprehend something of the nature of the sensibility of the Picts. There is no Pictish saga cycle, no religious lyric poetry and no great Pictish epic but the stone sculpture compensates for these sad deficiencies to a remarkable degree.

Pictish art as we know it was in its beginnings entirely functional. By incising a series of designs on the flat surfaces of free-standing boulders the artists were principally engaged in conveying a message to those who looked at them. These designs are repeated in virtually identical forms all over the Pictish area and it is generally agreed that they must, therefore, be symbolic. The distribution of the symbol-bearing stones covers all the territories which we know from the written sources to have been Pictish – from the Shetlands in the north to Pabbay in the west, the North Sea in the east, and the Forth–Clyde line in the south. It should be noted that symbol stones are found in the districts where there were brochs, in the far north and in the Hebrides, and that these areas must not be thought of as somehow less Pictish than the eastern districts. The fact that symbol stones were erected all over Pictland suggests that this was a late custom and the lack of symbol stones in Argyll bears this out. When the Scots won this district from the Picts symbol stones were not being erected, so that they must be dated to some period after the fifth century.

The symbols, which comprise abstract designs, animal designs and a few representations of objects, are stylistically very uniform. The curvilinear patterns and the stylisation of the animals have a

Figure 7 Pictish symbols

Figure 8 Pictish animal symbols

consistency which almost suggests that they were designed at one point in time by one school of artists. The designs are very beautiful, and the incision on the stones is even and controlled. Some of the most aesthetically successful symbols are found in the north and this could be interpreted as having a bearing on the place of origin of the designs or simply be taken as evidence for a particularly talented group of sculptors practising there. It has been suggested by Professor Charles Thomas that the stones are headstones, and that the symbols are the ancient tattoo designs, which he further believes indicated the personal rank of the tattooed individual. I have put forward a case for their being connected with ownership. In fact it is unlikely that the meaning of the symbols will ever be determined with certainty.

At a later period the symbols were used in conjunction with the cross. These monuments are properly dressed slabs with the sculptures first in very shallow relief which then gets heavier as the series progresses. An interlace cross is on the front of the slab and the symbols are usually, but not always, placed on the back. The remaining space is filled with all sorts of apparently random iconography such as hunting scenes, fantastic animals, classical motifs, and other unidentifiable figure scenes. Some of this iconography must come from portable ivories and textiles but some of it could well be illustrations of Pictish folk-tales.

Many of the features of the decoration of these cross-slabs can be paralleled in the great contemporary illuminated Gospel books of Durrow, Lindisfarne and Kells, and this provides a date of some time in the second half of the seventh century for their commencement.

Some writers have felt that many of the features of the designs on the earlier incised monuments also find their most natural analogies in these manuscripts and that some of them must therefore be as late as the seventh century. On the basis of the closeness of the resemblance in treatment of the Pictish animal designs and some of the animal evangelist symbols in three contemporary manuscripts, one of which is the *Book of Durrow*, I have suggested that the illuminators, seeking around for integrated animal designs for their animal symbols, lighted upon the already existing powerful Pictish animal designs. If this is so, then the symbol stones pre-date or are at least contemporary with the earliest of these Hiberno-Saxon manuscripts. Professor Thomas would release the early symbol stones entirely from their connections with the manuscript tradition and dates them even earlier. These matters cannot be discussed here but what should be emphasised is the extremely high quality of Pictish sculpture. The Picts were obviously naturally talented artists with a highly developed sense of line and composition. From the start they had no difficulty in laying out interlace designs and later they exploited brilliantly the resources of relief sculpture. Their repertoire, while clearly related to what was going on in England and Ireland, remained individual. Their interest in David iconography is so marked as to suggest the existence in Pictland of an illustrated Psalter. Their fondness for spiral designs of great complexity is not found in other contemporary stone sculpture. The nature of the cross-slab, itself a peculiarity of the Picts, allowed them space to produce an extended piece of secular narrative art such as the battle scene in Aberlemno churchyard, which is unparalleled. On the other hand the magnificent cross-slab from Nigg, aswirl with curves and bosses, is aesthetically very close indeed to the well-known Chi-Rho page in the *Book of Kells*. The figure sculpture on this slab also recalls the figure style of the Kells school.

The great monuments of Nigg, Hilton of Cadboll and the sarcophagus at St Andrews represent some of the most impressive monuments of the latest phase of Pictish sculpture. The sarcophagus bears no symbols but its David iconography and its enmeshed bosses surrounded by snakes link it firmly with a symbol-bearing monument such as Nigg. Many splendid crosses of this period, particularly in the north, survive in fragments only. Tarbat in Ross appears to have had a number of them and must have been a very important centre. A fragment, now in Elgin museum, of a figure of David virtually identical with the figure on the sarcophagus, is all that is left of what must have been a sculpture of comparable distinction. These crosses were clearly raised in considerable numbers by artists of superlative capacity for patrons of sensibility and taste and in themselves provide irrefutable evidence for the intellectual awareness of Pictish society.

The Picts, then, have left perhaps their most distinctive mark on Scotland in their sculptured stones scattered over the countryside. Did they contribute any other lasting effect on the later kingdom of Scotland? Pictish families, particularly in the north-east, may have persisted for many years after the Scots took over, and local methods of administration and land-tenure are unlikely to have been instantly uprooted. A close scrutiny of the sources for medieval Scottish history may reveal traces of this kind of Pictish continuity. At present, however, it can only be said, in sentimental vein, that if we Scots like to think of ourselves as something distinct from an Irish colony then it is the spirit of the tribes who went to make up the Picts that we must invoke.

CHAPTER 3

THE SCOTS OF DALRIADA

John Bannerman

'No Scot ever set his foot on British soil save from a vessel that had put out from Ireland.' Latin writers of the early centuries of our era, whether continental or insular, refer to the inhabitants of Ireland as Scotti or Scots, and to Ireland itself as Scotia. They spoke Gaelic, a Celtic language, which is a continuing part of our heritage, and Gaelic culture is increasingly recognised to have been an important factor in the preservation of our identity as a people. The term for a Scot in his own language was *Gàidheal* or Gael, although today it describes a Gaelic-speaking Scot only.

Population movements in Ireland in the fourth and fifth centuries resulted in settlements of Scotti along the western seaboard of the neighbouring island of Britain. In Scotland itself, the penetration was even greater. We find Scotti, apparently acting in conjunction with the Picts, harassing the Roman province of Britain in the vicinity of the Walls in the fourth century, and this should probably be seen in the context of traditional material, supported by place-name study, which tells of early settlements of Scotti, apparently from Munster, in the Pictish province of Circinn, now Angus and the Mearns, in the Lennox district of the British kingdom of Strathclyde, and elsewhere.

But the history of the Scots in Scotland begins with the foundation of the kingdom of Dalriada, mainly Argyll and its islands, in what was presumably once part of Pictland. It is not clear when the Scots of Dalriada in Ireland, which corresponded more or less to the present-day coastal area of County Antrim, began to cross the narrow stretch of intervening sea, but when their royal dynasty, in the person of Fergus Mór, son of Erc, forsook Dunseverick, their Irish capital, and took up permanent residence in Scotland around AD 500, it can fairly be assumed that their overseas colony was not only securely established but already overtaking in importance the mother country. It is arguable that the advent of Fergus Mór is the single most important event in Scotland's history. To this we owe two basic facts of life, that we are today Scots living in a country called Scotland. From Fergus Mór, with a few early exceptions, descend all subsequent kings and queens of Scots, including the present queen of Great Britain; pride in the antiquity of the dynasty was to be a unifying factor at periods of crisis in our later history.

An event of almost equal significance was the advent of yet another Scot from Ireland in 563, namely Columba, or, to give him his Gaelic name, Colum Cille, 'Dove of the Church'. He was a scion of the royal family of the Uí Néill, the most powerful people in Ireland of the time. He was to become the paramount saint of the Scots. And although the Scots, in their attempts – culminating in the Declaration of Arbroath of 1320 – to persuade the papal authorities that their church and state were independent of England, claimed the Apostle Andrew, brother of St Peter of Rome, as their patron saint, it was the *Brecbennach* of Columba, housed at Arbroath, then the premier monastery in Scotland, which protected the Scots at Bannockburn. Indeed, if Scots today were asked to name the most spiritually significant centre in their country, invariably the answer would be Iona, the small island off the west coast of Mull on which Columba founded his monastery.

The period during which Fergus Mór flourished may be calculated from the extant Irish annals, which incorporate a chronicle apparently compiled in Iona in the first half of the eighth century. The fullest versions are contained in the *Annals of Ulster* and the *Annals of Tigernach*. It is the most informative source for the early political history of Dalriada. Adomnan, abbot of Iona (d. 704), who wrote a life of Columba within a century of the latter's death in 597, was primarily concerned to prove the sanctity of Columba, but he has much to tell us not only of the saint's life and career but also of the history of Dalriada in his own time and earlier. The work is also a valuable commentary on the social and economic life of the area. The *Senchus Fer nAlban*, 'History of the Men of Scotland', a seventh-century compilation in origin, records the genealogies of the ruling families in Dalriada and is also in some degree a census of the military and economic resources of its people. The early eighth-century *Genelaig Albanensium*, 'Scottish Pedigrees', seems to be a continuation of the genealogical section of the *Senchus*. Finally, chronicles, which consist mainly of lists of kings of Scots with the lengths of their reigns, are extant from the eleventh century. The most important non-native source is Bede's *Ecclesiastical History of the English People*, completed in 731. Bede, a Northumbrian monk, was particularly interested in the church which emanated from Iona and which played such a large part in bringing Christianity to the Angles of Northumbria. However, although it is true to say that the Scots of Dalriada are the most fully documented of all the Dark Age peoples in what is now Scotland, there are and will continue to be many gaps in our knowledge of their history.

All the sources listed above mention Aedán, great-grandson of Fergus Mór, and king of Dalriada from 574 to about 608. He is easily the most considerable lay figure among the Scots until Kenneth, son of Alpin, in whose reign the political union of Scots and Picts was effected in 843–4. To some extent, one can judge this by the amount of information extant concerning his career. There are records of battles fought by him in the Isle of Man, in Ireland, in the Orkneys, in the Pictish province of Circinn, and against the Maeatae of central Scotland. The only real setback of his career was a defeat inflicted on him by the Angles of Northumbria at the unidentified Degsastán in 603. But the point to note here is that this battle was fought on Northumbrian soil.

Aedán's extension of the power and prestige of the Scots owed much to the support and counsel which he received from Columba. Columba's most significant act in this context was to win the friendship of, and apparently convert to Christianity, Bridei (Brude), over-king of all the Picts (d. 584), especially as Bridei had already inflicted a defeat on the Scots some sixteen years before Aedán's succession. Iona, Bede tells us, 'held for a long time pre-eminence over the monasteries of all the Picts, and was their superior in ruling their communities'. According to Adomnan, Columba consecrated Aedán king of Dalriada on Iona, the earliest documentary reference to a ceremony of ordination of a king of Scots in Scotland. We find him advising Aedán at the Convention of Druim Cett in 575 in the latter's dialogue with Aed, son of Ainmire, king of the Uí Néill, concerning the future status of Aedán's Irish territories. He is recorded as praying for Aedán's success in battle with the Maeatae, while Aedán is seen taking his advice as to which of his sons should succeed him as king of Scots. The importance of this partnership between church and state, demonstrated so clearly in Aedán's reign, cannot be over-estimated, it is a recurring theme which extends far beyond the period of Dalriada's existence as a separate entity.

In the *Senchus Fer nAlban*, three chief peoples are named in seventh-century Dalriada. The least important of these was the Cenél nOengusa, 'kindred of Oengus', who inhabited the island of Islay. The Cenél nGabráin, 'kindred of Gabrán', named for Aedán's father, occupied Kintyre, with Gigha, possibly also Jura, and Crích Chomgaill, 'the territory of Comgall', present-day Cowal, with its islands, certainly Bute, but probably Arran also. The Cenél Loairn, 'kindred of Loarn', occupied the territory so-called today and the island of Colonsay, and, by implication, dominated all the islands and mainland districts to the north of these not inhabited by the Picts. On the mainland, the boundary between them probably ran somewhere to the north of Ardnamurchan, while Columba is said to have baptised a Pict on the island of Skye. To the east, the ridge of mountains known in Gaelic as Druim Alban separated Scot from Pict. The strongholds of the Cenél nGabráin, at least around 700, were Dunaverty in the Mull of Kintyre and Tairpert Boitter, presumably near Tarbert, Lochfyne, while Dunollie, near Oban, and Dunadd on the Crinan Canal were the contemporary strongholds of the Cenél Loairn.

As the names of these peoples suggest, the structure of society was kin-based. The basic kin group was the *derbfine* or 'certain kin', which consisted of four generations of descendants including the common ancestor; that is to say, an ancestor, his sons, grandsons and great-grandsons. It was with the derbfine that responsibility for liabilities incurred by any one of its members lay, and all members of this group were heirs in respect of property, personal and landed. The ruler of each of the kindreds named above was a *rí* or king, with the king of the Cenél nGabráin overlord of Dalriada at this time. Succession to the kingship was decided within the derbfine of a king. A study of the application and occurrence in the Irish annals of the term *rígdomnae*, literally, 'material of a king', that is, a person eligible to succeed to the kingship, shows that dynastic

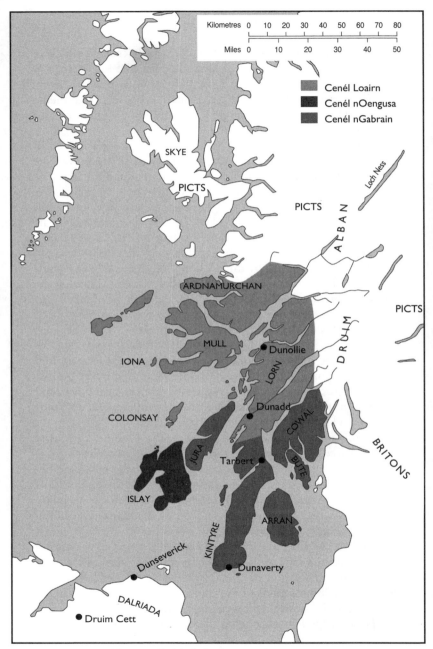

Figure 9 Dalriada in the seventh century AD

succession lay with members of the derbfine, the common ancestor of which had himself been a king. In the hope, often deferred, of avoiding internal strife among what would normally be a large number of eligible males within the royal kindred, a successor was appointed during the lifetime of the reigning king. He was called *tánaise ríg*, 'second to a king', from which derive the English terms for the system *tanistry* and *tanist*. The intention was to secure the person best fitted for the job. He was to be of age and sound in mind and body. It was therefore unusual for a son or grandson to succeed, although perfectly legal given the right circumstances, while the succession of a brother, a nephew or a cousin was more likely. This pattern of succession to the kingship of the Scots, with the later innovation, probably Pictish in origin, that it could pass through a female, was to obtain without interruption into the twelfth century and remained a factor in the succession stakes for some centuries thereafter.

The other free grades in lay society were the noble and the commoner. The noble was generally a close relative of the contemporary king or a descendant of relatives of earlier kings. All commoners were in a client relationship to the nobles and, as far as the *Senchus* was concerned, were expressed in terms of houses. Thus, the Cenél nGabráin had 560 houses or clients, while the Cenél Loairn and the Cenél nOengusa had 420 and 430 respectively.

From every twenty houses were to come two seven-benched boats, which probably meant that every twenty houses was to provide twenty-eight oarsmen, allowing for two to a bench as would be normal. The necessity for such a system of recruitment is testimony to the importance of naval power to the sea-girt inhabitants of Dalriada, already exemplified in the military expeditions undertaken by Aedán involving long sea voyages. The Gaelic *curach* was a word frequently used to describe the vessels which plied Dalriadic waters at this time; their lineal descendants, still so described, are in use today along the west coast of Ireland. Structurally, the *curach* consisted of a framework of wood covered with pitched hides, now tarred calico. In addition to oars, it had a sail. According to Adomnan, it was a ship of this kind which sailed northwards for fourteen days and nights, 'beyond the range of human exploration', before returning. The twenty-house unit of

Dalriada has echoes in the fiscal organisation of later medieval Scotland.

The *Senchus* also allows us to estimate in round figures the number of men which each kindred could muster for a *slógad* or hosting, 800 from the Cenél nGabráin, 700 from the Cenél Loairn and from the Cenél nOengusa 500. Thus, Aedán's armies, in so far as they were drawn from Dalriada in Scotland, cannot have numbered more than 2,000 men at any one time, although we do know that he had a contingent direct from Ireland at the Battle of Degsastán. One hundred of the 700 men which the Cenél Loairn could muster were Airgialla, the name for a group of peoples in a vassal relationship to the Uí Néill in Northern Ireland. It seems that they were of the Northern Uí Macc-Uais, a section of which had apparently settled in the islands dominated by the Cenél Loairn and were performing military service for the latter, a function which this people had already carried out for the Uí Néill in Ireland.

In conclusion, what strikes one most forcibly when examining in detail the system of society obtaining among the Scots of Dalriada and in contemporary Ireland is how often its constituent elements find their precise equivalent in the so-called clan system of later Scotland.

The culture of the Scots of Dalriada, as might be expected, mirrors that of contemporary Ireland. And indeed, Gaelic-speaking Scotland and Ireland constituted a single culture-province down into the seventeenth century. The obituary notices of famous people, especially of the professional and ecclesiastical classes, often represent them as being equally well known in Ireland and Scotland. Thus, in the *Annals of Tigernach*, Mael-dúin, bishop of the Scots (d. 1055), resident in the monastic community at St Andrews, is eulogised as 'the glory of the Gaels', that is, of the inhabitants of Scotland and Ireland.

The church in Ireland, and therefore in Dalriada, neither of which was ever part of the Roman Empire, was not imposed by conquerors but was truly missionary in character, recruiting from the beginning most of its members on the spot. And after some initial hostility, the most fertile ground for recruitment was the existing native learned classes. The result was a fusion of Christian and Mediterranean cultural influences with pagan and vernacular learning. The whole process received an even greater impetus, when, by the sixth century, the church had become predominantly monastic in character, a type of monasticism, moreover, at once ascetic and intellectual, promoting through the monastic school the education of laymen. It has been estimated that, by the eighth century, the proportion of literate laymen in the areas served by the Celtic church must have been abnormally high when compared with the rest of Northern Europe. It is significant that one of the earliest and most important extant poems in the vernacular is an elegy to Columba, the greatest of the educated religious of the Celtic church, probably composed around 600 by Dallán Forgaill, a lay poet said to be the most renowned of his time in Ireland. But more than that, Columba himself was, according to early tradition, a poet of note in the vernacular, and he was certainly a Latin scribe; Adomnan portrays him on the very day of his death in the process of copying a psalter.

But monastic scribes did not confine themselves to the mechanical process of copying the scriptures, they began to make original contributions to ecclesiastical literature, the most characteristic being saints' lives. One of the earliest and most interesting was the *Life of Columba* by Adomnan. Adomnan also wrote an account of the holy places in the Eastern Mediterranean from notes dictated to him by a bishop of Gaul who had travelled in the area and whom Adomnan had entertained on Iona for a time. His writings indicate a library at Iona of considerable resources, containing, among other things, works of Jerome and of Sulpicius Severus, Pope Gregory I's *Dialogues*, Athanasius' *Life of St Anthony*, Hegesippus, alongside Solinus and Virgil's *Aeneid* of pre-Christian antiquity, but the influence of the vernacular tradition is also evident, many of his stories demonstrating Columba's miraculous powers are based upon the oral literature of the time. And it was not long before the monastic scribes were recording in writing the native tradition as it stood. The result is that we have in Gaelic the oldest vernacular literature in Western Europe.

The single most important body of early vernacular literature preserved for us by the labours of the Celtic church monks were the sagas, particularly the Ulster Cycle with Cú Chulainn as its central figure; and also the cycle of sagas associated with Fionn and his son

Ossian whose names, by the nineteenth century, had become familiar far beyond the bounds of Scotland and Ireland. The typical product of the lay poet of the period was praise poetry, eulogy and elegy, aimed at the elevation of kindreds and the heads of kindreds. Even here the influence of the church is evident, for the metres were modelled on early continental Latin hymn metres, and they continued in use in Scotland into the eighteenth century. But more than that, the subject matter was considerably widened and includes what we would now call nature poetry, an extraordinary manifestation centuries before it appears in the literature of other peoples.

Deriving directly from the scriptoria of the Celtic church monasteries is the school of manuscript illumination, which has been described as 'the finest flower of Celtic art'. The traditional curvilinear treatment of ornament, incorporating fantastic animal figures and spiralling foliage, either present for its own sake or as a frame for representations of scriptural motifs, is generally thought to have reached its peak with the *Book of Kells*, a large Gospel book intended to lie on the altar. Begun, it seems, in the Iona scriptorium around 800, it was described by the *Annals of Ulster* in 1007 as 'the chief relic of the Western World'.

The style and artistry of the illuminated manuscript was reproduced on contemporary stone-work, sometimes so exactly as to imply direct influence of one on the other. Thus the great wheeled crosses of St Martin and St John on Iona have on them representations of the Virgin and Child surrounded by angels found elsewhere only in a page of the *Book of Kells*. The bosses standing out in high relief, which are so characteristic a feature of these crosses and, more particularly, of the cross at Kildalton in Islay, remind us of metal-work, an art in which the Celts, whether in their continental or insular setting, are generally recognised to have excelled. The Hunterston Brooch, which dates to the early eighth century, has few rivals for excellence in workmanship and is a fine example of the Celtic artist's propensity for making the most of a limited space with complex and detailed but perfectly proportioned ornament. Although found at Hunterston, Ayrshire, it is probably of Dalriadic origin. Nor should we forget, since we have already had occasion to mention it, the reliquary from Monymusk of the same period, which is in the form of a house-shrine made of wood, elaborately decorated with metal-work, and almost certainly the *Brecbennach* of Columba.

A surface crowded with stylised representation and ornament, at its best so delicately proportioned and imaginatively varied in treatment as to defeat totally the onset of monotony, and the love of clear and distinct colour, are perhaps the most characteristic features of the visual arts. But they are also present in literature, particularly in poetry, notable for the variety of literary ornament and metre. It is not unlikely that the music of the harp, for long the most highly regarded instrument among the Scots, if it had survived, would have exhibited the same love of decorative variation. It is certainly present in the classical music of the bagpipe, which had overtaken the harp in popularity by the seventeenth century. These are the factors which give the culture of the Scots in all its aspects a notable unity of form and purpose.

The political fortunes of the Scots of Dalriada took a backward step in the reign of Domnall Brecc, Aedán's grandson. It is recorded that he was defeated in battle on no less than four occasions. His opponents may have been Picts in 634 and 638 but, in 637, his participation in the well-known battle of Magh Rath in County Down against Domnall, son of Aed, king of the Uí Néill, seems to have cost him his Irish territories. Dalriada in Ireland was no longer to be ruled from Scotland. At Strathcarron about 642, Domnall Brecc met his death at the hands of the Britons of Strathclyde; a famous victory this and a stanza commemorating it, incorporated in the British poem *Gododdin*, ends with the words 'and the head of Domnall Brecc, ravens gnawed it'. This is the earliest certain record of hostility between Scot and Briton in Scotland.

Internally, the chief result of Domnall Brecc's disastrous career seems to have been to weaken the Cenél nGabráin, allowing the Cenél Loairn to move into the ascendancy towards the end of the century; Ferchar Fota (d. 697) was the first of their leaders to figure in the list of the kings of Dalriada. It seems also to have promoted a split in the Cenél nGabráin itself. The Cenél Comgaill, who inhabited Crích Chomgaill or Cowal and who were named for Comgall, Gabrán's brother and predecessor as king of Dalriada, had taken their place alongside the other three peoples of Dalriada by 700.

The Cenél Loairn's period of dominance was anything but a peaceful one for them. Internal troubles resulted in Selbach, their leader and king of Dalriada, destroying Dunollie, one of their own strongholds, in 701. Thirteen years later, he rebuilt it. Nor did the Cenél nGabráin allow the Cenél Loairn to hold undisputed sway over Dalriada, and although the latter normally held them off successfully, they defeated Selbach in a *bellum maritimum* in 719, the first sea-battle recorded in the history of the British Isles. Finally, as the leading people of Dalriada at this time, the Cenél Loairn had to bear the brunt of what seems to have been the first and last sustained campaign against the Scots by the neighbouring Picts under their king Oengus. This Pictish aggression culminated in 741 with 'the smiting of Dalriada by Oengus, son of Fergus'.

It has generally been thought that Dalriada remained under the heel of Pictland until the political union of the two countries about 843 and consequently it has been usual to express surprise that the union was effected by the king of Scots rather than a king of the numerically superior Picts. True there was no further reference to Dalriada in a political context until 768. But this was a battle between Picts and Scots in Fortriu, now Strathearn and Menteith, a Pictish province neighbouring on Dalriada. It seems that the prevailing pattern of aggression by the Scots at the expense of the Picts had already reasserted itself. The king of Scots involved was Aed Find of the Cenél nGabráin, and it may be taken that one result of the Pictish invasion of Dalriada was the elimination of the Cenél Loairn as a contender for political leadership in the country. Thereafter, Fortriu and Dalriada are closely connected, with kings of Dalriada who were sometimes also recorded as kings of Fortriu.

At the outset, this makes it less surprising that Kenneth, son of Alpin, of the Cenél nGabráin (d. 858), should have brought Scots and Picts together in a lasting political union. It has, however, been suggested that Kenneth may have had a valid claim to succeed to the kingship of the Picts in the female line. Other sources assert that the union was the result of military conquest by Kenneth, possibly aided by reinforcement direct from Ireland, and perhaps only after the Picts had been weakened by a defeat at the hands of a marauding Danish army. And indeed, there are frequent references to Scandinavian raids on both Dalriada and Pictland from the beginning of this century, so that a drawing together in the face of a common enemy is a not unlikely trend.

A combination of some or all of these factors would explain why the union took place when it did, but it does not explain the virtual disappearance of the Picts from history, a disappearance so complete that certain twelfth-century English chroniclers were able to make the extraordinary error of locating Picts in Galloway. The most likely explanation is that the Scoticisation of the Picts was well under way by the time of the union, which is in itself, of course, a fundamental reason for the union taking place under a king of Scots. Settlements of Scots in parts of Pictland, beginning, it seems, at least as early as the fourth century, must have played their part in the process but the most important factor was surely the introduction of Christianity to the Picts by the Scots. The linguistic and cultural penetration of Pictland following in its wake cannot be over-estimated. The new kingdom of the Scots became known as Alba in Gaelic and Scotia in Latin, names which are, of course, current today.

Just as did Fergus Mór three and a half centuries earlier, the kings of Scots went east, enabling them to take a firmer grip of their vastly extended territories. Their southern boundary was now the Forth–Clyde line. They took up residence at Scone, which became the *caput* or legal centre of Scotland. Centuries later, in his bid for the kingship of the Scots, Robert Bruce was careful to have himself crowned at Scone, but, because Edward I of England had already removed it to Westminster, could not be installed on the coronation stone of the king of Scots, generally known as the Stone of Destiny, which, tradition has it, was brought by the Scots from Ireland, first to Iona and then, presumably after the union, to Scone.

The kings of Scotia were of the Cenél nGabráin, but the ruling family of their erstwhile rivals the Cenél Loairn also seem to have shared in the eastward expansion. Thus, an eleventh-century mormaer (later *comes* or earl) of Moray derived his descent from Ferchar Fota of the Cenél Loairn. As the Cenél nGabráin expanded through the Perthshire glens linking Dalriada with Pictland, so the obvious and perhaps the only conceivable outlet to the east for the Cenél Loairn, situated as they were in Northern Dalriada, was up the Great Glen and into Moray. The later aspirations of the Men of Moray to elevate members of their ruling family into the kingship of the Scots, successful in the case of Macbeth (d. 1057) and of his successor Lulach (d. 1058), although both also had legitimate claims to succeed within the kin-based system of succession, may well have been inspired by the memory that the Cenél Loairn once competed with the Cenél nGabráin in the provision of kings of Dalriada.

The vacuum which may have been created in Dalriada as a result of the removal of the ruling families of the Cenél nGabráin and the Cenél Loairn seems to have been filled by the Airgialla, the people whom we saw subordinated to the Cenél Loairn in the seventh and early eighth centuries. It would be natural for them to increase in power and influence as the Cenél Loairn was weakened by internal strife and Pictish aggression in the first half of the eighth century. Whatever the case, Gofraid, son of Fergus, apparently a member of their ruling family, came over from Ireland with an army to assist Kenneth, son of Alpin, and settled in the islands. His descendants, at first submerged under Norse overlordship in the area, were to re-emerge in the twelfth century in the person of Somerled, 'king of the Isles' (d. 1164), who was, in turn, ancestor of the later Lords of the Isles.

In keeping with the partnership between church and state so evident in the time of Columba and Aedán, the administrative centre of the church moved east with Kenneth. Thus, in 849, a division of the relics of Columba seems to have been made, some going to the monastery of Dunkeld and some to the monastery of Kells in Northern Ireland. In the Celtic church, the authority of the founding saint went with his relics and the result was to split the Columban church in two. The reason for the removal of some of Columba's relics to Kells, which now became head of all the Columban monasteries in Northern Ireland, was the increasingly insistent presence in the waters between Ireland and Scotland of Norse sea-going raiders whose first attack on Iona had come towards the end of the previous century. This does not mean that Iona was abandoned. A monastic community continued in existence there. Iona itself remained the spiritual centre of the church and almost all the kings of Scots down to Domnal Bán, whose reign ended in 1097, are said to have been buried there.

A further shift of the administrative centre of the church from Dunkeld to St Andrews had almost certainly been accomplished by 943 when Constantine II, King of Scots, abdicated to become abbot of the Culdee monastery at St Andrews, and there it remained until the Reformation. No doubt the relics of Columba went too – this would explain how the *Brecbennach* came in time to be housed in the monastery of Arbroath, also on the east coast. But the fact that the monastic community at St Andrews belonged to the Culdee order is itself sufficient indication of the presence of the Columban church. The Culdees, that is, *Céli Dé*, 'Client of God', came into being as the result of a reform movement within the church in Ireland in the second half of the eighth century. Perhaps because there was a community of Culdees at Iona, as well as at St Andrews, the order seems to have been particularly strong in Scotland and their monasteries also included Abernethy, Brechin, Loch Leven, Monifieth, Monymusk and Muthil. At the first two of these are located the best-preserved examples of round towers in Scotland, again typical of the church in Ireland, where the earliest seem to date to the tenth century. They were built partly as bell towers but also for defence, particularly for the protection of the precious relics of the monastery.

A constant factor in the history of the Scots from the period of migration from Ireland right through to the twelfth century was their urge to expand into new territories. Immediately the union of Scots and Picts was effected, they turned their eyes southwards and Kenneth himself, we are told, undertook no less than six invasions of Lothian, still the northern part of the kingdom of Northumbria. In Indulf's reign (954–62), the Scots captured the stronghold of Edinburgh and, in 1018, Malcolm II won the battle of Carham which finally secured possession of Lothian for the Scots. About this time, and, presumably through a dynastic connection, Duncan, Malcolm II's grandson, succeeded to the British kingdom of Strathclyde. So that when Duncan became king of Scots on his grandfather's death in 1034, the bounds of Scotland were fixed more or less as they are today, although the border, as we know it, had still to be precisely defined.

The story of the continued expansion of the Scots can be read on the ground, as it were, in the spread of Gaelic place-names over the country. For the Picts, partly a Celtic-speaking people, the transition to Gaelic cannot have been too difficult. Nor yet for the Britons of Strathclyde, and here we should not forget an earlier and independent movement, beginning in the early tenth century, into Galloway and Carrick, perhaps from the Western Isles, perhaps from Ireland, of a people who, although of mixed Scotto-Norse origin, were already largely Gaelic speaking. But the evidence of place and personal names shows that even Lothian must have had a considerable Gaelic-speaking aristocracy by the twelfth century.

The Scoticisation of almost the whole of what we have come to know as Scotland by the opening of the twelfth century cannot be too strongly stressed. It survived the influx in this century of people and ideas which flowed from the Norman Conquest of England. Thus, in the fourteenth century, Robert Bruce, King of Scots but bearer of an Anglo-Norman name, was able to urge the Irish to join with the Scots and rise against English domination, reminding them that the Scots and Irish shared a common origin, common customs and a common language.

CHAPTER 4

BRITONS AND ANGLES

D. P. Kirby

WHAT can be termed the Forth–Tyne or Clyde–Solway province of Dark Age Britain formed the originally British (P-Celtic) territory of what was to become in large measure part of Scotland. Though the population may have been basically of non-Celtic prehistoric origin at the time of the Roman Conquest, Celtic Brythonic chieftains were probably in the ascendancy. By the early fifth century, at the end of the Roman period, older British folk-groups – the Damnonii across the valley of the Clyde, the Novantae and Selgovae of Dumfriesshire and Galloway, and the Votadini between the Tyne and the Forth – were evolving into primitive states, possibly as specifically frontier states with the military task of containing the attacks of Picts and Scots from the north and west.

Strathclyde, Rheged and the kingdom of the Gododdin emerge most clearly. The frontiers of Strathclyde reached to the '*Clach nam Breatann*' (Stone of the Britons) on the western side of Glen Falloch at the head of Loch Lomond in the north and nearly to Stirling in the east. From the fifth century Dumbarton was the capital of Strathclyde. The immediate vicinity of Stirling was known as Manaw of the Gododdin, and Stirling and Edinburgh were Gododdin strongholds. The heartland of Rheged appears to have been the Eden Valley, for example Carlisle. Traprain Law, near Haddington, is the classic site at present from North Britain, revealing in its treasure the interaction of Roman and native and apparently enjoying a continuous occupation into the Dark Ages. These kingdoms were all part of a network of British states which stretched across the whole of immediate post-Roman Britain.

In the course of the fifth and sixth centuries the Angles, Saxons and Jutes from North Germany and Denmark overran most of what is now England. Cornwall and the Lake District remained British as did Wales and North Britain. The Britons put up fierce resistance to the Anglo-Saxons but were unable to contain the incoming hordes. The struggle in North Britain is unusually well documented. The North British scene can be reconstructed from the British writings of Gildas in the sixth century and Nennius in the early ninth, from the extant pedigrees of North British ruling families, and from the British bardic compositions of Taliesin and Aneirin which are generally believed to date to the late sixth century. It is clear that the North British area by the time of the Anglo-Saxon onslaught was at least nominally Christian. This is evident from archaeological excavations at Whithorn, for example, and, as the period progresses, Ardwall Isle, from the distribution of early inscribed Christian stones such as the famous 'Peter' stone at Whithorn or that at Yarrowkirk which commemorates two otherwise unknown princes, and from the bardic poems with their references to 'Heaven' and 'Easter'.

The Britons would be conscious that they were Christians when confronting the pagan Picts, and the missionary activities of the Whithorn-based Ninianic Church in the fifth century may have been intended to tame the enemy. But the Scots were Christians with their own priests. St Columba founded Iona in 563. For a relatively recently converted people like the Britons, as with other primitive peoples on other occasions, there must have been tremendous psychological tensions in having to resist at one and the same time both pagans and Christians. The Britons nevertheless achieved considerable success. They managed to confine the Picts and Scots above the Forth and the Clyde. It is not clear who was the dominant British leader at any one time. Coel the Old, in the early fifth century, was the progenitor of many northern dynasties including that of Rheged. Ceretic of Dumbarton, whom St Patrick reproached for his slave-raids on Ireland, and who was approximately Coel's contemporary, was the ancestor of the kings of Strathclyde. Later on Arthur must have been a leader of some significance. The Welsh annals date his death at Camlann to 537 and Camlann could be Birdoswald on Hadrian's Wall. Nennius locates one of his battles in the Caledonian forest, which, if true, would place this particular campaign in the heart of Southern Pictland, and it is possible to see Arthur as one of the commanders primarily responsible for checking Pictish and Scottish advances. His alleged connection with what is now southern England (with South Cadbury, for example, or Cornwall) is much more tenuous.

In the 580s and 590s one of the principal warriors among the North Britons is said by Nennius to have been Urbgen (or Urien), lord of Rheged, in Taliesin's words 'Golden King of the North'. By this date the main antagonists to the North Britons were the Angles of Northumbria. Established in Yorkshire or Deira from the fifth century, a new Anglian spearhead under Ida struck inland from Bamburgh and Lindisfarne in the mid-sixth century to establish the kingdom of Bernicia (which ultimately became part of Northumbria). It was against the successors of Ida in Bernicia that Urbgen led a great North British coalition, including Rhydderch, king of Strathclyde (afterwards remembered as the patron of St Kentigern). Urbgen was slain during a subsequent siege of the Angles on Lindisfarne by a rival British leader, Morcant, ostensibly one of his allies and perhaps a king of the Galloway area. The death of Urbgen appears to have been followed by widespread disintegration of the British kingdoms of the north. Under the attack of a succession of very able kings of Northumbria, drawn primarily from Bernicia, the major British states, with the exception of Strathclyde, collapsed. The Votadini counter-attacked only to be defeated at Catraeth (Catterick), a catastrophe comparable perhaps to the calamity which befell the Scots at Flodden many centuries later. The epic British poem describing the disaster at Catraeth is known as the *Gododdin* of Aneirin. Even Aedán, king of Dalriada, was defeated in 604 when he came to the aid of the Britons. In 638 the Northumbrians captured Edinburgh and in 642 Stirling. At the same time the Bernician royal family seems to have acquired Rheged by a diplomatic marriage. In this tremendous upheaval many Britons evidently fled south into Wales and hence the earliest Welsh literature is dominated by 'the men of the North', as they were known, and recalled the deeds of Arthur, Rhydderch and Urbgen and many others, not least Merlin. Later, in the romances of the Middle Ages, Melrose, for example, became Mons Dolorosus; the homeland of Tristan was Loenois (Lothian); and Carlisle appeared as one of Arthur's great courts. The legend lingered on and, though the reality was probably grim, the magic has not yet entirely lost its spell.

With no fundamental linguistic differences and not least because of the western seaways, the Britons of Wales were able to maintain contact with the Britons of Strathclyde. A stray stanza in the *Gododdin* records the defeat and slaying in 642 of Domnall Brecc, King of Dalriada, by the Strathclyde Britons, and the Welsh annals show that events in Strathclyde might occasionally be recorded in Wales down into the early eleventh century.

Moreover, Anglian settlement across North Britain was, with the exception of East Lothian, probably not very intensive, certainly not in the further western regions. In Galloway and Dumfriesshire the pockets of densest settlement were in the vicinities of Whithorn and Hoddom. The seventh-century Northumbrian palace, with timber halls and other buildings enclosed with a palisade, at Yeavering in the Cheviots, was in the centre of a British complex. An apparently British hall, recently excavated near Dunbar, together with a subsequent Anglian hall on the same site, both with structural features related to the Yeavering buildings, suggests that the craftsmen at Yeavering drew in part on native British tradition. In this connection it is interesting that Rhun, son of Urbgen, may have worked as a missionary in the vicinity of Yeavering in the 620s. A rectangular timber hall, 55ft by 18ft, of undoubted British construction and dating to the sixth or seventh centuries, has recently been excavated at Kirkconnel in Dumfriesshire. Early Anglian colonisation in the border counties was essentially in the valleys and of limited proportions. Such linear earthwork defensive constructions as the Catrail in Roxburghshire or the De'il's Dyke in Dumfriesshire and Ayrshire may have been British attempts to restrict settlement and expansion. Moreover, across most of this area there survived a rural economy and a social pattern similar if not virtually identical in kind to that in Wales and Scotland. Taxes were traditionally levied in cattle; and pastoral, semi-agricultural settlements depended for survival on summer grazings away from the house dwellings. This is a fundamental aspect of agrarian development in North Britain which has really only begun to be explored in the light of later medieval documents. The evidence would certainly indicate, however, that the Angles failed to colonise this region intensively enough to obliterate Celtic custom. Perhaps a situation again prevailed here as on the eve of the Roman Conquest in which an older population and society survived but under the dominance of a minority alien aristocracy.

The cultural development of much of North Britain under Northumbrian domination was shaped by this Anglian élite. Examples of early British monumental sculptural art survive from Whithorn, but Anglian styles of sculpture and ornamentation, characterised essentially by the animated vine-scroll, dominate from Nithsdale and Hoddom to Abercorn on the Forth. Anglian sculpture is pre-eminently represented, of course, in the famous crosses of Ruthwell in Dumfriesshire and Bewcastle in Cumberland, with their naturalistic Mediterranean figures and their Northumbrian decorative motifs. It always seems odd that these masterpieces should be on the borders of Northumbria, but perhaps major works elsewhere in more developed areas have been destroyed. It is not easy to delineate any evolving British strand among the surviving monuments of North Britain. It may be that much British monumental art has been destroyed, or perhaps the Britons mainly drew on the artistic ideas of neighbouring peoples. Apart perhaps from the odd fragments with interlace decoration not particularly Anglian in character, the sculptured stones of Govan, for example, an important British artistic centre on the lower Clyde, all date to after AD 900 and draw essentially on late Pictish or Anglian traditions with some Scandinavian (Viking) influence. The so-called 'disc-faced' or 'disc-headed' crosses of Galloway also belong to this age and are moulded by Irish and Viking styles, while south of the Solway, in the Lake District, at the same period, are some pure Viking pieces and the Scandinavian impact is dominant. Artistic links between these crosses of the Lake District and Galloway suggest contact by sea, cutting out the Solway basin and apparently placing that region for a time rather on the fringe of developments.

What made possible the cultural dominance of Northumbria was, not unexpectedly, the influence of the Northumbrian Church. The Synod of Whitby (664) by no means obliterated the formative Dalriadic influence on Northumbrian ecclesiastical life which retained a Celtic element that could accommodate itself to the administration of North Britain. Though the later medieval cathedral appears to have destroyed all traces of Ninian's foundation at Whithorn, Abercorn on the Forth, which was a Northumbrian bishopric from 681 to 685 for the temporarily subject Picts, was of Irish appearance and design and consisted basically of a large, roughly oval, enclosure. Whithorn was established as a see for the Britons of Galloway around 720 and survived as such into the ninth century. There were ecclesiastical contacts between the Northumbrians and the Picts and between the Northumbrians and the Scots, and the Northumbrians were instrumental in bringing the Picts and the Scots to an acceptance of the Roman Easter in the early eighth century. But on the Strathclyde Britons they could not prevail. It was not until 768 that the Britons in Wales accepted the Roman Easter. The date of Strathclyde's acceptance is unknown. In fact, very little as yet is known about the church in Strathclyde. Only with the appointment and consecration of Bishop John in 1114–18 does a see at Glasgow clearly emerge.

The Northumbrian scholar Bede wrote in 731 that, though the Picts and the Scots were then at peace with the Angles, for the most part the Britons who were not under Northumbrian control opposed them through inbred hatred. These would be the Britons of the kingdom of Strathclyde. Feelings ran high on both sides. In 786 visiting papal legates to Northumbria reprimanded the Angles for adopting British fashions of dress, thereby imitating in this way the life of those whom they had always detested. For a time, in the 670s, the Britons of Strathclyde, together with the Picts and the Scots, had been under military subjection to the Northumbrians but this overlordship was ended when the Northumbrians were defeated by the Picts in 685 at Nechtansmere (Dunnichen). Bridei, King of the Picts, the man responsible for the victory at Nechtansmere, was a son of Bile, formerly King of Strathclyde. The Strathclyde Britons for long played a significant part in the power politics of the north. It was the Strathclyde Britons under King Teudebur who defeated the seemingly invincible Pictish King Oengus in 750; and it was necessary for Oengus to ally with the Northumbrians to avenge this insult. The Northumbrians annexed the plain of Kyle in Ayrshire, however, and it is likely that Dalriadic Scots were migrating into British territory before Kenneth mac Alpin conquered the Picts. A daughter of Kenneth mac Alpin married Run, the son of Artgal, King of Strathclyde, and Run's son, Eochaid, was joint King of the Scots from 878 to 889 with Giric son of Dungal.

This reversal to the Pictish principle of succession through the mother is strange. Perhaps Constantine I, son of Kenneth, had such a danger to the male line in mind when he was responsible for the slaying of King Artgal in 872. By no means all the names of the kings of Strathclyde in this period are known. The only dynastic pedigree to survive from Strathclyde is that which traces the ancestry of Run, son of Artgal, back through Teudebur and Bile to Ceretic.

One early Irish writer described the capture of York in Northumbria by the Vikings in 866 as the beginning of great suffering and misfortune for the Britons. In 870 Dumbarton was indeed captured by the Vikings after a siege of four months and its riches and countless captives taken away. On the whole, however, Strathclyde itself seems to have been on the sideline of Viking movements. It must have been the Britons particularly of what is now south-west Scotland who suffered most. As late as 875 the bishop of Lindisfarne and his community were in the vicinity of Whithorn, attempting unsuccessfully to obtain a crossing into Ireland and greater safety. They returned to Bernicia and established their bishopric first at Chester-le-Street and then in 990 at Durham. But after 875 a darkness falls on Galloway which is primarily illuminated by the evidence of place-names. These reveal that from around 900 onwards Norse settlers were striking into this region from south of the Solway, together with Irish-speaking immigrants from Ireland known as the *Gall-ghaedhil* (foreign Gael) who gave their name to Galloway. There must have been quite a ferment. If the archaeologist could wish for some of the Dumbarton riches of 870, so the historian could wish for a detailed contemporary account of what was happening in Galloway and Dumfriesshire in the early tenth century. On the one hand, Viking art is conspicuous. On the other, a dynasty, which seems to have been predominantly Irish, must have established itself, for in 1034 is recorded the death of Suibne, son of Kenneth, King of the Galwegians. In addition, the tenth and eleventh centuries, again judging from the evidence of place-names, witnessed a British resurgence both in Galloway and Dumfriesshire and in the Lake District, south of the Solway, suggesting that Britons were also moving into these areas from Strathclyde and colonising afresh among the Vikings and the Irish. And, finally, there were the Scots.

Galloway was not to come securely under the control of the Scottish kings until the 1160s, but the threat to Strathclyde and the Lake District from the successors of Kenneth mac Alpin was more immediate. The MacAlpin kings had conquered what had been southern Pictland in the mid-ninth century but it is doubtful if they exercised any real authority north of the Mounth, over Moray. They therefore looked southwards for expansion. By the reign of Indulf (954–62), Edinburgh had been reoccupied. Further territory in Lothian was ceded to Kenneth II around 973 and in 1018 the Scots, probably under the personal leadership of Malcolm II, won a great victory over the Bernicians at Carham on the Tweed which established the Tweed as the new frontier. Northumbrian Angles north of the Tweed would either flee south or become absorbed within the Scottish kingdom. Malcolm's successors repeatedly tried to advance further. Duncan I, his grandson, carried out an abortive attack on Durham, not long before he was slain in Moray in 1040 by Macbeth. Duncan's son, Malcolm III (1057–93), who was able to make capital out of the Saxon resistance to the Normans in the north after the battle of Hastings, ravaged as far south as the Tees and the Cleveland hills. But no permanent success was ever achieved beyond the Tweed, not even by David I or William the Lion. A similar process of territorial expansion went on in the west and it was this which affected Strathclyde.

The native ruling family of Strathclyde may not even have survived the death, between 900 and 943, of Donald, King of the Britons, for his successor is named as Donald, son of Aed, in all probability the brother of the reigning king of the Scots, Constantine II, son of Aed. If the medieval chronicler John of Fordun is to be trusted at this point, Donald was succeeded by his son Owen, and in this way Strathclyde passed under the control of an offshoot of the Scottish dynasty. In 945, in an attempt to obtain a peace settlement with the Scots, Edmund, King of Wessex, granted Cumbria to Malcolm I, King of the Scots, on condition that Malcolm become his helper by land and sea. But what was ceded? Cumbria, from *Cumbri* (fellow-countrymen), was a name which could be applied to Strathclyde. Indeed, the British language of this whole region is known to linguists as 'Cumbric'. Strathclyde and Cumbria, in fact, were used interchangeably. Now in 945 Edmund had recently sustained a

serious onslaught from the Vikings at York and had only just managed to push his way northwards; he can have been in no position
to cede the valley of the Clyde to the king of the Scots, whose
kinsmen were probably in a strong position there already. Edmund
must have granted land south of the Solway, in modern Cumberland. The boundaries of this Lakeland province appear to have
been the Rerecross on Stainmoor and the River Duddon to the
south. This would be a strategic area for intercepting Viking communications between Ireland and Man, Galloway and Yorkshire.
It was later Scottish tradition that heirs-apparent to the Scottish
kingdom were given British territory to govern. The descendants
of Owen for their part did not press their claims to the MacAlpin
kingship but hostility was latent. In 971 Culen, King of the Scots,
was slain, probably at Abington, by Rhydderch, brother of Donald,
son of Owen, King of Strathclyde. The two families were demonstrably drifting apart. When the heirs-apparent of the MacAlpin
kings were sent to reign among the Britons, therefore, they must
have gone elsewhere than to Strathclyde proper, and the likelihood
is that they went to the British lands south of the Solway. The last
king of Strathclyde was probably Owen the Bald, son of Donald.
When he died in 1015, this particular branch of the MacAlpin
family, which had been making Strathclyde their own, evidently
died out or failed to maintain itself. It was in consequence probably
the whole British area of Strathclyde, as well as the lands south of
the Solway, which Malcolm II granted to his intended heir, Duncan;
and it is significant corroboration of this general extension of
Scottish influence into British territories that Malcolm III, son of
Duncan, is styled in a twelfth-century Anglo-Norman chronicle,
frequently using older material, as 'son of the king of the Cumbrians'.
Moreover, Gaelic place-names in Strathclyde, some representing
settled, others pastoral, communities, appear to go back long before
1015 and spread steadily outwards across Lothian. Early Scottish
settlement of this area was of quite significant proportions.

The arrangement with King Edmund afforded the Scots a very
desirable footing south of the Solway, and helps to explain their
eagerness to acquire land along the east coast, possibly to the Tees.
To have successfully annexed all this territory would have created
a very different Scotland from that which did emerge. Had this

southern land been permanently acquired, there might have been no determined drive by later Scottish kings to assert their authority over Moray and the Gaelic uplands. It was the repulse from England which threw the Scottish kings back at the Highland massif. The new Norman knights were like storm-troopers, for whom neither the Saxons, the Welsh, nor the Scots were a match. In 1092 William II (Rufus), King of England, came north to Carlisle and fixed the Solway as his northern boundary. Again, like the Tweed, this line of demarcation was never to be effectively challenged. The next year Malcolm III perished in a skirmish at Alnwick. The Scottish kingdom plunged into civil war to emerge under the sons of Malcolm and Margaret insecure at home and under embarrassing vassalage abroad to the Norman kings of England. The sons of Margaret were still lords of Cumbria above the Solway before succeeding as kings of the Scots, and it was the introduction of feudal tenure and the creation of a territorial diocese at Glasgow by David as earl of Cumbria in the period 1107–24 which opened up this British region, before any other part of Scotland, to the impact of Norman French society.

Archaeological advances are greatly extending our knowledge of the early British church in North Britain or in what is now southern Scotland. The science of place-name study is revealing, ever more clearly, the movements of peoples and the origin of incoming settlers. The historical records take us some way towards reconstructing the essentially dynastic history of Strathclyde. But we need to know much more about the later history of the church in these British areas from the eighth to the eleventh centuries, and much more about the secular and material culture of the Britons before we can fully appreciate the significance of native Scottish influence on the general development of the region that was to become the launch-pad for the introduction of feudalism into medieval Scotland. Here, in fieldwork and topographical survey, as throughout all Scotland, the enthusiasm of local societies, in co-operation with the technical skills of archaeologists, historical geographers and historians, can make a very real and vital contribution.

CHAPTER 5

THE EARLY CHRISTIAN CHURCH

Charles Thomas

CHRISTIANITY, seen as one of several Mediterranean religions introduced to Britain in Roman times rather than as the revelation of divine truth, began to affect Scotland at a comparatively late phase, and its initial progress there was slow. This does not impute any special strength to heathendom, in this case the polytheistic beliefs surviving from later prehistory. It is more likely to reflect the difficult internal communications and sparsely populated state of the country, two conditions inimical to the rapid diffusion of any new idea.

The profound changes in Scottish life between (say) Calgacus and the Caledonians in the first century AD, and Queen Margaret and her circle in the eleventh, could be attributed to a variety of factors – some demographic, others political or even climatic. The contribution of Christianity to this process, here as elsewhere, is most readily detected in the sphere of literacy, language, craftsmanship and the social order. Despite the relative paucity of documentation, we can nonetheless reconstruct in rough outline the story of Scotland in Early Christian times, since much of it can be inferred from the evidence of archaeology and the history of art. In this chapter, a personal version of such a reconstruction will be offered, but in the guise of historical narrative, not as a disjointed catalogue of archaeological details.

The first individual Christians in Scotland may very probably have been legionaries, auxiliaries or camp-followers from the eastern provinces of the Roman Empire, as early as the second century. As individuals, they have left no trace. Our story properly commences a little later, around the close of the fourth century, and in the person of Scotland's first saint, Ninian. The earliest record of

Ninian of Whithorn (whose real name was perhaps Niniavus) occurs in Bede's great *Ecclesiastical History* early in the eighth century; and the passage has to be appreciated in its true context. A little before 700, the Angles of Northumbria – that vigorous and gifted people to whom Bede himself belonged – had pushed their kingdom westwards across what are now Dumfries and Galloway. They had therefore acquired in the process several existing religious centres, including Whithorn in Wigtownshire. Bede is retailing a tradition then current at Whithorn (where the community might well have included British, Anglian and even Irish brethren) which he would have received from some such correspondent as Pecthelm, the Anglian bishop. Bede tells us that 'Nynia' was a Briton, a bishop who had been regularly instructed in the faith 'at Rome' (in the Roman manner?), and that he had built at Whithorn a church of stone called, in Latin, *Ad Candidam Casam*, 'At the White House'. This church and the bishop's see were named in honour of St Martin. While modern students discount any direct connection with Martin of Tours, who died in the 390s, the general ambience of Ninian's career as portrayed in two later sources – a narrative miracle poem of the late eighth century and Ailred of Rievaulx's life in the twelfth – would support a late fourth-century date.

Was this the first Christian settlement in Scotland? Why should it have been at Whithorn? Archaeology provides partial answers. The long coastal shelf of Dumfries and Galloway, as the distributions of Roman coins and small finds now show, was increasingly inhabited during the Roman centuries by people conversant with Roman material culture. Expansion westwards into this fertile tract from the great border settlement at Carlisle, and refugees from the major barbarian assaults on Hadrian's Wall and its hinterland, might be among the explanations for a pattern which looks like more than merely the outcome of trade. Recent excavations below the east end of Whithorn Priory church revealed, under the medieval burials and infill and under still-earlier burials of the Anglian period, the crushed remnants of an east–west long cist cemetery of Early Christian character, itself apparently having disturbed cremations associated with Romano-British pottery. A native, part-Romanised settlement at Whithorn in the third century, embracing Christianity during the fourth, petitioning for its own bishop (from Carlisle?) late in that century, and being supplied (from the same source?) with Ninian, who constructed his original church in the now-Christian local burial ground, is a hypothesis which would accord with these slender archaeological and historical clues.

During the next two centuries, almost all our evidence for any Christian life (or death) is drawn from south of the Forth–Clyde line, in the form of inscribed memorial tombstones. These can be very approximately dated by the style of the Roman capital lettering, by the evolution of a basic Christian motif called the *chi-rho* (anagram of the first two Greek capital letters of *Christos*, 'The Anointed One', like our modern letter X with a P superimposed on it), and by precise linguistic forms of some British Celtic personal names. The distribution shows us a rather leisurely spread from south to north – from the later fifth century in the Rinns and Whithorn, to the beginning of the seventh just south of the Forth – and at least one such stone, that at Yarrowkirk which names two local princes, implies a measure of success in converting the ruling families of the region.

What kind of church organisation does this indicate? Ninian was a bishop. A stone from Kirkmadrine in the Rinns of G a l l o w a y names two *sacerdotes* – literally 'priests' but at this period equally translatable as 'bishops' – and two more from the Peebles area, one long since lost and known to us only from a medieval report, actually mention *episcopi* or 'bishops'. We sense the force of Bede's remark that, as he puts it, Ninian had been 'regularly instructed'. This is a diocesan and episcopal church, like the Church of Rome, and later, the Episcopal Church in Scotland. One might take a further, tentative step and suggest from the groupings of these early memorials, as well as from early traditions and place-names attached to selected churches, that diocesan areas did exist at this stage. If so, there is some general correspondence to what we believe to have been the secular tribal areas, by now the post-Roman kingdoms of North Britain – Strathclyde, Gododdin, Rheged, and in the long basin of the Tweed a lost kingdom which may underlie the Bernicia of Anglian Northumbria.

North of the Forth–Clyde line, some at least of the Picts may have been introduced to Christianity; even if we now find it hard to credit unreservedly Bede's statement that the southern Picts (the

Picts living south of Aberdeen and the Mounth) had been converted by Ninian in person, harder still to accept more recent views which would make Ninian a peripatetic missionary roaming as far afield as the Moray Firth and the Northern Isles. On the eastern coast, the ascertained distribution of large lay cemeteries containing oriented long cist graves, a few of which are demonstrably sixth century and the majority of which are certainly Christian, spreads north of the Lothians around the coast of Fife and the mouth of the Tay. Are these the graveyards of scattered communities of Christian Picts? Was Abernethy, certainly a church site of great antiquity, founded in this context? On the west coast, if we choose to accept that the king Coroticus to whom, about 450, St Patrick of Ireland addressed a minatory epistle was the ruler of Strathclyde with his citadel at Dumbarton Rock, then we must face an implication. Patrick compares the soldiers of Coroticus (who had recently slain or enslaved some Christian converts) with 'the Scots and apostate Picts', that is, with barbarians. If 'apostate' here means anything stronger than just 'un-Christian', it implies backsliding from a notionally converted state; and this, if located at all, would surely be on the north bank of the Clyde.

In the Glasgow region during the latter part of the sixth century we encounter our second realistic figure, Kentigern or Mungo, today mainly remembered as the patron of Glasgow's magnificent cathedral. There is no cause to reject the entry in a somewhat later North British chronicle, the *Annales Cambriae*, that notes the death of Conthigirn(us) under the year 612. In the medieval life of the saint by Jocelin of Furness, the original graveyard surrounding the first church on the site of St Mungo's is claimed to have been consecrated by St Ninian. If by this we understand 'founded in connection with the diocesan episcopal church stemming from Ninian and Whithorn' I see no real reason to reject this tradition either.

In fifth-century Ireland, the Patrician church, as with the sister church in western Britain (Cumbria, Wales and the south-west), seems to exhibit a diocesan episcopal character. Its links were transmarine, with the church in Gaul, to a lesser extent with Spain, and in some important respects directly with the Mediterranean. At the end of the fifth century, a very different kind of Christian outlook, born in the desert lands around the east Mediterranean, was transmitted to the British Isles. Monks (*monachi*, 'solitaries') – in the sense of individual Christians who had taken personal vows of poverty or chastity or solitude – formed an early feature of Christian life. Communities of such monks sharing a communal existence with components of work, worship, prayer, education and missionary activity grew partly out of enforced retreat to the deserts in the face of Roman persecution (before AD 313), and partly – notably as the movement's popularity gained ground – out of complex reactions to the worldliness of the church under the later empire. In such monasteries, the abbot and not the bishop was ruler, and provision for lay Christians was not on planned territorial lines. A diocesan structure involving bishops who controlled defined diocesan areas from fixed urban sees became increasingly irrelevant to those adhering to monastic ideals.

It is now highly doubtful whether full monasticism, inspired by St Martin of Tours' two pioneer establishments in north-west Gaul, did first take root in British soil at Whithorn in the late fourth century. Whithorn does appear to have become a conventional monastery by Bede's day, but this change can be ascribed to Irish Christian activity in Galloway two centuries after Ninian. The small building whose restored foundations protrude from below the east end of Whithorn Priory is much more likely to have originated as a subsidiary monastic chapel in the seventh century than to represent Ninian's supposed 'church of stone'. Monasticism possesses its own distinctive field-archaeology, absent from earlier Whithorn, as it is also absent from Ireland during the fifth century. Where approximate dates can be supplied for the archaeological traces of our first monastic establishments, such dates are won with difficulty from fragments of wheel-made pottery from the Mediterranean imported alongside the fresh ideas of monasticism itself. On this score we detect, not surprisingly, a sea-borne spread from south to north. The earliest datable foundation (about 480 to 500) seems to be Tintagel on the north Cornish coast. Scarcely later are those on the south Welsh coast. A few decades later, we find monasteries in Ireland, particularly the Irish midland plain and its river-system extensions.

The picture is complicated by a non-religious factor, that of internal migrations and new colonies which took shape, in both Britain and Ireland, during the third to seventh centuries. Irish groups were settling in areas like Pembroke and Argyll, where new dynasties were founded. Friction between the incomers and existing populations must have been related to the availability of desirable land and to densities of settlement.

The settlement in western Scotland – historically of interest because the extra-national name of the Irish colonists (*Scotti*) later became applied to the whole region – must be seen in terms of migration in strength, late in the fifth century. It sprang from what is now Ulster. It was from this province also that Columba or Columcille, an aristocratic recruit to the first age of insular monasticism, was drawn. By the middle of the sixth century, the Dalriadic settlers (as they are known) in Argyll may have contained in their ranks descendants of Irish families first converted in Patrick's day; we do not know this, but it was in part to provide a religious focus for the settlement that Columba (born about 521) and his companions founded their monastery on Iona in AD 563.

While by no means the only extension of Irish monasticism to the Irish colonies – and we tend to overlook St Moluoc at Lismore, and later St Maelrubha at Applecross, to say nothing of less distinct figures working in west central and south-west Scotland – Iona was unquestionably the most influential. We possess a stylised *Life of Columba* written about 690, a century after Columba's death in 597, by Adomnan, the ninth abbot of Iona. A continuous connection was maintained with Ireland, whither indeed (at Kells, County Meath) the Iona community returned during the Norse onslaughts of the early ninth century. There was a close relationship with the Dalriadic ruling houses, as well as external contact with royal circles in Pictland and Northumbria. Finally, the founder himself was, at various times, the subject of widespread cults involving church dedications, relics, and devotional literature.

We can fairly say, then, that Christianity in the far west and north of Scotland (including the western and northern isles) stems in the main from 563 and later. Archaeologically it is represented by a typical monastic church, with enclosed monasteries of varying size on islands, promontories and high ground; with isolated enclosed chapelries and cemeteries; with a huge series of grave-markers, cross-marked slabs, free-standing crosses and pillars; and with all the minor material culture of a missionary church.

While most natives would have been British speakers of ultimate prehistoric origin, ranging socially in far-flung communities from the descendants of prosperous broch-centred farmers to crofters and fishers at bare subsistence level, the Irish clerics and their parties would have encountered – probably in Skye, certainly in Orkney and Shetland – Pictish settlers spreading out from north-east Scotland. The Christian missionaries apparently contacted Orkney from the late sixth century, with Shetland somewhat later than this. At the height of the fashion for *deserta* and really isolated asceticism, many small islets hardly capable of supporting life were pressed into service as hermitages; still other Irish brethren sailed across near-Arctic seas as far as Faroe and Iceland, if not indeed further.

The conversion of the Picts, the political centre of whose loosely strung kingdom was in Columba's time near Inverness, is historically ill-defined. Overlooking for the minute any earlier contacts between the church of St Ninian's day and the Picts in Fife, or Dunbartonshire, we do possess Adomnan's record of visits undertaken by Columba to the Pictish king, Bridei, and to districts 'across the ridge of Britain'. In the next hundred and fifty years, it is likely that Christianity spread slowly through Pictland on lines similar to those that we infer for the western seaboard, but we have no direct information; nor, in that extensive region south of the Moray Firth and north of the Tay, has the field-work necessary to establish the appropriate sites of such a missionary church yet been undertaken.

Northumbria, in the early seventh century, comprised two regions or sub-kingdoms – Bernicia in the north, and Deira in roughly part of Yorkshire. Dynastic quarrels had led to the exile of some Bernician princes, in Pictland or among the Irish settlers in Argyll. Oswald, who returned to unite the realm after a notable victory at Heavenfield (by Hadrian's Wall), must during the years 617 to 634 have had much contact with the Irish monastic mission. He spoke Old Irish, was presumably baptised, and may even have stayed at Iona. In 635, he resuscitated the spark of Christianity in Northumbria, of which more below, by inviting Aidan, an Irish monk from Iona, to act as bishop and to found a new monastery at Lindisfarne (Holy Island). The repercussions of this move went far beyond the following thirty years of Irish-type Christianity in this northern English kingdom.

In 597, St Augustine and his small mission, with the blessing of Pope Gregory the Great, had landed in Kent with the aim of converting the pagan English. Gregory's elaborate scheme for the division of the country into two provinces, Canterbury and York, with subordinate dioceses and an independent bishopric at London was not in the event immediately realisable. Outside the relatively civilised kingdom of Kent, the only early extension took place as a result of a Christian Kentish princess marrying Edwin of Northumbria. The accompanying Christian entourage, headed by Paulinus, did succeed in baptising Edwin on Easter Day in 627, in supervising a mass baptism of the Deirans, and in building various churches; but Edwin's untimely death in battle a few years later and the pagan devastation which ensued virtually extinguished this little candle. When Christianity came again to Northumbria, it did so through Bernicia, not Deira, and not primarily as a diocesan episcopal church on orthodox Roman lines. There was a strong, perhaps dominant, element of monasticism derived from the western world of the ascetic and scholarly Irish church.

In lowland England, the 'regular' Roman church of the fourth century, as far as we can detect with its hierarchy and structure in line with imperial practice, was almost entirely erased by the Anglo-Saxon settlements during the fifth century. Gregory and Augustine, through their mission, sought to re-establish this link with the metropolitan heartland. Success was eventually to crown their efforts, and we recall that the present constitution of the Church of England is broadly on this Gregorian model. In the powerful and brilliant Northumbria of the seventh century, however, it was not until the decisions of the Synod of Whitby in 663 (or 664) had been taken that the Northumbrian church turned finally towards Rome, the continent, and in the direction of medieval Europe.

This is relevant to Scotland, particularly the Lowlands, about which it can be said that Edinburgh has been an English-speaking centre since the seventh century. Between 635 and 663, and probably later, whatever remained of the old Ninianic Christian province in the south of Scotland had been enriched by a variety of new monasteries within the ambit of Lindisfarne. In the case of at least two – Old Melrose in a bend of the Tweed, Abercorn just west of Edinburgh – it may be significant that these retained their British place-names throughout, instead of being given English ones (like Hexham, Jarrow, Whitby or Monkwearmouth). Were these two like Whithorn the diocesan churches of sub-Roman times?

The full circle of Irish influence, ecclesiastical contact and borrowings between Northumbria and Pictland, was not closed until a century later. There were certain procedural divergences between the Roman church, which stemmed continuously from the age of the apostles and the early Mediterranean centuries, and the so-called Celtic church, that early offshoot leaning towards monasticism and surviving in much of Ireland and parts of north and west Britain. Apart from such minor questions as the shapes of clerical tonsures, the number of bishops needed regularly to consecrate a new bishop, and the method of computing annually the date of Easter, there was the wider problem of the status of bishops – in Celtic lay eyes not necessarily as important as abbots, and within the monasteries often subordinate to abbots who were not themselves also bishops. Bede, writing of Iona, could draw attention to the 'unusual arrangements' current there, in which 'the island has an abbot for ruler who is a priest, to whose authority all the kingdom, including even bishops, must be subject.'

It was, however, the controversy over Easter that influenced the course of the church in Pictland. In 663 or 664, at Whitby, the Northumbrian church moved to the Roman method of computing Easter, and presumably this would have held good within that part of Pictland – Fife, and some uncertain area northward – which from the mid-650s to 685 formed part of the Northumbrian kingdom as a result of conquest. The Pictish church must then, like Oswald's brother Oswiu and his royal wife Eanfled, have had the embarrassment of two distinct dates for Easter according to the way in which these had been reckoned.

In 685, after the notable Pictish victory at Nechtansmere in Angus, the Northumbrians were forced to retreat south of the Forth, abandoning Abercorn and other places. The Pictish church was left to its older parent, the Iona of Columba. About 690, however, Adomnan of Iona (who had twice visited Northumbria and enjoyed much prestige there) accepted the Roman method of computing Easter. Despite difficulties then raised at Iona, where the community did not follow suit until 716, Adomnan's action won over most of the Irish foundations. Around 710, the Picts, as Isabel Henderson has pointed out in a previous chapter, accepted the Roman Easter as well, and as if this were symbolic of entry into the wider world of the Roman church, cast off the ecclesiastical domination of Iona, expelling certain Columban monks. Whatever form the church in Pictland now assumed, and as a kingdom with some kind of tribal substructure it may well have moved in the direction of fixed territorial dioceses retaining monasteries only in distant and isolated areas, we can attach to this post-710 period a new phenomenon. This is the appearance of a very notable strain of artistic endeavour, especially in fine metal-work and relief sculpture, that brings into a single east-coast continuum not only Northumbria, Pictland, the far north of Scotland and the northern isles, but also to the south the converted English kingdoms beyond the Humber and (through Northumbria) the continent.

What has now become Scotland, then, on the eve of the first Norse raids and settlements around 800, presents to us a complex and fascinating picture of provincial Christianity – a picture drawn from a number of sources, and one which was built up through a series of fortuitous events. We have noted the fact that Oswald happened to be exiled within reach of Iona; the fact that one church chose to calculate Easter through a nineteen-year equinoctial cycle and another through an eighty-four-year table; the fact that a late Romano-British community at Whithorn was in a position to have its own bishop; and (we could add) the fact that a type of monasticism evolved in the eastern Mediterranean happened to fit into the social structure of Early Christian Ireland rather more readily than urban-centred dioceses. We can attempt a necessarily simplified summary of the position in the late eighth century.

From Galloway and Clyde-mouth, in a long ragged chain right up to the archipelagos of the far north, monasteries of varying importance from Iona downwards still flourished – ruled by abbots, and staffed by brethren of Scottish (that is, Irish), North British, Pictish and even English descent. One might cite such cases as Whithorn itself, Kingarth in Bute, probably Govan, Iona, Lismore, Applecross, Birsay and Deerness in Orkney, and Papil in Shetland. Not all are known and fewer still are explored. A multitude of much smaller 'eremitic monasteries', with bare handfuls of

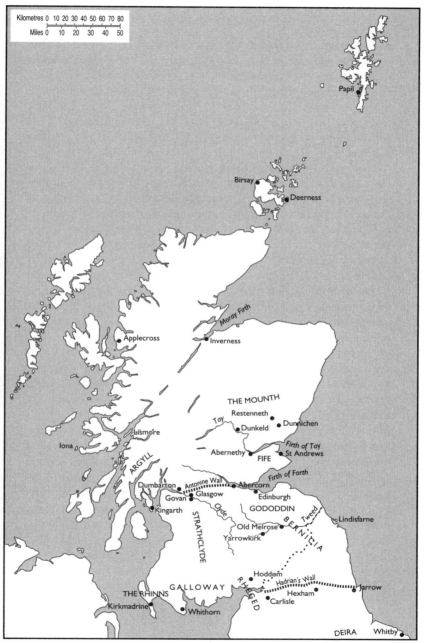

Figure 10 Early Christian centres

monks, have to be added, together with isolated hermitages, the equivalent of mission stations in the shape of enclosed cemeteries with cells for clerics, and perhaps even the counterpart of later domestic chapels for ruling families. There is still no firm evidence that this remnant of western Christianity was, except in a very wide way, diocesan, and the old monastic *paruchia* (roughly, the enforceable sphere of influence of a given major monastery) may have been the practical unit.

Over most of Scotland, nonetheless, north of the Forth and Clyde, the church in Pictland is seen to be moving closer to regular episcopal foci (such as Abernethy, St Andrews, and perhaps Dunkeld) and to a corresponding diocesan structure. In southern Scotland, we see but the northern aspect of that portion of the English church connected with now-enlarged Northumbria; with some rearrangement of its dioceses, but since the Synod of Whitby closely in line with the continent. To the west, that long-lived North British kingdom of Strathclyde, whose religious side found expression later still as the medieval diocese of Glasgow, alone has some claim to more or less continuous status, through the chair of Kentigern, from Ninianic times.

There are of course gaps in this picture. The Christian history and archaeology of disturbingly extensive areas (for example, Ayrshire, or the north-west beyond Argyll) is still hardly known. Nor was this a static picture. As with every other known church, maturity had brought its own problems, and earlier in the eighth century Bede had given hints of the need for reform in many ways. Asceticism would always possess some peculiar hold on the Celtic mind and the Culdee movement represented a peculiarly lasting offshoot from Columban days and the first wave of monastic customs. In 795, Norse devastation commenced at Iona; internally, the Scots and the Picts were being nudged by historical currents towards a form of unity, attained first during the stormy reign of Kenneth mac Alpin in the middle of the ninth century. The church in Northumbria was itself an obvious target for Viking plunder, nowhere more so than in such exposed places as coastal Lindisfarne. Iona, despite Kenneth mac Alpin's adherence to the cult of Columba (he himself was buried there, and the Relig Oran graveyard seems first to have taken shape as a sacred enclosure on this occasion), entered a period of decline. Whithorn at the end of the ninth century became a momentary refuge for the monks of Lindisfarne who were attempting to flee to Ireland. It was on this occasion that the Lindisfarne Gospels, immersed in their shipwreck, were miraculously cast up on a beach near Whithorn; but after this, Whithorn too fades into obscurity, not relieved until the see was revived in the early twelfth century.

Above all, perhaps, we get the impression that in Scotland we have a clear case of the story of Christianity being in large measure inseparable from the country's political and social history. Despite our sadly inadequate knowledge of the parts played by individuals in this development, the impression is as true of Scotland between the Romans and the Vikings as it is of more recent centuries in Scottish history. The archaeology of this period, largely dominated by the remains of Christianity, is rich, exciting, informative and only imperfectly explored; further work cannot fail to throw much light on contemporary Ireland, Pictland and northern England. Of those names that we do know, Columba for sure, and one would like to think Ninian as well, must be placed besides Patrick and Augustine as Christian figures of destiny.

CHAPTER 6

THE NORSEMEN
David M. Wilson

THERE is to this day a community of taste and spirit between Scotland and Norway which must owe its origin to the geographical situation of Scotland in relation to the western seaboard of Scandinavia. Lerwick, in Shetland, is as close to Bergen as it is to Aberdeen and, ever since the Viking Age, there has been constant traffic between Norway and the mainland of Shetland – an island which forms the first of a series of stepping-stones which trace the path from the north to Scotland and to the Irish Sea. While there are minimal traces of Scottish–Scandinavian contacts before the Viking Age, such connections are not adequately documented until the Norsemen arrived to raid and settle the rich lands to the south.

The foreign activities of the Norsemen were many and varied; their Scottish adventure was but one facet of their kaleidoscopic career in most of the known world in the years between, say, 790 and 1080. In the east, Swedish traders reached towards Baghdad, while in the west Danish kings felt strong enough to face the military might of the empire of Charlemagne, and Norwegians sailed the Atlantic, discovering America, Iceland and Greenland and settling with greater or lesser success in most of the North Atlantic islands. The Scottish career of the Norsemen was merely a prolonged and varied episode in a complicated series of manoeuvrings in which the Scandinavians sought to gain riches or political power outside their own country. The story of the Norsemen in Scotland cannot be taken in isolation: reference must continually be made to events both in Scandinavia and in other western countries.

The evidence on which this story is based is often difficult to evaluate. Although this is a historical period, and written sources are available, some of these sources are more reliable than others. Their quality naturally varies in a period of 300 years. In the ninth century, for instance, contemporary British sources are often very

1 Ring of Brodgar, Orkney

2 Broch of Mousa, Shetland

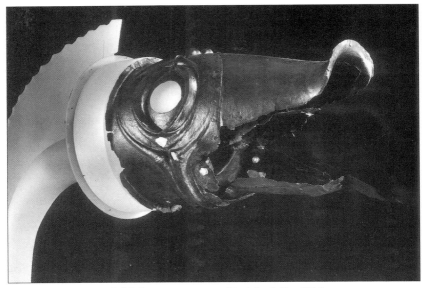

3 Celtic bronze trumpet, Deskford, Banffshire

4 Roman distance-slab, Hutcheson Hill, Glasgow

5 opposite and below
*Pictish symbol stones
at Glamis manse and
Aberlemno churchyard*

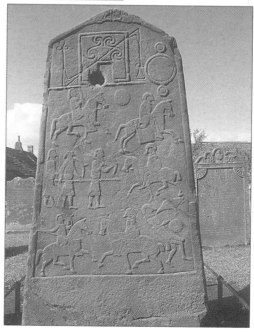

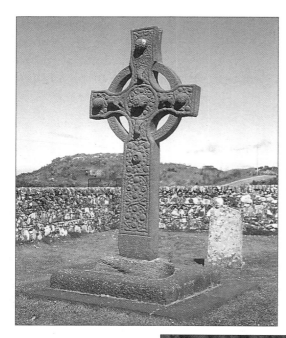

10 *Kildalton Cross, Islay*

11 *Anglican Panel (detail) from Jedburgh Abbey*

12 Mote of Urr, Kirkcudbrightshire

13 Part of Norse settlement, Jarlshof, Shetland

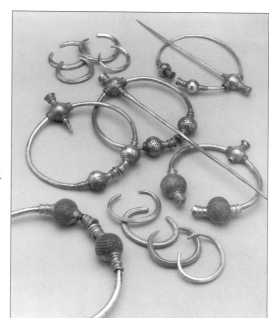

14 *Viking hoard,
Skaill, Orkney*

15 *Norman church, Leuchers, Fife*

16 *Dirleton Castle, East Lothian*

17 *Caerlaverock Castle, Dumfriesshire*

18 (a) Bute or Bannatyne mazer

18 (b) Detail of the Bute mazer

19 Lochindorb Castle, Morayshire

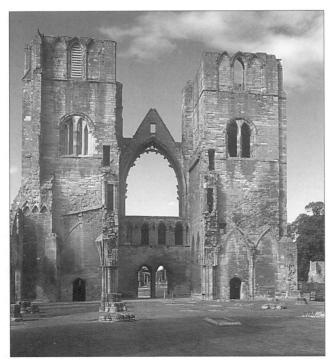

*20 Elgin
Cathedral,
Morayshire*

21 Tomb of the Wolf of Badenoch in Dunkeld Cathedral

22 Threave Castle, Kirkcudbrightshire

Dine bernard stuart Lord vsobeny eftoffier capitaine et Conmendur generalt de Narmee de Charles Roy de france quant il ailla de Napoli

23 *Sir Bernard Stewart, Lord d'Aubigny*

24 *James III – early portrait coin*

25 Angel figures playing
musical instruments,
Rosslyn Chapel, Midlothian

26 James IV
(Mytens' copy of a
contemporary
portrait)

27 Andrew Myllar's
printing device

one-sided: if we are to believe the *Annals of Ulster*, for example, the most important late eighth- and early ninth-century attacks on Scotland were those on the Christian monastery at Iona which was founded by St Columba. The annalists (probably because an Iona chronicle was used as a source by the Irish annalists) omit all references to attacks and settlements in the islands and in the northern areas of Scotland, attacks which we know from other sources to have taken place. It is unfortunate that, until the very end of the Viking Age, there are few Scottish historical sources for the Norse activities, while the Scandinavian sources (of which the most important is undoubtedly the *Saga of the Orkneys*) were mostly written down long after the events which they record, and must often be treated as less than reliable. Careful evaluation of the historical material – Anglo-Saxon, Irish, Scottish and Scandinavian – enables us, however, to build up an outline against which evidence from other fields of study can be laid. Two other disciplines – the study of place-names and archaeology – provide the only other major sources for the Norse settlements of Scotland. The former is, in Scotland, in an embryonic stage and the latter is extremely one-sided – only six major Norse settlement sites, for example, have been thoroughly excavated in Scotland (two in Shetland, three in Orkney and one in Caithness), whereas the sites of more than fifty graves or cemeteries have been recovered from the Norse areas of the country.

The reasons for Norse activity in Scotland were diverse and obscured by lack of evidence. Basically, however, two traits can be discerned; first the acquisition of movable wealth which could be taken back to the homeland and, second, the acquisition of land for settlement. Neither must be over-emphasised and both could be carried on by one man in the course of his lifetime; in the *Saga of the Laxdalers*, for example, Ketil Flatnose said that 'he preferred to go west across the sea to Scotland because, he said, he thought the living was good there. He knew the country well, for he had raided there extensively.'

The raiding activities of which Ketil spoke can occasionally be revealed by archaeology, both in Scotland and in Scandinavia. In Scandinavia, objects of Scottish manufacture found in ninth-century graves reflect in some cases the raids of the first Vikings. It is sometimes difficult to distinguish between Irish and Scottish metal-work; but a number of Pictish brooches, for example, of the same form as those found in the St Ninian's Isle treasure, have been uncovered in ninth-century Norwegian graves and tell of Viking adventures overseas. In Scotland the graves of the Norse raiders and traders tell of the early years of their appearance in this country, while the hoards of treasure reflect the story of their 300-year period of high influence. The St Ninian's Isle hoard, buried in the last years of the eighth century or in the early years of the ninth century, was presumably one of the earliest treasures hidden against the initial Norse onslaught. Like such hoards as those from Croy in Inverness-shire and Rogart in Sutherland, it was probably hidden by a Pictish family at the time of a threatened attack and never reclaimed because of the death or captivity of the original owners.

The later hoards (hoards like that from Skaill in Orkney, which contained a large number of silver penannular brooches, as well as coins which date its deposition to about 950) may well represent the family treasure of a settler in the new lands who fell victim to some internecine Norse quarrel of a type often recounted in the Scandinavian sources. Nearly thirty hoards of the Viking Age have been found in Scotland, but the vast majority belong to the latter category, and probably only about three to the St Ninian's Isle group. The hoards, however, indicate the troubled nature of the times and by their distribution show the areas that most interested the Scandinavians – namely the northern and western islands, the west coast and the most northerly counties of the Scottish mainland.

A similar and perhaps more significant pattern is demonstrated by the distribution of Norse graves in Scotland. These are all found within the same area and no graves are found on the east coast south of the Moray Firth, with the exception of a single burial at Errol in Perthshire. Examination of Norse place-names has shown a like distribution and indicates clearly that the Scandinavian settlers never permanently penetrated the rich heart of Pictland – the area that became the kernel of the Scottish kingdom after the Dalriadic Scottish king, Kenneth mac Alpin, with the aid of Norse relatives and friends from the west and from Dublin, conquered the remains

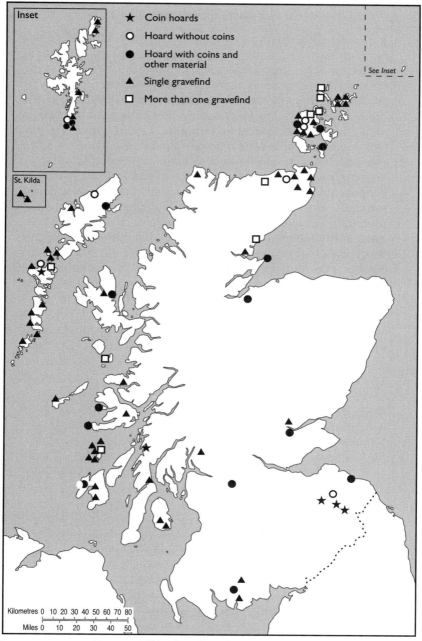

Figure 11 Viking hoards and graves in Scotland

of the Pictish kingdom in a long series of campaigns in the mid-ninth century.

The graves have an added interest in that their contents show the type of people who came from Scandinavia to die in Scotland. The objects found in the burials show that they represent the first hundred years of the Norse presence and, although the vast majority are male graves containing weapons, a good number are the graves of women who wore Scandinavian fashions. The Norsemen, then, were already confident enough in the early ninth century to begin to bring their women to Scotland and to settle the new lands permanently. Most of the graves are found singly: cemeteries are rare and only at Pierowall on the Orkney Island of Westray has a substantial cemetery been recognised (seventeen graves have been established from existing records; perhaps twice that number have been uncovered at the site since the eighteenth century). No Scottish grave can be dated to the tenth century and we may assume that, as elsewhere in the Norse areas of Britain, the settlers gradually adopted Christianity and eschewed their ancient pagan customs of which the most obtrusive archaeologically was the rite of burial with grave-goods. There is a hint at one or two sites, particularly at Ackergill (where one of the graves in a cemetery contained a chain of Norse type), that the Norse adopted the cist-grave inhumation rite of the native population and also respected Christian burial places – a feature which is paralleled, for example, in the Isle of Man. At a much later date – in the eleventh century – a few grave-stones decorated with Scandinavian ornament were set up (examples have been found at Kibar on Barra and at Dòid Mhàiri, Port Ellen, Islay); such monuments are, however, very uncommon. From such material it is clear that already in the ninth century the Norsemen were settled in the areas which they held until the collapse of Norwegian power in Scotland.

There are many indications that they were willing to adopt features from their new country. Although they brought their own law, they were willing to adopt a new religion, Christianity, and even early in the Norse period we have seen how they adopted and respected Christian burial practices. In minor things they were also influenced by local conditions: although they brought their own women with them they soon adopted local fashion in dress; the

British ring-headed pin, for instance, is a common dress-fastener in Scottish Norse graves.

Norse settlement sites are also found but it is hard to generalise concerning them as most of the finds are from the northern isles or the northernmost counties. Excavations currently being conducted in North Uist and elsewhere are producing definite evidence of Scandinavian settlement in the Western Isles. Although a number of sites in this area have been identified in the past as Norse, the North Uist is the first to provide more than a hint of Scandinavian influence. On the other hand, a site in Shetland, romantically named Jarlshof by Sir Walter Scott, provides us with one of the most completely excavated Scandinavian settlements in the west Norse world.

Like its Norwegian and Icelandic counterparts, Jarlshof is a large farm (villages were apparently rare in Norse areas at this period) and is set on the edge of a bay with a gently shelving beach (ideally suited for drawing up ships) on the southern tip of the mainland of Shetland. The site has a long history, for it was continuously occupied from the seventh century BC until the last house to be built there was sacked by the notorious Earl Patrick Stewart in 1609. Excavations of a desultory sort were carried out at the site during the early years of this century, but systematic excavation was not started until the 1930s and by the time the site was completely cleared, shortly after the Second World War, a considerable complex of buildings of Viking Age date had been uncovered.

Basically the Viking Age site was a single farm. In its earliest phase (dated to the first half of the ninth century by the excavator, the farm consisted of a long dwelling-house, 70ft by 20ft, with slightly bowed sides divided into two rooms and with a central hearth in the main room, the hall. At some distance from the house were a series of byres and other ancillary buildings, all enclosed by a boundary wall which survived from the pre-Viking Age settlement of the site. The house is adequately paralleled in other Atlantic communities – in Iceland, for example, or in Greenland – and was presumably the house of a reasonably wealthy family. That the family became more prosperous is indicated by the gradual development of the farm over the next 400 years; the buildings being added to or repaired and the whole dwelling-house being ultimately replaced by a completely new structure, until, in the final phase, an elaborate house and a number of outbuildings were clustered together and surrounded by the tumble-down ruins of earlier structures.

The farm was self-supporting and the excavator has suggested that, from a pastoral–agricultural economy in the early phases of the settlement, fishing began to play a more dominant role in the eleventh century, for line- and net-sinkers are found in some numbers in the later period of the Norse farm. A certain number of exotic objects of Scandinavian or Scottish origin were found in the course of the excavations, but the vast majority of the large number of finds reflect the humdrum round of everyday life – cooking pots of soapstone, querns, sickle blades, pins, spindle whorls for spinning and so on. The great quantity of soapstone on the site reflects a major industry of the Viking Age, for, at a period when the rest of Europe was using pottery, people of the western Scandinavian areas made elaborate vessels from soapstone. Traces of a soapstone quarry, in which the cores of soapstone bowls are still to be seen in the living rock, have been recognised some fifteen miles north of Jarlshof at Cunningsburgh, and it is possible that some of the objects quarried here found their way to Jarlshof and even further afield.

Objects made of soapstone are also found in great quantities at the only other Norse settlement so far excavated in Shetland – Underhoull on Unst, the most northerly island of the archipelago. This farm seems to have been built in the early ninth century on the site of a pre-existing settlement, and may well have survived for two or more centuries. The main building consisted of at least two rooms in a longhouse rather smaller than that at Jarlshof (measuring 55ft by 15ft). Although the site was by no means as rich in finds as Jarlshof, its size and situation, near to the shore in a small bay in Lunda Wick, together with the fact that it is situated on the edge of one of the most fertile areas in Unst, would suggest that the family who farmed here were reasonably substantial farmers even though they may not have had the wealth or social position of their Jarlshof contemporaries.

Farms of comparable status have also been excavated at three other sites in Scotland: at Skaill in Deerness and at Aikerness in

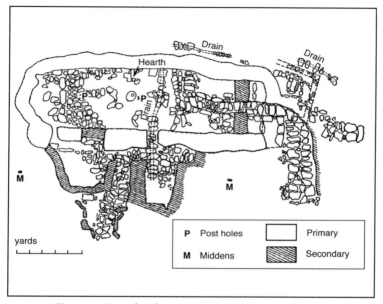

Figure 12 Norse longhouse at Underhoull, Unst, Shetland

Orkney, as well as at Freswick in Caithness. But the most important settlement site other than Jarlshof is the great complex of structures on Birsay, a tidal islet off the north-west tip of the Mainland of Orkney. Here, on the site of an early Christian monastery, was established a farm which ultimately grew into a complex establishment consisting at one time of the palace of Earl Thorfinn (who died there in 1065) and later of the palace and cathedral of the bishop of Orkney. The site was finally downgraded when the new cathedral in Kirkwall received the shrine of its patron saint, St Magnus, from Birsay in the middle of the twelfth century. By then the earl was already living in his castle in Kirkwall and, although the bishop retained a major house on the mainland opposite the islet of Birsay, he too was soon to move nearer to his cathedral. With a few insignificant exceptions no building took place on the site after 1200 and the work of archaeologists has revealed an unique series of buildings, both secular and lay, which span the whole of the Norse period.

Unfortunately, the finds from the site have not been published and a discussion of the excavation is only available in a most summary form so that any description can only convey a rough idea of the building sequence. On the slope above the foundations of the stone-built cathedral, outside the area recognised as the bishop's palace and a little to the south of it, are preserved today two houses exactly equivalent to those found at Jarlshof and elsewhere; the excavator has implied that they formed part of a complex of a ninth-century farm. If this is the case, it is interesting that the settlers respected the site of the pre-existing church (we know it is a church from various inscribed and decorated Pictish stones); perhaps they buried their dead in the cemetery alongside the bodies of the previous owners; whether such be the case or not the church preserved its identity and it ultimately became the site of the cathedral of the diocese. Here can be seen that respect for sacred places, even if they were not of the pagan Norse religion, which has been noticed earlier and which is an outstanding feature both in Scotland and in other lands settled by Scandinavian invaders. The new church was endowed in the middle of the eleventh century by Earl Thorfinn the Mighty on his return from a pilgrimage to Rome. A range of buildings, together with the church, form a square courtyard partially surrounded by a cemetery. These buildings – which may be interpreted as the bishop's palace – seem to have been built in the twelfth century. A major building complex to the east, partly collapsed into the sea, may represent the remains of the earl's house, for we know that Earl Thorfinn, for example, spent a good deal of time here. The interpretation of the various buildings on the site – some of which are large and very impressive – is a matter of controversy, but two large halls have been tentatively identified.

Birsay is a splendid memorial to the wealth of the Orkney earldom in the period of Norse rule; but other uninvestigated sites, such as that at Westness on Rousay, may yet reveal impressive buildings – at least as large as those found at Birsay. Birsay is the only place in the Norse world where a semi-royal and episcopal complex survives. Gardar in Greenland provides us with the only comparable episcopal site so far excavated.

No site remotely resembling Birsay has been found on the west

coast of Scotland or in the Western Isles – indeed such sites probably never existed. Iona functioned from time to time as a bishop's
seat during the Norse period, but the cathedral of the diocese was
at Peel in the Isle of Man (the title of the Manx bishopric – Sodor
and Man – to this day enshrines the Norse bishopric, the word
'Sodor' referring to the *Suthreyjar*, the southern isles or Hebrides).
Little of Norse origin remains at Iona other than a runic inscription, the odd grave slab carved in a Scandinavian style and the
graves of a few kings of the Isles. The politics of western Scotland
in the Norse period are complicated, as the area seems to have been
under the nominal control of different people at different times, the
King of Dublin, the King of Man and the Earl of Orkney being the
chief contenders for the overlordship of the area. We may presume
that there were grand houses – even royal houses, like that of Somerled of Argyll – in the area, but they have never been identified
archaeologically and even more humble Norse dwellings have not
been recognised. We have seen how the graves and hoards demonstrate a firm Scandinavian presence in the west and there seems little
reason to doubt the strategic importance of this area in relation to
the important mercantile route between Norway and Dublin. The
settlers of the islands and of the west coast and their descendants
controlled this major trade artery and drew their wealth from it.

The Viking Age proper is considered as finished by the end of
the eleventh century, but Norwegian political power continued in
various parts of Scotland until much later. The Hebrides – with
Man – were abandoned to the Scottish crown as late as 1266. The
northern isles were officially Norwegian for an even longer period.
Orkney was pledged to the Scottish crown for 50,000 Rhenish florins
in 1468 as part of the cash dowry of Margaret, daughter of Christian
I and wife of James III; while in 1469, in connection with the same
marriage, Shetland was pledged for 8,000 florins. Neither pledge
was redeemed. But long before any of these events people who
lived in areas which had once been under Scandinavian control
considered themselves as Hebridean, as Shetlanders or as men of
Argyll, not as Norsemen; they hardly considered themselves as
Scots – many of them to this day are, for example, Orcadians first
and Scots second. In Shetland the view is expressed that all that ever
came from Scotland was 'dear meal and greedy ministers'.

It is in Orkney and Shetland that the Scandinavian element in Scotland's make-up is still seen to this day. Not because there are a large number of huge blond 'Vikings' in these islands – this well-fostered image seems ludicrous even to the casual observer – but there are many minor contacts. An Orkney drifter's skipper will listen to the Norwegian weather forecast – in Norwegian. Scots-women are often met with in west-coast fisher communities in Norway, married out of Kirkwall or Scalloway. A Norwegian lifeboat is stationed in Lerwick and there are Norwegian consulates in the islands. If one digs deeper one finds more fundamental traces of Scandinavian contact: the ancient Norse 'udal' law of the northern isles is still occasionally upheld in the Scottish courts and the names of tools and fishing equipment have a Scandinavian ring. Until 250 years ago a language – Norn – was spoken in the northern isles which was basically a Scandinavian tongue.

For Scotland as a whole, however, the traces of Scandinavian influence can easily be explained by the geographical setting of the two areas on the edge of the Atlantic. Place-names, loan words and church dedications are the only real survivals of the Viking Age. Other features are no more significant of an 800-year-old contact than is the presence of an Icelandic consul in present-day Edinburgh. Those who would argue to the contrary can only be accused of romanticism.

CHAPTER 7

ANGLO-FRENCH INFLUENCES
G. W. S. Barrow

MACBETH, the warrior king who nevertheless found time to journey to Rome and 'scatter his money like seed to the poor', brought the first Norman knights to Scotland. Refugees from the Anglo-Welsh border country, they fought for Macbeth at the Battle of Dunsinnan Hill (1054) and were cut down by the king's rival and supplanter, Malcolm Canmore, and his Northumbrian allies. The Scots cannot have been much impressed by these newcomers, with their hauberks and war-trained horses, any more than were the Irish by the sight of their first Norman invaders a century later: 'ninety heroes dressed in mail, and the Gaels put little store by them'. The Scots learned their mistake sooner, though not quicker, than the Irish. Already in 1072 King Malcolm had met the greatest of all the Normans, William the Conqueror, at the ancient Pictish centre of Abernethy on the Tay, only a few miles south of the spot where Osbern 'surnamed Pentecost' and Hugh and their unnamed fellow-Normans had been slain. There, in the presence of the great host William had brought from the south, the King of Scots bowed to the duke of the Normans – now five years king of conquered England – and became his vassal. There was no Scottish Hastings, and the Normans attempted neither to dislodge the native dynasty nor to take over the country. But from 1072 until the death of the last of the Conqueror's sons in 1135 the kings of Scotland danced for the most part to the Normans' tune.

The ascendancy of the Normans from 1050 to 1150 was a European phenomenon which has never been satisfactorily explained. In the course of this century the Normans had made themselves practically the equal of the kings of France in their own small duchy and actually masters of Sicily, southern Italy, England, Scotland and much of Wales, and they had played a decisive part in the great Frankish push into the Near East and the lands of the old Roman

Empire based on Byzantium. Within another thirty years they had added Ireland to their list of conquests. Scotland might have been conquered and overrun by them, as befell England; penetrated piecemeal with a long series of conquests in miniature, as happened in Wales; or half-conquered, without full assimilation, as proved to be the fate of Ireland. In any event, Scotland could never ignore the Normans, nor be ignored by them. But what in fact occurred was not complete conquest, nor piecemeal conquest, nor half-conquest. Through the dynasty of Malcolm Canmore (which was able to hold the Scottish throne almost without a break from 1058 to 1290), Scotland came to terms with the Normans. It is true that they were in the ascendant politically and militarily for ninety years (1124–1214); but it was an ascendancy under the crown, a crown which never completely ceased, even in its most 'Normanised' phase (1153–1200), to be responsive to native custom and native political institutions. Consequently, Scotland was never brought permanently within the ambit of a continental empire (the fifteen years' explicit overlordship of Henry of Anjou, 1174–89, was not typical), nor did French ever become the universal official language, as it did, for example, in England. All through the twelfth and thirteenth centuries the real linguistic struggle in the Scottish kingdom was not against French but between the two principal native vernaculars, a form of northern English ('Scots'), which eventually won, and a form of Irish ('Scottish Gaelic'), which eventually lost. It is noticeable that when in the late thirteenth and early fourteenth centuries the Scots government wished to correspond with the French government they wrote in Latin; only when communicating with the English government did they have recourse to French, or what passed for French south of the border.

When we use the name 'Normandy' we call to mind the pleasantly rolling, well-wooded, apple-growing, dairying duchy on either side of the lower Seine, stretching westward to take in the fertile Côtentin peninsula. When we think of 'Normans', however, the image is of grim stone *donjons* and brutal mailed knights. The contrast forms one of the unresolved paradoxes of history. Perhaps we should reflect that Normandy, while rich enough to support the fierce military aristocracy implanted there by the Viking invasions, was yet not so rich that its people – especially its younger sons, trained for war from childhood – had no incentive to venture forth in search of land and fortune. The Norman expansion was merely part of a general outward migration from the provinces of the north-western Franks – northern Burgundy, Lorraine, Flanders, Picardy, Normandy itself, Maine, Anjou, Poitou and even Brittany, Celtic in speech and custom but politically dominated by the Norman duke. A trickle of men from these regions was perhaps beginning to enter Scotland before the death of Malcolm Canmore in 1093. His long reign of thirty-five years had seen a strengthening of Scottish links first with the Scandinavians of the far north (Malcolm's first queen was the widow of an earl of Orkney) and then, more significantly, with the Anglo-Saxon kingdom to the south.

It was in 1068 that extraordinary accidents of history had brought to the shores of Malcolm's kingdom as a political refugee, Edgar the Atheling ('heir'), the legitimate pretender to the English throne whose hopes had been dashed by the Norman Conquest, and his sister Margaret. Although they had been born and brought up far away in Hungary and their experience of England had been confined to a few years, they represented in the eyes of countless Englishmen the prestige and the lawful succession of the old West Saxon dynasty. Soon after they had fled to Scotland King Malcolm married Margaret as his second wife. This proved to be a momentous match, though not in terms of Anglo-French influence, for Margaret's Englishness was somewhat remote and there was almost nothing Norman or Frankish about her ancestry or background.

Queen Margaret was one of those meteoric characters of history who leave their mark regardless of patterns and trends. The fact that her marriage with Malcolm Canmore brought about an increase in Anglo-French influences in Scotland was mainly the accidental result of her ambition to rescue the Scots from what she considered to be their woeful ignorance and barbarity – not for nothing had she been brought up in Hungary in the generation after Saint Stephen had christianised the previously pagan Magyars. She herself was obviously regarded popularly as a saint long before her formal canonisation (1249). She provided that the main Forth ferry – the Queensferry as it was called in her honour – should be free for poor pilgrims, and she brought Benedictine monks, the first to be established in Scotland, from Canterbury to a new church at Dunfermline, which her youngest grandson King David I afterwards enlarged and promoted as Dunfermline Abbey. Margaret died in 1093 soon after hearing the news of her husband's death.

Almost as soon as King Malcolm and his Hungarian queen were dead, the Scots revolted against this foreign immigration (small-scale though it must surely have been), and would only allow Malcolm's heir, Duncan II, to keep the throne if he promised to introduce no more Normans or Englishmen to perform military service for him. Again one may see the close parallel with Ireland a century later, where Dermot Mac Murrough, King of Leinster, who had brought in the first Normans, was made – in vain – to promise not to bring in any more and to repatriate those he had brought as soon as possible. The anti-foreign reaction lasted for only three years. In 1097, Edgar, Duncan II's half-brother, gained the throne with the support of troops supplied by William Rufus, the Conqueror's son. Unmarried, Edgar was succeeded in turn by his two younger brothers Alexander I and David I. This remarkable span of sixty years during which the crown was held by a single generation gave stability to Scottish royal government in a crucial period when powerful and rapacious Norman kings of England might well have been tempted to dismember or even swallow up the smaller and much weaker northern kingdom. Norman penetration of Scotland began in earnest in the time of the three brothers Edgar, Alexander and David. It became particularly intensive under David I (1124–53), two whole generations after the Norman conquest of England. David held wide estates in the English midlands (the 'Honour of Huntingdon'), so that he had many ready-made Norman vassals, tenants by knight-service who would be glad of the chance to add to their lands and would expect to hold estates newly acquired in Scotland by the same military service which they were used to in England. This Norman penetration of Scotland took an outward and visible form about which we know a good deal. It also had a more inward, invisible effect which can hardly be traced at the time it was happening, but which can be seen through its ultimate results in medieval Scottish society.

The visible normanisation consisted of the settlement of powerful Anglo-Norman and Anglo-Breton and Anglo-Flemish barons, with their accompanying knights and servants, in the country between the Cheviots and the Clyde–Forth line, with a handful of outlyers in Fife and even in Moray, which fell into David I's direct possession in 1130. In Strathclyde and the south-west generally (save for Galloway and Nithsdale) David seems to have granted out existing territorial units of government or lordship, perhaps in some cases former petty principalities resembling the cantreds and commotes of Wales. In the east, in Lothian, Berwickshire, Tweeddale and Teviotdale, the incoming Normans seem to have been given smaller estates resembling more closely the manors of midland and northern England. The barons would hold their new lands by knight-service, and one of their first tasks would be to compel the inhabitants to build the earthwork and timber castles of the 'motte-and-bailey' type – 'motes' as the Scots soon learned to call them and still would if the Ordnance Survey and archaeologists had not taught them otherwise. One of the most splendid examples in southern Scotland is the great Mote of Urr (Kirkcudbrightshire), built probably for Walter of Berkeley, chamberlain to King William the Lion, not long after 1165. More typically these motes were fairly small structures, shaped like Christmas puddings, scores of which may still be seen, scattered widely across the Scottish countryside, especially in the south. Good examples, close to main roads, are on the golf course at Carnwath in Lanarkshire (a castle of the de Somervilles since David I's time), at Duffus in Moray (surmounted by a later stone tower), and at Inverurie, at the confluence of Urie and Don, where King William the Lion's brother David built the 'Bass of Inverurie' as his motte castle probably in the 1180s.

In southern Scotland before 1153 the pattern of Norman settlement was thus mainly determined by grants from the king of sizeable blocks of royal demesne in favour of military vassals, most of whom came from the Scottish king's English lands. Robert de Brus (Bruce) was given Annandale for ten knights' service; Ranulf de Sules (Soulis) Liddesdale; Hugh de Morville – King David's constable – Cunningham and Lauderdale; Robert Avenel: Eskdale. These families came originally from western Normandy, had benefited in a small way from the Norman Conquest of England and now gained much more land and power as 're-exports' to Scotland. Brix (whence Bruce) and Morville are near Cherbourg,

Soulles (whence Soulis) is near St Lô. Some other famous families introduced under David I clearly had a Norman origin, but it is not always easy to give them a location south of the Channel. One family prominent on the Honour of Huntingdon had already, by the early twelfth century, taken its surname of Lindsey – Lindsay – from the largest division of Lincolnshire, where they were lords, under the earls of Chester, of the rich manor of Fordington. Lindsay is thus an English name, but the family's earliest known forenames, Baldric, Walter, William and Drogo, point unmistakably to a Norman origin, at least on the paternal side.

Men from far afield, with no ties of tenure, were also drawn to Scotland by King David's generous patronage. From Shropshire, for example, came Walter, younger son of a Breton named Alan son of Flaald who had been highly favoured by Henry I. Walter son of Alan joined King David's service about 1136 and was made steward – chief officer of the household. He was also given the lordships of Renfrew and North Kyle (Walter's Kyle) in Ayrshire. It was probably also the king who arranged a marriage for Walter with a lady named Eschina of London. Doubtless Eschina was a 'Norman' on her father's side, but through her mother she was apparently the granddaughter of a member of the ancient Northumbrian aristocracy of the border country, Uhtred son of Liulf lord of Mow. Walter and Eschina were ancestors of the Stewarts, a long and still-continuing line: their direct descendant in the sixth generation took the Scottish throne in 1371 as King Robert II. Walter himself was typical enough of the continental settlers of good family who were favoured by David I: not in fact Norman, but the younger son of a man who had acquired lands in several parts of England in the wake of the Norman Conquest. And of course Walter brought with him in his train a whole group of followers, knights, esquires, serjeants, archers and household servants, with their womenfolk, many of whom settled on lands provided by their lord in what later became the counties of Ayr and Renfrew. Among them was one Richard Wallace (*Walensis*, 'the Welshman'), a castle-garrison serjeant in Shropshire, who has probably left his Christian name in the Ayrshire parish of Riccarton, 'Richard's village'. We shall never know whether Richard's family were called 'Welsh' because, though Normans, they lived among the Welsh in Shropshire, or because they really were Welsh but had adopted the Anglo-Norman way of life. The Wallaces prospered in the great Stewart fief of south-west Scotland, and William Wallace, a younger son of a cadet branch of the family established at Elderslie in Paisley, has given the surname an immortality equal to that of the Stewarts themselves. Even the grandfather of Walter son of Alan, the dimly obscure Flaald from Dol in Brittany, has won his own kind of immortality as the equally dim Fleance of Shakespeare's *Macbeth*.

The beginnings of the great Scottish house of Stewart may be seen as a microcosm of the whole era of Norman settlement and colonisation in Scotland. The king grants high office and rich lands to the head of the new family, who in turn settles his followers in lesser fiefs, many to be held by military service. As part of the process castles are built, religious houses and hospitals are founded and endowed, parish churches established or enriched, and trading towns or 'burghs' are planted and given the necessary municipal and trading privileges. All of this can be seen going forward in the time of the first Stewart, Walter son of Alan (*c.* 1136–77) and his son and successor Alan (1177–1204). Walter built – or received from the king – the first castle of Renfrew, and probably built another at Dundonald. Paisley Priory – afterwards Abbey – was founded in 1163 for Cluniac monks from Much Wenlock in Shropshire, chiefly in honour of Saint James the Great whose shrine at Compostella was then approaching the height of its renown. (It was only later that the ancient local cult of Saint Mirren of Paisley reasserted itself.) Walter also founded a hospital for lepers at Morriston in Berwickshire and contributed to the endowments of St Peter's Hospital in York, as well as to famous Scottish abbeys of royal foundation at Kelso and Melrose. His son and grandson, Alan and Walter II, continued these benefactions and made other gifts to monasteries and churches further afield – Coupar Angus Abbey, Canterbury Cathedral (in honour of Thomas the Martyr) and the well-known pilgrimage church of the Holy Rood at Bromholm in Norfolk, whose mother-house at Castle Acre had been befriended by their forebear Alan son of Flaald. As for towns, Renfrew began as a royal burgh and after passing into the Stewart's possession may have been rather over-shadowed by Rutherglen and Glasgow. Nevertheless, it seems to have enjoyed a modest prosperity, and the same is true of the family's other burgh, Prestwick in Ayrshire, which kept its ancient constitution for many centuries. Of the towns which grew up on the Stewarts' estates, it seems likely that Paisley flourished most vigorously from an early date, but rather surprisingly it did not become a burgh until 1488.

If this first phase of 'Norman' settlement in Scotland, always and rightly associated with David I, had been the whole story, we should still have to recognise it as a formative influence on our history. It had, after all, familiarised the Scots with the feudal system of landholding which is still the basis of Scottish land law; it had brought new forms of government by means of royal castles and burghs, sheriffs, justiciars and knight-service baronies; it had established contacts between Scotland and the latest currents of intellectual and religious life pervading western Christendom in the twelfth century; it had, above all, given added strength and a new direction to the ancient Scottish kingship and thus in a real sense created, or at least made possible, the medieval Scottish kingdom which endured till 1638 despite the shock of Flodden and the strains set up by the Reformation and the union of the Scottish and English crowns in 1603.

But when King David died, an old man, at Carlisle in May 1153, a second and even more thoroughgoing phase of Anglo-French influence was yet to come. From 1153 to 1214 the throne was held by two of David's grandsons, Malcolm the Maiden and William the Lion. Unlike their grandfather, who had no Norman blood, Malcolm and William were the sons of a Norman mother, Ada de Varenne, herself descended from a Capetian king of France. They were strongly imbued with the prevailing ideals of the Frankish world to which they were obviously proud to belong. This was a world of professionalised knightly warfare, of chivalry, of courtly love and *chansons de geste*. It was also a world in which a passionate and often tender Christian faith could sometimes be qualified by an uncertainty as to whether Christ was inspiring raw barbarian warriors to find room in their hearts for Christian love, for compassion towards the poor and the sick and protectiveness towards women and children, or whether, on the contrary, Christ was being enlisted within an order of knighthood which for all its Christian invocations displayed strong features of Germanic paganism.

It was not just that Anglo-French influences were intensified under these francophile rulers. They were also spread much more widely across the Scottish kingdom. Knights' fees were created in Galloway and Nithsdale (untouched by David I), and, with more permanent effect, north of the Forth, in Fife and Gowrie, in Angus and Mearns, in Aberdeenshire and Moray, and even as far north as Sutherland. Settlers were encouraged to come not only from the English estates of the Scottish kings (a reservoir which may have begun to dry up), but also direct from Normandy, from over-populated Flanders, and from almost every part of England, especially Northumberland, Yorkshire, the Welsh borders and Somerset. Under Malcolm IV's direction Clydesdale was feudalised with a colony of Flemish adventurers who have given their personal names to such places as Houston, Thankerton, Symington, Wiston, Lamington, Roberton – as well as to places not in the Clyde Valley such as Symington in Ayrshire and Lockerbie in Dumfriesshire. One notable family originating in French Flanders, in the region of Béthune, was that of de Quincy. Robert de Quincy first came to Scotland at the end of Malcolm IV's reign. By the time his grandson Roger had died in 1264, the last male representative of the main line of the family, the de Quincys had acquired vast estates in many parts of Scotland, the hereditary constableship and an English earldom. And even though the de Quincys themselves may have left little or no trace on Scottish society, many of the descendants of the men they brought with them – for example the Beatons and Bethunes whose ancestor was one Robert de Béthune, an original companion of Robert de Quincy – must be living in Scotland today or will have gone to form part of the Scottish component in areas of British settlement scattered across the world.

A brief list will show how many famous Scottish surnames would be missing if King Malcolm and King William had not pursued the same policy as their grandfather and with even more vigour: Agnew, Hay, Moubray, Sinclair, Ramsay, Boswell, Landells, Bisset, Menzies, Lovel, Barclay (Berkeley), Vallance (Valognes), Montgomery, Colville, Fraser, Gourlay, Grant, Carvel – these and many others have become thoroughly acclimatised and naturalised in Scotland since the first bearer of the name got a toehold north of the border through the favour of our two 'normanising' kings, of whom a near contemporary said, wrongly and rather unfairly, that 'they held only Frenchmen dear and would never love their own people'. Some families seem to have become naturalised very quickly indeed, so that it is not always easy to trace their continental origin. At first glance it is impossible to see behind the homely Perthshire name of Muschet the Norman village of Montfiquet, near Bayeux, from which came Richard de Montfiquet, the first of the Scots Muschets. Sometimes a Norman surname might be dropped altogether, although this was rare, for the Normans seem to have been proud of their surnames. Two of William the Lion's most prominent knights belonged to a family named de la Kernelle, who must have come from La Carneille near Argentan. While junior branches of the family kept the surname until it emerged as Carvel or Carvill, the senior line, holding the knight's fee of Guthrie in Angus, seem to have taken the name of Guthrie from their lands at an early date. There are several instances where greater families brought lesser ones in their train and yet it has turned out to be the lesser family which has survived and prospered while the greater has dwindled or been extinguished. Thus the de Soules family brought the first Hays and Agnews; the Bissets brought the Grants; and the long extinct family of de Normanville brought the family of de Mesnières or de Meyners, which we now call Menzies. The most startling example of rise and fall is of course provided by the great family of Cumin, Comyn or Cumming. Their Scottish career began when King David I arranged a good match for Richard Cumin, nephew of his chancellor William Cumin (certainly a Norman, but of quite humble origins). By the middle of the thirteenth century the Comyns had become the most powerful baronial clan in Scotland, with enormous estates in Galloway, the Borders, Aberdeenshire and the Highlands, two or three earldoms and a guaranteed place in the king's councils. A hundred years later, mainly because of the family's opposition to Robert the Bruce, there was little left of all this Comyn empire save for the Cummings of Altyre (Moray) and the Cumines of Rattray (Aberdeenshire) who have carried on the family name down to the present.

It would be wrong to think of the age of Anglo-French influence in Scottish history as nothing but a matter of family trees and clan pedigrees, fascinating though these have always been to all Scots.

The structure of Scottish government in the Middle Ages was a unique amalgam, not yet fully explored or understood, in which very diverse elements, Celtic, English, Scandinavian and Frankish, were compounded – in precisely what proportions it may never be possible to determine. But it would be absurd to deny or under-estimate the value and importance of the Frankish or French contribution. The feudalism of Scotland was Norman or Anglo-Norman and the knights' fees and motes had their counterpart in the Scottish setting of some of the Norman-French poetic romances, and in the confident way in which the new settlers renamed Edinburgh Tanebroc or (more romantically, after the Arthurian stories which they had been delighted to adopt) Le Chastel des Pucelles, the 'Maidens' Castle'; Dumbarton 'Chastel de Dounbretaigne'; Roxburgh Castle 'le Marche Mont' (Marchmont); even Carstairs 'Chastel Tarres'. The royal household, at the heart of government, was French in conception: the king attended by his steward, chancellor, chamberlain, butler, constable and marischal, while in the country at large the king's justice was administered by justiciars, a characteristically Norman institution. When Frenchmen began to settle in Scotland in significant numbers, around 1100, they found a king, unanointed and uncrowned, mormaers only slowly becoming earls, clan chiefs called toshachs, a ministerial lesser nobility of thanes (here and there identified with toshachs), hereditary dempsters or judges, secularised abbots and other clergy and a social organisation which was at least partly tribal. This pattern was not changed, still less abolished, overnight. But its archaic Celtic and Anglo-Celtic character was far less prominent by the later thirteenth century than it had been at the start of the twelfth, and the most powerful solvent in the whole process of change was the presence of ideas brought directly or indirectly from the continent, especially from the Frankish territories of northern France.

Nowhere was this more striking than in the church. The very first of the orders of 'reformed' Benedictine monachism to cross the Channel were the monks from Thiron, near Chartres, who came in 1113 to Selkirk and moved fifteen years later to establish their great abbey at Kelso. The Cistercians came to Melrose as early as 1136, while the order was still under the direct influence of Saint

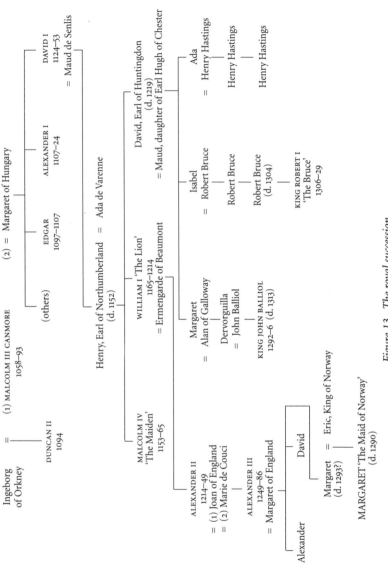

Figure 13   The royal succession

Bernard. The Augustinian canons of Cambuskenneth Abbey (1140) came from Arrouaise in Picardy, those of Jedburgh Abbey (*c.* 1138) probably from Beauvais, while the monks who set up the priories of Beauly west of Inverness and Pluscarden near Elgin, about 1230, came from the remote house of Val des Choux founded in the forest north of Dijon at the end of the twelfth century, and belonged to an order which had daughter-houses only in France and Scotland. The secular clergy also were much influenced by new blood and new brooms from the south. A recognisable diocesan organisation was established and in 1192 brought into immediate dependence upon the papacy. Dozens and scores of parishes were created, and in many cases must have been provided with small stone churches of which so few still remain: Leuchars in Fife and Dalmeny in West Lothian being among the best of the handful of survivors. For a century from *c.* 1130 Anglo-Norman or French bishops predominated in the Scottish church, and one of the last of them, William Malvoisin from the district of Mantes near Paris, ruled the principal Scottish see St Andrews from 1202 to 1238, and probably did more for the unity, discipline and morale of the church of Scotland than any other single bishop of the twelfth or thirteenth centuries.

Anglo-French influences did not make Scotland either an English or a French country, nor the Scots an English or a French nation. They permeated deeply and permanently, so that the Scotland which successfully resisted the onslaught of Edward I and his son was a very different country from that on whose shores Margaret of Hungary, afterwards Saint Margaret, had landed as a refugee in 1068. Yet the inhabitants of Scotland must have retained a basic continuity, and could reject as well as absorb if it suited them. In 1163 Walter, the first Stewart, granted his monks of Paisley Abbey a tenth of the venison from the hinds and does taken locally in what his charter calls *fermeisun*, that is the close season (French, *fermer*) after 11 November, when stags are protected but hinds are not. By the later Middle Ages the monks of Paisley, blithely misreading their founder's charter, were referring to their estates of 'Ferrenes', and today the Fereneze Hills above Barrhead are a reminder of the fact that all influences in history reach, eventually, the point of exhaustion.

CHAPTER 8

THE MAKING OF SCOTLAND

A. A. M. Duncan

O N 15 June 1215, when John, King of England, was among recal-citrant barons at Runnymede, somewhere in Scotland the young king Alexander II – the 'red fox', King John called him – received a welcome gift from one of his barons. For on the death of his father, the aged King William, his enemies had 'entered Moray, namely Donald bán the son of MacWilliam and Kenneth mac Heth, and the son of a certain king of Ireland, with a numerous band of evil-doers. MacTaggart attacked them and mightily overthrew the king's enemies and cut off their heads and presented them as new gifts to the new king . . . And because of this the lord king made him a new knight.' The families of MacWilliam and MacHeth, with a claim the one to the throne, the other to the earldom of Moray, had been thorns in the flesh of the Scottish kings for almost a century, representing the faded vision of a kingdom with strong provincial loyalties, pre-eminently Celtic in language and institutions but nonetheless held and exploited with its dependent Anglo-Saxon provinces south of the Forth by the warrior kings of the royal dynasty – the only kingdom of size and significance in the otherwise frag-mented Celtic world.

This eleventh-century promise had faltered and failed as the twelfth-century kings accepted men from England and France into their service and friendship and French language and culture, pre-eminent throughout Western Europe, into their court. The achievements of this band of incomers discussed in the previous chapter were out of all proportion to their numbers because their way of life was adopted enthusiastically by the native aristocracy everywhere save in the far north. Moray and Ross had yielded consistent support to the dissident MacWilliam and MacHeth families, invading presumably from Ireland, but in the 1180s these rebels had been suppressed with the aid of the men of Galloway under their lord, baptised Lachlan but calling himself by the French euphonym Roland.

About 1210 William Comyn was favoured by the king with the heiress of Buchan as wife and the title of earl, this in time to provide a valuable contingent against the rebels in Moray. In 1228 his son was similarly active and was rewarded with a great lordship in Badenoch and Lochaber with control of Strathspey which had proved a route for the king's enemies as well as his avenging armies. This senior branch, the Red Comyns (from their heraldic colour, while the earls of Buchan, a junior line, were the Black Comyns) established themselves in the mote at Ruthven near Kingussie, and in the second half of the century built the simple stone castles of Lochindorb and Inverlochy and even intruded themselves into Athol, where, much to the annoyance of the earl, they built a castle at Blair. In this way the Grampian massif was, if not controlled, then at least policed, for the king of Scots.

'Celtic' risings continued until the 1230s but that of 1215 with which we began was the last of importance and it was suppressed by a Celtic aristocrat of Ross, MacTaggart – 'son of the priest' – lord of the ancient but laicised Celtic monastery of Applecross. The king who had found the native earls of Dunbar, Fife, Strathearn and of the other southerly provinces apt for assimilation to Anglo-French culture now found himself a more strongly Celtic agent in the home of resistance. His reward was to be made a 'new knight', token of acceptance into the social order of French-speaking chivalry. A few years later the title earl of Ross was conferred upon him, while that of earl of Sutherland was given to a junior branch of the family of Flemish origin which had settled in Moray about 1150 and had taken Moray to be its name. These new earls enjoyed an independence of action attributable to remoteness from the wealthy Lowland zone where the king generally resided. Yet when in 1222 the men of Caithness burned their bishop for his insistence upon his tenth penny it was the king who led an army to kill the ring-leaders, cut hand and foot from eighty bystanders and fine the whole delinquent community. For this offence against God's servant endangered the standing of the whole kingdom and the immortal soul of its king; if he wished, his hand could fall heavily in redemptive punishment upon any part of his realm, however remote.

Or almost so. Only in Argyll had the native aristocracy seemed immune from royal control, while the western isles were part of the Norwegian not the Scottish kingdom. In forty-five years from 1221 to 1266 both passed to Scotland. In 1221–2 the Clyde basin and in 1249 mid-Argyll and Lorn were subdued by naval expeditions. From 1244 the king's aim was to recover the isles from Norway but because of a royal minority (1249–61) the campaign was postponed till 1262 when the Scots invaded Skye from Ross. The Norwegian king's retaliatory expedition in 1263 with its indecisive skirmish at Largs merely made the Scots more determined and by 1265 only the Outer Isles were unconquered; the Norse surrendered them by the treaty of Perth in 1266.

Late in the thirteenth century a map-maker seeking to draw out the 'kingdom of Scotland' would have shown its bounds from Tweed (including Berwick) to Solway, a southerly dip to include Man, the whole mainland and western isles to the Pentland Firth, but not beyond to the northern isles. The Isle of Man passed to England from 1296, and Berwick in effect from the same date; the northern isles became Scottish in 1468–9 but gradually lost their Norse speech from the fourteenth century to the seventeenth. But although all would have agreed that this was the kingdom, our map-maker might well have looked puzzled if we had commented on the inclusion of Man in 'Scotland'.

In the twelfth and earlier centuries Scotland (Scotia) was the land north of the Forth, while to the south lay Lothian on the east coast and Cumbria (alias Strathclyde) on the west. The kingdom took its name from that part which had extended its rule over the rest and 'kingdom of Scotland' certainly included all three parts. But only in the thirteenth century had Scotland come to mean not only the lesser part but also the whole land (and in some spheres the older usage lingered on into the fourteenth century). Moreover if David I and his successors were 'king of Scots', they had inherited this use of 'Scots' from a much earlier age when it meant the men of Scotia; writing of 1216 the Melrose chronicler speaks of Alexander II invading England from Scotland 'with his whole army excepting the Scots from whom he took money' (in place of army service) and of 1217 he speaks even more clearly of 'a general army, namely of English, Scots and Galwegians', where the English are the men of

Lothian. The English certainly did not distinguish in this way – all were Scots – and this limited usage of 'Scots' was perhaps becoming old fashioned. But it is striking how among the many citations of barons, greater men, good men, or army, 'of Scotland' there are to be found so few Scottish examples of 'Scot' or 'Scots' before the troubled times of the 1290s. Men sensed first of all a king and kingdom, and second a land, Scotland, because these could be seen and they had a function in at least the politics of the time. But why unite in one abstraction a wide diversity of languages and ways of life by speaking of the inhabitants of Scotland as 'Scots'? What function did they have in common except obedience? It is not fortuitous that they appear regularly in only one phrase, and in second place there: king of Scots.

One group which had much in common was the wealthy landowners whose cultural affinities were expressed in the building of castles. In the Lowland zone which includes the central belt but also stretches up the east coast, along the Moray Firth and as far north as Dornoch, different styles were employed according to the taste and resources of the builders. At Kildrummy the Earl of Mar, at Dirleton the de Vaux, and at Bothwell the Morays, favoured a strong round donjon with walls of enormous thickness; elsewhere the castle of enceinte, a curtain wall with a large stone gatehouse enclosing a courtyard with (vanished) wooden buildings was perhaps more general than surviving examples (for example Inverlochy, Lochindorb, Mugdock) would suggest. But at least equally numerous is the residence of much more obviously peaceful character, the hall-house, a two- or three-storey stone house with windows and no strong military features (such as Rait or Morton). Now although industrialisation has removed many buildings of these kinds, we have recently come to recognise an increasing number of them, clearly attributable to the thirteenth century. Castles in the north are documented in Easter Ross and Easter Sutherland; in the west they are found in mainland Kintyre, Argyll, Lismore and Mull. From Dunaverty at the Mull of Kintyre to the hall-house at Aros on Mull, and including such a masterpiece as Dunstaffnage and such remote strongholds as Tioram and Mingarry, Argyll is now recognised as a province whose leaders fully deserve their contemporary description of 'barons' as well as the modern one of 'chiefs'. They knew how to demand, and get, the best in prestigious housing and were in no cultural or political backwater. Yet beyond Ardnamurchan point, in Tiree, the small isles, the outer isles, in Skye and on the long ragged coast from Castle Tioram northward, there is no sight of such buildings. There are monasteries in Argyll, but none in the north-west; many recognisable early church buildings in Argyll but few if any beyond. All of which shows that at the highest social level Argyll was part of Scotland in a real sense while the outermost northern and north-western fringe was not. But this common culture was found only at the highest social level. The men of Argyll doubtless retained the pre-eminent social functions of the kindred and its head in the same way as the men of Galloway whose insistence upon their 'liberties' and upon the 'law of Galloway' lasted well into the fourteenth century, resisting the castles, sheriffs and juries foisted on them by the king after the unified lordship of Galloway broke up in 1234. Nonetheless the *Gaidhealtachd* was split into those in Buchan, Strathspey, Athol, Argyll and Galloway whose lords accepted the ways of Lowland Scotland, and those beyond who knew them not. Among the latter Gaelic speech and Norse-derived place-names are still strong; among the former English speech and Gaelic-derived place-names are general. In such ways we betray our forbears.

Moreover, the modern eye which discerns the strength of the castles of the landowning class may mislead the imagination into a notion of 'feudal anarchy'. In fact, as the hall-house suggests, thirteenth-century society was remarkably peaceful. Of royal castles we know most and can recognise that they were built as safe storehouses for wealth and produce, and as intermittent residences often sited for the king's hunting. Men were called to garrison them in time of crisis and the king's agents rode in and out upon his business, but for much of the year their only full-time resident was the castle janitor. Before Scottish independence was compromised in 1291 two crises shook the otherwise peaceful, even sedate, political life of Scotland which these castles ensured. One was a struggle for power among barons during the minority of Alexander III (1249–61) which reveals the existence of those cliques and ambitions which trouble any government when its controlling head, whether thirteenth-century king or modern president, is unable to rule. The immense power of the Comyns under the late king cast them in the role first of reformers of the state (dominated by the ambitious Alan Durward), then of a closed oligarchy swept away in its turn by leading magnates of moderate views. Striking, however, is the reliance of both the Comyns and their opponents upon the help of the English king in bringing about their palace revolutions; to all he was a man to be trusted, with a disinterested concern for a peaceful Scottish kingdom so long as it made no alliance with France. And broadly this Scottish judgement was justified. Yet when Alexander III (who had, we might say, a vested interest in separateness) took over government he is found pursuing a policy of greater independence, buying out an English family which had inherited the constableship and a monastery with English ties. Some English landowners retained major Scottish interests but by the late thirteenth century almost all Scottish barons were conscious of their overriding allegiance to the Scottish king, and the strong tide of Anglo-French cultural influence was on the ebb. Unfortunately among the exceptions were two English barons, holders of wide Scottish estates, Balliol and Bruce (grandfather of King Robert I), upon whom in 1286 and more clearly in 1290, devolved the right to the Scottish throne. These men were almost certainly to blame for selling out the kingdom's independence to Edward I in 1291, but they did so after Bruce had caused years of crisis (1286–90) in which the Scottish barons had again showed themselves trusting of the good intentions of the English king in holding him in check. The treaty which they negotiated, if carried into effect, would have anticipated the union of 1603 by uniting two kingships in the person of one king who would have lived in England.

But the ruling caste in Scotland was no longer French in manners and customs as it had been in 1200. The French romance about his ancestor commissioned by Alan, Lord of Galloway before 1234 had no successors and there is scant evidence of what the aristocracy read. One or two pointers may be significant: there was a recrudescence of interest in the Celtic past, so that an earl of Fife could give the surname Macduff as a forename to his son: showing the interest in things Celtic (and the incomprehension!) of an essentially non-Celtic people. And there was no use in documents of French. In English government and baronial life French was the language of communication but the Scots employed it only to write to England – except for Bruce who thus again betrays his English loyalty. We reason that most Scottish magnates by the late thirteenth century preferred to speak not French but that northern English known as Scots and thereby strengthened social bonds with their English-speaking dependent lairds as well as political understanding with England.

The causes of this change were doubtless complex. Yet undoubtedly of great importance was the commercial and urban development sustained by the great European boom of the twelfth and thirteenth centuries. Expanded population, consumption and production demanded an efficient means of exchange and offered rich profits to any state which exploited its opportunities. Urban privileges were given from the time of David I and a policy of encouraging foreign settlement in the towns was so successful that from Berwick to Inverness or even Dingwall the English tongue filled their streets. Perth, situated at a river crossing and also at the place where the Tay becomes tidal and thus accessible to small sea-going vessels, was at a nodal point of communications. The original town may have lain between the castle and the kirk. But at some time, presumably in the twelfth century, a larger scheme was laid out and Perth became the most important town in Scotland after Berwick. Its institutions like those of other Scottish burghs had English names; the main thoroughfares were known as 'gaits', something to 'gang' along. Like other Scottish towns Perth had a provost, a royal agent, at its head. At Berwick, however, the town grew so prosperous on the wool trade to Flanders that the king (doubtless for a reward) allowed its merchant gild to take over burgh government and Berwick the 'Alexandria of the north', alone of Scottish towns had a mayor, the 'great man' of the gild at its head. Yet because seafaring techniques were rudimentary most European trade was still coastbound, while the great centres of population and markets lay to the south of Scotland. Both these factors effectively bound Scottish trade to use English waters and ports and Scottish commerce was to a large extent an extension of English trade – which strengthened the already pronounced English character of Scottish town life.

Townsfolk were few but their influence great, for they were opportunity to any with a need to buy or sell. They took with them the language of commerce, English, into all their dealings. In Lothian they would find that all spoke English but in Fife, Angus and Gowrie the language of business gradually ousted the languages of the aristocrat, French, and the peasant, Gaelic. By what stages this happened is obscure but the struggle between the two principal

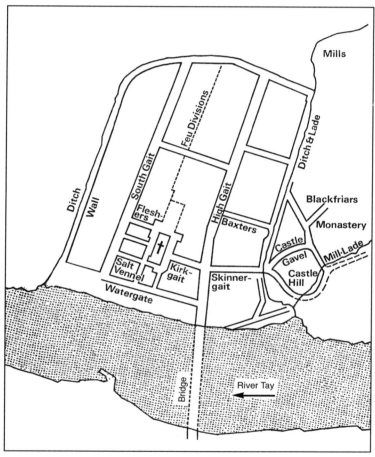

Figure 14 Medieval Perth. (The bridge was built before 1220 to replace a ford. The straight line of the Feu Divisions suggests that the two main streets were laid out at the same time.)

105

native vernaculars, Scots and Gaelic, was resolved in victory for the former and by the end of the thirteenth century Gaelic speech outside the Highland line was probably limited largely to Galloway and Buchan. We can be as sure as of anything in our history that William Wallace and most of his men ordinarily spoke Scots. And if our map is to express the personality of Scotland this is another characterisation that must appear upon it: there was a *Gaidheal-tachd* which was a little larger than the Highlands and much larger than the outermost north-western fringe which escaped Anglo-French influences. Yet it was shrinking.

Perhaps because Gaelic was still widespread enough to be spoken by some with a Lowland way of life, contemporaries offer few comments upon distinctions of speech. There seems to have been little of that Anglo-Saxon hostility towards Celtic speech as sheer perverseness best corrected by unsparing chastisement, which has been prevalent since the fifteenth century. What they do speak of are social and legal distinctions within society between free and unfree. Sales of 'native men' have survived in numbers from the early and mid thirteenth century; these were men unable to leave the status, duties and obligations to their lords into which they had been born. In the twelfth century pursuit of the fugitive 'native' is common enough to show that he was a real asset to his lord. He, his wife and children must work on the land and pay rent at the will of the lord who was free to sell them to another and refuse to sell to them the freedom which they might offer to buy. Yet if this is the theory to which legal documents subscribe, it is doubtful that it remained the fact as the thirteenth century progressed. It is dangerous to generalise for geography imposed many variations. Change was most rapid near the ready markets of the larger towns, and remote areas were probably very conservative. Moreover so limited were the means of communication that regional variation could be drastic. Rains washing out a harvest would raise the cost of the winter loaf but poor roads and carts prevented the law of supply and demand from operating to relieve famine, which must often have caused a heavy mortality. Yet the overwhelming impression given by the sources is one of economic prosperity and social mobility.

Certainly by the end of the thirteenth century it was the land they held (and not their birth) which imposed servitudes upon many peasants. In Lothian, where we are best informed, these servitudes were limited to mowing and harvest works; the rest had been compounded into the payment of rent. Moreover there was wide variation in the economic position of individual peasants, from the husbandmen with a hundred or more acres each down to the poorest cottager without even a garden, and the wage labourer hiring himself out to other more fortunate peasants. So far as the lord to whom their rents came was concerned (lay aristocrat or ecclesiastic), such peasants may have been unfree, subject to his will in his court, but the reality of the lord's power was surely economic rather than legal. Both lord and peasant wished to maximise their returns from the land which the latter held of the former, which meant frequent adjustments of rent and changes of tenancy, not rigid holdings and unwanted labours. It meant that the richer peasant (whose tenure was still insecure) must guard his precious gains in a harshly competitive society and an environment where nature is notoriously unsmiling. The poorest peasant must die under the dike in winter's cold after a bad autumn's rain. And those between must make shift as best they could to meet the lord's demands in rent, for if they failed there was assuredly another willing to take their cottar house and land.

This was no static society of the old-fashioned picture-book Middle Ages. Population grew and with it pressure on resources. The lord's share of the village field shrank as his peasants' ploughs took over more and more to fatten the lord's rent book. New land was broken out, much of it marginally productive. Great flocks of sheep grazed hill pastures and profits from their wool financed castle and monastery building. The rich were almost certainly getting richer; many middling families were able to make satisfactory provision for younger sons – that is, they too were in real terms better off though some certainly went to the wall. Among the peasantry too economic distinctions were perhaps accentuated so that the rich peasant and poor laird were indistinguishable. These consequences of two centuries of economic expansion, of lively demand for bread and cloth, produced a society which even in Scotland had stretched its resources to the limits imposed by its technology. But in the process legal servitude (which may have meant slavery even as late as the eleventh century) had shrunk from serfdom inherited in the blood to unfree tenures with modest obligations on the holder. The last we hear of personal unfreedom in medieval Scotland is in Moray in 1364 but on the eve of the war of independence in the 1290s it was already much diminished.

On 27 April 1296 at Dunbar a 200-year phase in the history of Scotland came to an end with the defeat of its aristocratic leaders in battle, the subsequent abdication of their king John (Balliol), and the imposition of direct English rule under Edward I. For a decade the barons had struggled with the unfamiliar problems of government and the vexed one of settlement of the royal succession. In 1290 they had agreed to a union of the Scottish and English kingships by marriage but had stipulated that the kingdom was to remain distinct: Scots were to hold the great offices of state, and they were not to have to go for law or administrative act outside the bounds of the kingdom.

These terms are revealing. They show that these men thought not of a nation of Scots but of a kingdom, of a territory whose magnates were bound in allegiance to a common king. Their last king had defended the independence of the kingdom because independence was personified in his own position. But those bound in allegiance to him had no such vested interest. With an absentee king their interest was in protecting or even increasing their own influence in decision-making processes by retaining them in the kingdom. In 1249–59 the barons had compromised the king's position while jockeying for power with English help, and in 1290 they abandoned the king's position while seeking to protect their own. They were not successful in doing so and in 1296, again setting aside the king (this time because he was too weak), they took up arms in defence of the right to do the kingdom's business within the kingdom. These words are perhaps too harsh a description of the unconscious attitudes of honest men trying to do their best in the unfamiliar role of interim rulers with a responsibility for the kingdom in wardship. Great lords in Buchan, Fife or Kyle where their social prestige and royally conferred offices made them unquestioned leaders, they were regarded by all as *the* community of the kingdom. This indeed is what they called themselves – not the Scots, but the community of the realm, and it was this community and the whole tradition of a baronial political class which went down to failure at Dunbar.

Economic strength had long been more widely spread among other landowners – great and small lairds, freeholders and even rich peasants. So long as king and baronage ruled effectively they had no political claims. Now all was changed for the English garrisoned Scotland, threatening taxation and military call-up as well as practising extortion and bad debts. Unlike the baronage these classes knew nothing of the English king, had no lands in England and no acquaintance with overwhelming English resources. But they knew from long habits of obedience that they were of Scotland and they too now laid claim to be part of the community of the realm. They sustained through many vicissitudes, a struggle against the English in which the word 'freedom' recurs ever more insistently. This is not to deny that the aristocracy played a significant part nor to suggest that anything democratic was born in these years. The politically significant increased from a few tens of barons to a few hundred of knights. A few thousand freeholders and husbandmen were active in the army and so achieved military importance. But the condition of most men changed slowly and (to them) imperceptibly; doubtless a deep pool of peasant ignorance and indifference remained undisturbed in many areas. Yet enough had changed. Two centuries of growing wealth and able and effective kings had created Scotland, the notion of a kingdom which, however disparate its languages and cultures in different regions and at different social levels, was nonetheless bound in allegiance to one king. A few years of political blundering and the risings of William Wallace, Andrew Moray and Robert Bruce, the king, demanded action from hitherto silent social groups. Their war was conducted with cries about the nation race and people of Scots which at least in intensity had no precedent and which must reflect popular beliefs and slogans. 'Nation' stressed their birth in the kingdom, 'race' their descent within the kingdom, and 'people' their social comprehensiveness in the kingdom; but all these words were (and strictly still should) be used of a people not of a land. By invoking in these three words their standing to act, they also created, for the kingdom, the Scots.

The Scottish Nation

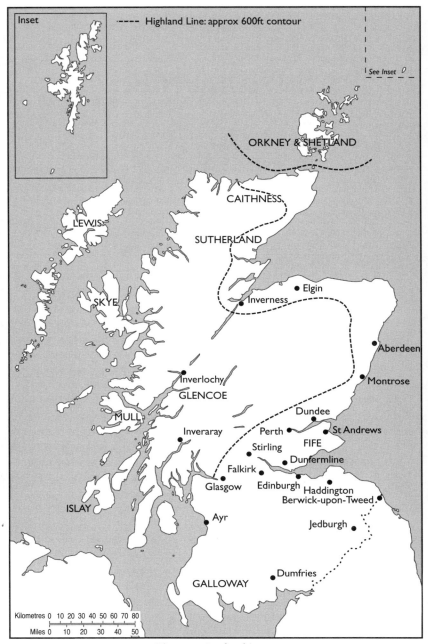

--- Highland Line: approx 600ft contour

See Inset

ORKNEY & SHETLAND

LEWIS

CAITHNESS

SUTHERLAND

SKYE

• Elgin
• Inverness

• Aberdeen

Inverlochy •
GLENCOE

• Montrose

MULL

• Dundee

Inveraray •

Perth •
• St Andrews

Stirling •
FIFE

• Dunfermline

Falkirk •

Glasgow •
Edinburgh •
Haddington
Berwick-upon-Tweed

ISLAY

• Ayr
Jedburgh •

GALLOWAY
• Dumfries

Kilometres 0 10 20 30 40 50 60 70 80
Miles 0 10 20 30 40 50

Figure 15   Scotland in 1707

CHAPTER 9

WARS OF INDEPENDENCE

G. W. S. Barrow

O N a night of storm in March 1286 Scotland lost the last king of her ancient dynasty, Alexander III. Ten years later, almost to the day, his kingdom was plunged into war with England, her larger and richer neighbour to the south, a war which was to endure with comparatively brief intervals of peace or truce till the fifteenth century. These long years of war and hardship gave the Scottish nation a consciousness of its own identity stronger than anything previously known. Yet the name usually given to them, the 'Wars of Independence', is a misleading modernism, which would have seemed incomprehensible to Scots of the thirteenth or fourteenth centuries. Far from coming to a sudden awareness of their separate identity in 1296 and striving to throw off long centuries of foreign rule, the Scots were alarmed at the prospect of their ancient and separate kingdom being relegated to the status of a feudal barony held by the English crown or, worse still, being perhaps abolished or at least swallowed up by a more powerful and recognisably different political lordship. It would be truer to call them the 'wars of preservation', or even 'wars of conservation'.

Undeniably, a sense of nationalism was accelerated in both Scotland and England at the turn of the thirteenth and fourteenth centuries by the wars waged between the English Edwards and the Scots kings, Balliol and Bruce. But nationalism was already an irreversible tide in European history. It was an accident, indeed quite literally an accident, which made the Anglo-Scottish wars one of the earliest test-beds of conflicting nationalism. Nevertheless, with hindsight we can justifiably say that despite long years of peace and friendly relations the kingdoms of England and Scotland were shaping inexorably, during the thirteenth century, towards a conflict which would be different from the old, almost casual, feudal strife, which would in fact be more profound, more bitter,

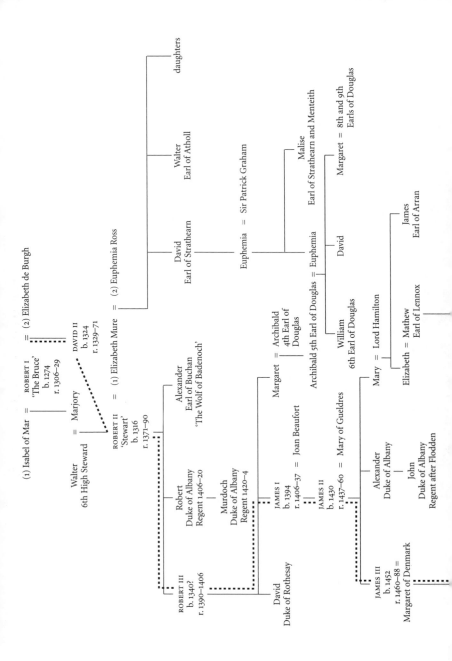

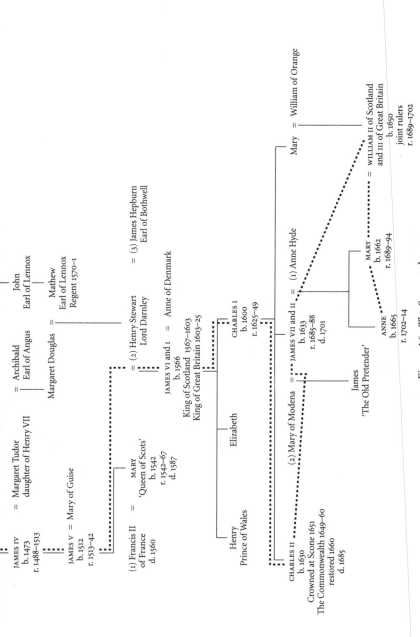

Figure 16 The Stewart dynasty

and much more difficult to resolve. European kingship of the high Middle Ages had, it is true, emerged out of feudalism; but it had taken on a vigorous life of its own, drawing its strength from a balance between external aggression and internal peace-keeping and law-giving. Slowly, but very surely, the west European monarchies became 'national'. The more 'national' they were the more success-ful they were and, barring accidents, the longer they were likely to survive.

Barring accidents; there was the rub. The Capetian dynasty of France, a perfect example of a monarchy which had first adapted itself to feudalism and then adapted itself to nationalism, was at the height of its power and prestige when in 1328 Charles IV died and, for the first time for over 300 years, there was no direct male heir of the Capets. More than a century passed before the French monarchy became effectively 'national' once more. Succession problems have always been the classic starting-point of far-reaching conflicts which have had little or nothing to do with the technical details of succes-sion itself. So it proved with Scotland in 1286. King Alexander's heir, acknowledged by the Scots lords in a remarkable proof of their political maturity, was King Eric of Norway's little daughter Margaret. By 1290 plans for her to marry the heir to the English throne, Edward of Caernarvon, were complete. A cautiously defensive marriage treaty had been ratified (Birgham–Northampton) and it is clear from its contents that it had been drafted largely by the Scots with the purpose of protecting the separate identity and special interests of the Scottish kingdom. All these plans, with their mixture of hopefulness and mistrust, were frustrated when the Maid of Norway died on her way to Scotland. King Edward I, called upon to preside over a settlement of claims to the Scots throne put in by thirteen competitors, insisted upon his 'superior lordship' over the northern kingdom being acknowledged by all the parties, and particularly, once the choice had fallen (no doubt correctly) on John Balliol, by the new king of Scots himself (December 1292).

Even if Edward I's demands had been of the most perfunctory and nominal kind, King John's position would have been difficult. But the English king insisted on the spirit and the letter of feudal law and something more besides. This misjudgement is all the more remarkable in a man who in these same years could rouse the patriotism of his own people with the warning that the king of France was bent upon the invasion of England and had threatened to 'wipe out the English nation from its land, if his power were equal to a scheme of such horrible iniquity, which God forbid'. The Scots magnates – bishops, earls and great barons – had already come to see themselves as the natural leaders of a 'community of the realm' of Scotland. The phrase, while it could bear different shades of meaning, is best understood as denoting the corporate unity of the kingdom and its people insofar as this was not, or for some reason could not be, comprehended in the king himself. As the wretched Balliol was pricked harder and harder by the feudal goad, the Scots plough which he had been elected to pull took on a life of its own, dug itself in, and refused to cut the furrow mapped out for it by the masterful King Edward. A council of twelve took the government of Scotland out of King John's hands, appealing to the papacy for moral, to the king of France for physical, support (July 1295–February 1296).

King Edward's fury evidently reflected the extent to which he had misjudged the Scottish situation. A large English army crossed into Scotland at Coldstream on 28 March 1296 and moved down the Tweed to take and sack Berwick, Scotland's richest town, with much slaughter and destruction. A month later King John's own army, the chivalry of Scotland reinforced by a sizeable infantry force, was scattered with heavy loss on a hillside south of Dunbar. The English advanced methodically northward, securing castle after castle and driving the hapless Scottish king and his now discredited councillors before them until they were forced to surrender early in July, at Brechin and Montrose. King Edward pressed on as far as Elgin, displaying the English royal banner farther north than it had ever been seen before. While King John, who had been compelled to abdicate, was led ignominiously to captivity in the Tower of London, the English forces scoured wide areas of the central and eastern Highlands before returning south for a great 'reconstruction' parliament at Berwick in August. At this parliament an English administration for Scotland was established, and almost 2,000 of the more substantial and prominent Scotsmen and Scotswomen gave in their fealty and homage to the English king – though it is unlikely that more than a small proportion of this great roll-call actually came to Berwick to perform the ceremonies in person. Even so, that summer had witnessed an impressive demonstration of King Edward's power and an apparent vindication of his belief that the kingdom of Scotland – which he had not yet abolished – was properly subordinate to the crown of England and would remain so.

With the next two years a pattern emerged which was to repeat itself again and again in Anglo-Scottish relations. Against a fairly consistent background of English demands for suzerainty over Scotland a number of elements or groups may be distinguished in the Scottish foreground. On the one hand, there were a few great nobles and gentry, presumably with their dependants, who saw English overlordship as a permanent reality – for whom, in other words, Edward I and the Plantagenets had effectively taken the place of the vanished Scottish dynasty of former ages. Two earls of Dunbar (until 1315) belonged to this group, and so, invariably, did the earls of Angus, who were de Umfravilles from Northumberland. Comparable with this small group, yet in a significantly different position, were a number of the nobles from the Isle of Man, the Hebrides and the west Highland seaboard, who had not yet become reconciled to the fact that since 1266 this wide region had been brought within the Scottish kingdom and must look to Perth and Edinburgh for its government rather than Bergen or (more often than not) to nowhere in particular. Such were the Macdougalls, lords of Lorn, the senior representative of the great house of Somerled (d. 1164), certain individuals among their kinsmen the Macruaries and Macdonalds, and a few powerful families of the west who had close links with Ireland, such as the Macsweens of Knapdale, builders of Castle Sween. These west highlanders and islanders can hardly be seen as especially 'pro-English', at least not on principle; rather were they suspicious of and hostile to effective royal government in the west from whatever source it might come. And in any case, their attitude was greatly complicated by the fierce rivalry among the descendants of Somerled which was a dominant feature of Hebridean politics until the 'lordship of the Isles' became a reality in the later fourteenth century.

The majority of Scots nobles, despite their homage to Edward I in 1291 and 1296 which they were very soon to explain away as having been taken under duress, seem to have believed that the kingdom of Scotland, as they and their forebears had experienced it in the twelfth and thirteenth centuries, not only had a right to exist but would survive military defeat and the fall of King John. They were, however, divided in at least two ways. First, there were the handful of the greatest nobility, the dozen or so earls and one or two others such as the hereditary steward – the 'Stewart' – and the lords of Annandale (Bruce), Badenoch (Comyn) and Douglas (Douglas). These great magnates were unavoidably close to the crown, whether Scottish or English, and many of them had English possessions. They were ill-equipped for any but the most formal, feudal kind of war and if they were defeated their education had trained them to accept defeat. Below them, and often attached to them by tenure, affinity or that personal service which made many young men join a great lord's 'meiny' or following were the lesser lairds, gentry and substantial freeholders. In Scotland a much higher proportion of this class were tenants-in-chief of the crown than in England. One of the most striking facts about Scotland after 1296 is that most of these men did not immediately switch their traditional allegiance to the crown to Edward I and his son. On the contrary, they quickly became the very mainstay of the Scottish struggle against English rule. Sir Thomas Maule of Panmure held Brechin Castle against Edward I in 1303 when much Scottish resistance had elsewhere collapsed. Sir William Oliphant, whose defence of Stirling Castle in 1304 forms one of the most splendid chapters of British military history, insisted that he held his command 'of the Lyon', that is, of the crown of Scotland. A Berwickshire knight, William de Vieuxpont, was arrested at Blaye near Bordeaux in 1300 while spying on English shipping movements; he was said to be 'of the company of William Wallace'. In 1306 Sir Malcolm of Inner-peffray, a vassal of the Earl of Strathearn, was as conspicuously bold and prompt to support Robert Bruce's bid for the throne as his lord was tardy and timid. A few years later, three lairds from very different parts of Scotland, Gilbert Hay of Errol, Neil Campbell of Lochawe and Alexander Seton of Seton, met near Stirling and swore a solemn oath to defend the liberty of the Scottish kingdom, and of its recently crowned King Robert I, against all mortal men, French, English or Scots, 'until the last moment of their lives'.

Towering above the rest, of course, yet coming from the selfsame milieu in Scottish society, is the great figure of William Wallace, who stood out in 1297 as the champion of the community of the realm and of what he also called 'the liberty of the kingdom'. Wallace was a son of the tenant of Elderslie, beside Paisley, a small fief held of the Stewart as part of his great lordship of Renfrew. The Stewart and the bishop of Glasgow were in fact Wallace's earliest patrons, but he soon showed that he would take a very independent and much bolder course of action.

As well as this horizontal division among the Scots nobles there was a more damaging vertical division. Despite the church's exhortations and the law's sanctions, feuds and vendettas (certainly not peculiar to Scotland) were endemic. But among the Scots they were especially bitter and intractable after 1292 since they were inextricably bound up with the dispute over the succession. Balliol versus Bruce was also, often automatically, Comyn versus Stewart, Macdougall versus Macdonald, Abernethy, Buchan, Ross, Strathearn versus Atholl, Douglas, Mar and Soulis. From 1296 to 1308 the war of the Scots against the English was at the same time an internal struggle, sometimes actually a fierce civil war, to settle the question of whether the great family of Comyn, dominant for much of the thirteenth century, should keep its old lead in Scots affairs, or whether the smaller family of Bruce with its many powerful allies should oust the Comyns once and for all. In the end, as every schoolboy knows, the Bruces emerged triumphant; but not without the struggle leaving behind it a legacy of internecine bitterness which it would take many generations and many more years of English hostility to efface.

The two last groups to be considered in the Scottish pattern are the church and non-noble class, burgesses, small farmers, servants of various kinds, pastoralists and fishermen, the landless and the unfree. Contrary to a belief about the medieval church which is still widely held, the Scots clergy of this period did not speak with a single voice, nor did they rise above the feuds and squabbles which beset the laity. Indeed, the church no longer enjoyed the almost unchallenged moral authority which it had possessed in the twelfth century. At the same time, it remained an indispensable and enormously influential part of society. Its leaders, the bishops and the greater abbots, took a natural place in the counsels of the community of the realm, and its highly trained administrators, lawyers and writers were expected to put their skill at the service of government. The six regents or 'Guardians' who had governed Scotland from 1286 to 1291 included two bishops, and not only these Guardians but their successors, Balliol's council of twelve, William Wallace in 1297, and the various combinations of nobles and ecclesiastics who followed Wallace from 1299 to 1304, all took pains to see that bishops and abbots were appointed who would serve and support the community of the realm against foreign attack. And while the bishops and other clergy undoubtedly took sides or were partisan already by birth and environment, so that Fraser of St Andrews was pro-Balliol, Wishart of Glasgow pro-Bruce, nevertheless it is undeniable that the Scottish church as a whole maintained a consistently 'national' attitude and did much in its preaching and writing to propagate 'national' feeling. Bishop David of Moray taught his flock that there was as much merit in fighting the English as in warring against the infidel Saracens. In 1296 an obscure Edinburgh priest named Thomas solemnly 'excommunicated' King Edward I with bell and candle as he led his conquering army into the Scottish capital. The English and Scottish clergy of this period foreshadowed unmistakably the sharply nationalist divisions of the western church which became so familiar at the time of the Great Schism of 1378–1417 and at the Councils of the fifteenth century.

It is much harder to gauge the feelings of the common people, for they have left no poetry or chronicle and very little in the way of record. They did not form a single, still less a self-conscious class. As a general rule, servants looked to and followed the tenantry, tenants the gentry, gentry the nobles to whom they were bound by ties of employment, tenure, regions or kinship, or a mixture of these relationships. It would be wrong to think of the wars of independence as a struggle involving only the noble orders, save for the slaughter and destruction which certainly did not spare the poor and humble. When a well-informed contemporary such as Walter of Guisborough tells us that English invaders of Annandale in 1298 were attacked by the local peasantry and that 'the common people of the land' followed Wallace as their leader and ruler, it behoves us to take his words seriously. Again, John Barbour, whose report of personal names and similar details is so exact, was surely not writing fiction in his tale of the West Lothian small farmer ('husband') William Bunnok, 'a stout carle and a sture, and of himself dour and hardy', who wrested the castle of Linlithgow from its English garrison by wedging in the gateway a waggon of hay crammed with armed countrymen. Episodes like this, however picturesque, do not tell us much, but there is a consideration of general importance to bear in mind when we are trying to assess the part played by the non-noble class. For centuries the Scots had been familiar with a universal obligation to perform military service, especially for the defence of their land in an emergency. The men who were thus called up, in earldom after earldom, equipped with spear and axe and bow, were not squires and knights and lairds but the ordinary adult male population of the burghs and countryside. For example, we are told that four husbandmen were the tenants of one ploughgate of land in Bowden, Roxburghshire, in 1327. They had to find one man equipped with armour who in turn would be the leader of thirty archers recruited from the barony of Bowden as its share of military service in 'the lord king's army'. It was thus that the common man would serve on occasions when 'the order was given for every man to go forth and defend his head'. Wallace and Bruce both made good use of the 'common army of Scotland'.

By the autumn of 1297 the English had been driven out of Scotland. The great rising led by Andrew Murray ('de Moray') in the north and by William Wallace in the south had produced an army which took the English administration by surprise and at Stirling Bridge on 11 September inflicted on its forces a defeat all the more crushing for being scarcely credible. Men on foot, largely unarmoured, did not beat knights in battle, nor Scots the English; now both rules had been dramatically broken. Murray and Wallace, moreover, were young men, showing their elders how the community of Scotland should be led. Murray, who might have emerged as a brilliant military leader, died soon after the fight, probably from a fatal wound. For nine months Wallace was supreme, knighted by one of the leading earls (Strathearn?) and ruling as Guardian in the name of the wretched King John Balliol. Scots nobles taken to Flanders by Edward I hurried home to stiffen the national resistance, but they either would not or could not take the leadership from the popular champion. His test came at Falkirk on 22 July 1298, when he chose to fight an essentially defensive, static battle with his immovable infantry 'schiltroms' against Edward I's much more mobile and experienced force of cavalry, archers and slingers. Instead of being under the sluggardly leadership of the Earl of Surrey, as at Stirling Bridge, the English army was led by King Edward in person, at the height of his career and prestige. When his Welsh auxiliaries threatened mutiny, his terse response was: 'We shall beat both the Welsh and the Scots in one day'. The Scots suffered a crushing defeat with heavy casualties, and Wallace, escaping with many of the other leading men from the field, was forced to yield his command to an aristocratic committee.

The outstanding personalities of Wallace and Bruce have always prevented us from seeing that the dark years from 1298 to 1306 were at least as important for the success of the Scottish struggle as the highlights of Stirling Bridge, Falkirk and Bannockburn. Two young noblemen, John Comyn (the 'Red Comyn') and Robert Bruce, came to the forefront. Comyn was son – soon to succeed his father – of the lord of Badenoch, chief of a powerful and ramifying baronial clan. Bruce (also soon to succeed his father, lord of Annandale) was in his own right Earl of Carrick. He inherited the next best claim to the Scottish crown after Balliol's. It was soon clear that they could not work in harness and in 1302 Bruce, ever mindful of his claim to the throne, deserted his former comrades still supporting Balliol and came over to Edward I. No less important at this stage than Comyn and Bruce were William Lamberton, bishop of St Andrews, John de Soulis, Simon Fraser, the chancellor Nicholas of Balmyle and the Bologna-trained Scots jurist Baldred Bisset, who prepared the Scottish case when the dispute with England was put before the papacy in 1301. Bisset emerges from these rather obscure years as a forensic champion of his country much as Wallace had emerged as its soldier champion. And Wallace himself was by no means *hors de combat*: he pleaded the Scots cause at the French and papal courts and after he returned to Scotland (1303?) he joined Fraser in some very effective guerilla warfare, of a kind which he perhaps ought to have concentrated on in 1298. Abandoned by their French allies and by the papacy, the Scots were overwhelmed by Edward I's last massive campaign against them in 1303–4. Comyn and other leaders surrendered on terms, Stirling Castle fell after a brutal siege, hundreds of prominent Scots were once again compelled to do homage to the English king and eventually, in the autumn of 1305, a new administration was set up, the basis of which was that Scotland was no longer a kingdom but merely a territory directly subject to the English crown – comparable perhaps to the present-day status of the Isle of Man and the Channel Isles. Before this had happened, Wallace, who had never submitted or acknowledged English overlordship, was captured and executed as a 'traitor' (24 August 1305). There were others, too, who refused to submit: John de Soulis among them, and probably a number of leading churchmen, for whom exile in France was the unavoidable lot.

Neither the settlement of 1305 nor the execution of Wallace had accomplished the conquest of Scotland. In February 1306, Bruce and his old rival Comyn met in the Greyfriars Kirk at Dumfries and quarrelled violently over a proposal that Bruce should be made king of Scots; in the quarrel Comyn was slain, and Bruce, with the obviously pre-arranged co-operation of the bishops of St Andrews and Glasgow, secured his hold over a number of vital south-country castles and was then (25 March) crowned at Scone. Almost at once he was worsted by an English counter-attack, and for nearly a year he skulked in hiding in Ireland and the Hebrides. Six months before Edward I died at Burgh on Sands in Cumberland (7 July 1307) Bruce returned to his own earldom of Carrick on the Scottish mainland. From this precarious base, employing a combination of enormous patience, reckless courage and ruthlessly savage guerilla attacks, Bruce built up a position of such strength that by late May he had beaten an English army in the field. Before the end of the year the English had abandoned much of their hold over Scotland, leaving Bruce free to concentrate on defeating his numerous and powerful internal enemies – especially the Comyns in the north-east and the central Highlands and the Macdougalls in Argyll. Rapid marches foreshadowing the campaigns of the great Montrose, brilliant surprise attacks and the systematic razing of captured castles showed that the new king was a military leader of genius. Despite a residue of doubt and bitterness arising from the supplanting of Balliol claims and the killing of the Red Comyn, the country rallied to Bruce as it had done to Wallace. And compared with Wallace, Bruce had three notable advantages: he was a crowned king, by an undoubted hereditary right; he possessed more versatility and skill as a general; and instead of confronting Edward I – 'Hammer of the Scots' – at the height of his powers he had to deal with the insouciant, pleasure-loving Edward II, whose hostility towards the Scots, though fierce enough in spirit, was fitful in application.

The years from 1309 to 1313 were spent in retaking Scottish castles occupied by the English in 1306 and in carrying the war – in the shape of destructive, terrorising raids – far into the north of England. Plunder was seized as far south as Beverley and Knaresborough, and large sums of 'blackmail' were levied from towns and country districts willing to pay heavily to avoid a visit from the Scots. Although Edward II had some good commanders who knew Scotland well, men such as Aymer de Valence and Henry de Beaumont, the English were never able to regain the initiative in this period. Consequently for them as much as for King Robert the year's respite given to the Stirling garrison in 1313 by his younger brother Edward Bruce posed an inescapable challenge to a battle which in the long run was likely to prove decisive. Had the English won, it is hard to see how the ancient Scottish monarchy could have survived, and though the Scottish nation might have done so it would not have become a nation-state and its development over the following centuries would surely have followed a very different path from that which our history did in fact follow. A Scots victory, on the other hand, while it would not bring immediate peace or the terms which King Robert wanted would mean that the English kings had lost the initiative in Scotland for good.

All the same, Bannockburn (Sunday and Monday, 23–24 June 1314), a full-scale pitched battle on confined ground against an enemy vastly superior in numbers, armour and weaponry, was the last kind of warfare that the Scots wanted. Its outcome, making every allowance for Edward II's poor generalship, was due to a genius for leadership and military tactics in Robert Bruce which long before his death had been recognised throughout Europe. There is no reason to believe that the Scots who bled with Wallace at Falkirk or were led at Halidon (1333) by Archibald Douglas or at Neville's Cross (1346) by King David II were less courageous or determined than their compatriots – in some cases the same individuals – who filled King Robert's schiltroms at Bannockburn. But 'Good King Robert', despite his chequered beginnings, possessed the magic of a commander who wins his battles. He knew exactly how best to seize on every weakness of an enemy, to be more highland than the highlanders when fighting on the slopes of Ben Cruachan yet, on more level terrain as at Bannockburn, to deploy his schiltroms aggressively as though they were moving human 'tanks' instead of keeping them fixed as Wallace had done.

Had Edward II been taken prisoner at Bannockburn a lasting peace would almost certainly have followed the battle, and papal and international recognition of King Robert's position would have been a matter of months, not years. As it was, Edward escaped, to lead or despatch armies against the Scots on several more occasions, but unable to prevent the Scots recovering Berwick, the last town in Scotland still in English hands, in 1318. It was nearly ten years after Bannockburn before Robert I was reconciled with the papacy, twelve years before he could renew the Franco-Scottish alliance of 1295–6, badly shaken by Philip IV's abandonment of the Scots in 1303, and it was almost fourteen years before an English king – by now the fifteen-year-old Edward III – and parliament could be persuaded to make what was intended to be a definitive, permanent peace. The Treaty of Edinburgh–Northampton (17 March 1328) annulled English claims to overlordship, recognised the Scottish kingdom under King Robert – with its boundaries as they had been in Alexander III's days – as 'separate, whole, free and in peace without subjection', provided for a marriage between the child David Bruce, King Robert's late-born son and heir, and young Joan of the Tower, Edward III's sister, and stipulated that the Scots should pay the English £20,000 'for the sake of peace'.

Robert I died, aged fifty-five, a year after peace had been made with England, surely with every reason to hope that this peace would be lasting and would bring back the fruitful harmony which had marked the relations between the two countries for most of the two centuries from 1093 to 1296. Despite the almost incessant warfare of much of his reign, King Robert was remembered not only as the champion, the Judas Maccabaeus, of his people but also as a humane and just ruler and strong lawgiver. When in 1320 the Scots barons addressed their famous letter to Pope John XXII (the 'Declaration of Arbroath') they acknowledged in memorable words the separate existence and character of 'this poor little Scotland, beyond which there is no dwelling-place', and in speaking of 'our laws and customs which we shall maintain unto death' and of the freedom of the kingdom which they would defend as long as 100 remained alive, they were not only echoing words which had been used by the Treaty of Birgham, by Wallace, by Baldred Bisset and by the lairdly trio of Campbell, Hay and Seton; their phrases capture for us an instant in the evolution of the Scottish nation as it had been slowly but surely developing during the twelfth and thirteenth centuries. It was King Robert's grasp of the needs and true character of this feudal kingdom emerging into a national state which gave his reign lasting importance.

The legacy of Robert the Bruce may have been glorious, and doubtless it grew more glorious in retrospect. The actual situation in which Scotland found herself at his death was pregnant with disaster. The new king was a boy of five. Through his much older half-sister Marjorie, David II had a nephew eight years older than himself, Robert the Stewart, who would have become king in 1329 instead of 1371 had his uncle never been born. Despite the Stewart's undoubted shortcomings, it would surely have been better for Scotland to have had an adult ruler to cope with the dangers of the 1330s. John Balliol, who died in 1313, had left a son Edward. From his base in England, the younger Balliol almost at once made a bid for the throne with the help of a few nobles whom Robert I, for good reasons, had disinherited. The last of the great men of King Robert's heroic days, James lord of Douglas and Thomas Randolph Earl of Moray, were dead, to be succeeded in the leadership of the community of the realm by an assortment of nobles, many of whom were sadly inept and incompetent. In successive years, 1332 and 1333, two full-scale Scots armies were cut to pieces and their leaders slain by invading forces, respectively under Edward Balliol and Edward III in person, who showed ironically enough that they had learned and remembered more of the great Bruce's tactics than the Scots themselves. By rights, Dupplin Muir, after which Balliol had himself crowned king of Scots, and Halidon Hill, after which Edward III reasserted an overlordship which his own solemn treaty of Edinburgh had disavowed, should have seen the total dismemberment of Scotland and consigned the struggles of Wallace and Bruce, Soulis and Lamberton, to oblivion. But the idea of the community of the realm was not forgotten. Five fortresses, Dumbarton, Lochleven, Kildrummy, Castle Urquhart on Loch Ness and Loch Doon in Galloway, held out bravely against the invaders. The boy king was shipped to France in safety and installed at Château Gaillard, with the abbot of Kelso as his tutor and a handful of noblemen and bishops to form his court. At home Sir Andrew Murray of Bothwell, son of Wallace's colleague mortally wounded at Stirling Bridge, held the time-honoured place of Guardian, and painfully reverted to the Fabian guerilla tactics of King Robert's early years. In 1335 he inflicted a resounding defeat on Balliol's chief supporters in Scotland at the battle of Culblean in Aberdeenshire, and though he could not stop Edward III twice more returning to invade the country, the Scots under his and Robert Stewart's leadership had recovered their nerve and their strength so successfully by 1341 that it was thought safe to bring King David back home. By this time Edward III's ambitious energies had been diverted to France. A country which harboured his enemies could also be a rich source of plunder. The Scots historian Andrew Wyntoun has a good story to illustrate the mood of Scotland during this grim decade: no one dared resist the occupying Englishmen who were everywhere in strength; only the children, too young to choose between good and evil, when asked whose men they were answered 'richt apertly' they were King Davy's men –

> They knew no fear their mind to say
> for their king was a child as they.

The 40s and 50s were the nadir of 'King Davy's' long reign. After the French suffered the crushing defeat of Crécy (August 1346) Philip IV called on the Scots to fulfil the spirit of the Auld Alliance by invading England. In October, King David led his army in an ill-judged and impetuous raid south of the Tyne, and at Neville's Cross, outside Durham, the Scots were calamitously defeated. The king himself was captured, and his nephew the Stewart, whose conduct on the field of battle was regarded by English observers as frankly treacherous, fled safely back to Scotland to assume once more the position of Guardian. A crippling ransom was imposed for David II's release, and six years passed before the Scots king could even return briefly, on parole, to try to hasten the collection of the money, variously fixed at ninety or a hundred thousand merks (approximately £67,000). When in 1356 the Scots seemed to be back-pedalling on the deal, Edward III, with characteristic brutality, devastated the south-eastern counties in the 'Burnt Candlemas'.

Perhaps not surprisingly, David Bruce has had a bad press among historians. It is refreshing and salutary that his character and conduct have recently found some sympathetic defenders. Rather than compare him with his father it might be fairer to place him beside his Stewart successors down to James V, for the problems he had to face were more like their problems. Kingship faced new and severe challenges from the mid-fourteenth century. An uneasy baronage struggled to defend its old pre-eminence, the middle class emerged with new strength, the whole of society was shaken by pestilence, a questioning of the customary forms of religious life, and agrarian and social upheavals. Yet kings, like other politicians, are judged by results. David II set an evil precedent when he allowed the Franco-Scottish alliance to push him into an ill-timed invasion of England, and the Scots under his own command suffered a disastrous defeat. The ransom which resulted had to be negotiated under the shadow of renewed English threats to Scottish independence. And, to complete a sorry chapter of failure, King David was unable to bequeath to his sorely tried kingdom an heir of his own blood and lineage. The royal Bruces died with him.

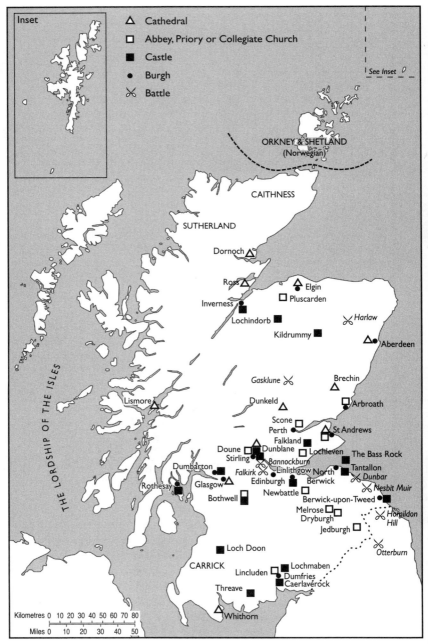

Legend:
- △ Cathedral
- □ Abbey, Priory or Collegiate Church
- ■ Castle
- ● Burgh
- ✂ Battle

Inset

ORKNEY & SHETLAND
(Norwegian)

CAITHNESS

SUTHERLAND

See Inset

Dornoch △

Ross △

Elgin ● △

Inverness ● □ Pluscarden

Lochindorb ■

Kildrummy ■

✂ *Harlaw*

Aberdeen △ ●

THE LORDSHIP OF THE ISLES

Gasklune ✂

Brechin △

Dunkeld △

□ Arbroath

Lismore △

Scone □

Perth ●

St Andrews △

Falkland □

Doune □ Dunblane △

Stirling ■ ✂ *Bannockburn*

Lochleven ■

The Bass Rock ■

Tantallon ■

Dumbarton ● ■

Falkirk ✂

Linlithgow □

North Berwick ■ ✂ *Dunbar*

Glasgow ● △

Edinburgh ■

Nesbit Muir ✂

Rothesay ●

Newbattle □

Berwick-upon-Tweed ●

Bothwell □

Melrose □

Dryburgh □

✂ *Homildon Hill*

Jedburgh □

Loch Doon ■

Otterburn ✂

CARRICK

Lincluden □ Lochmaben ■

Dumfries ●

Caerlaverock ■

Threave ■

Whithorn △

Kilometres 0 10 20 30 40 50 60 70 80

Miles 0 10 20 30 40 50

Figure 17 Medieval Scotland

CHAPTER 10

CROWN IN JEOPARDY

Ranald Nicholson

O N 7 October 1357 David II returned to Scotland, a free man after almost eleven years of tedious captivity. Four days before, the treaty of Berwick had settled his ransom at 100,000 merks, to be paid in ten yearly instalments. As security twenty-three noble hostages were delivered to Edward III. When a council met at Scone on 6 November it ratified the treaty (which brought Scotland a much-needed truce) and made provision to meet the ransom instalments. The initial measures proved to be insufficient and had to be supplemented by the raising of the great customs levied on Scotland's chief exports – wool, fleeces and hides. In 1358 the rate of duty was doubled; in 1359 it was trebled; in 1368 it would be quadrupled, and the rate of £1.33p then levied on each sack of wool would remain constant until the sixteenth century. Thanks to various financial expedients the first ransom instalment was duly paid at midsummer 1358 and the second instalment was belatedly paid in 1359; but no further instalment would be paid until 1366.

This was hardly a result of insolvency: David rapidly brought order out of the financial chaos that had existed during the lieutenancy of the Steward. In 1362 the chamberlain (no great noble but a civil servant, Walter of Biggar) accounted for receipts of £7,380 and his account showed a surplus of £4,544; by 1363 the king had a deposit of 5,000 merks in Stirling Castle. But if David was able to pay his ransom he was not eager to do so. Despite the stringent conditions of the treaty of Berwick he hoped to evade his obligations by assiduous diplomacy: in a number of visits to the English court he cultivated a special relationship with Edward III on the basis of their mutual interest in chivalry.

This, however, blinded neither side to national interest. By November 1363 Edward's patience was exhausted. From David he wanted more than fair words. At Westminster, where the two kings and their privy councils held negotiations, two memoranda were drafted. The first of these reopened the question of the Scottish succession: Edward would make no demand for the residue of the ransom, would release the Scottish hostages and restore occupied territory on the Borders, provided that he were recognised as David's successor in the event of the latter's dying without legitimate offspring; if Edward thus became 'king of England and Scotland' he would undergo a second coronation at Scone and the separate identity and territorial integrity of Scotland would be carefully preserved. The second memorandum envisaged that a childless David might be succeeded by one of Edward's younger sons, in which case the English concessions would be fewer.

Edward's proposals had been ingeniously formulated. An alteration in the succession did not, in theory at least, diminish the independence of Scotland, which, according to the first memorandum, would have had the status that it came to possess after the union of the crowns in 1603; and David had little desire to preserve the succession for his heir presumptive, Robert the Steward, who had deserted him at Neville's Cross. Even so, David did not commit himself to accepting the proposals: playing for time he hoped that he might foil both Edward and the Steward by producing offspring of his own.

On 4 March 1364 parliament met to debate the Westminster memoranda. Some spoke in favour of the first of these, some in favour of the second, and the king does not appear to have influenced the discussions, though he may (for the sake of diplomacy) have given a show of annoyance when both memoranda were ultimately rejected and the Steward's position as heir presumptive was preserved.

No specific diplomatic crisis followed. Instead there was a sense of impending crisis for the next few years as parliaments and councils met in rapid succession to hear the reports from each embassy sent to England. Edward demanded impossible conditions for the peace or long truce that the Scots desired. The best that could be achieved was a second ransom treaty in May 1365, harsher than the first: it reduced the yearly ransom instalments to 6,000 merks (£4,000) but increased the total ransom to £100,000, and the truce was assured only until 2 February 1370, when either side might renew the war on six months' notice.

The situation changed in 1369 when France, having recovered from the disasters of the previous decades, reopened hostilities with England. In June David went with a Scottish embassy to England and came back with a third ransom treaty much more favourable to the Scots. The ransom was now set at the original figure of 100,000 merks and credit was given both for the 20,000 merks paid under the first treaty and the 24,000 paid under the second; the remaining 56,000 merks were to be paid at the rate of 4,000 a year for the next fourteen years, during which time the truce would continue. By June 1370 David was again in London; but despite his apparent friendship with Edward he had sent Sir Archibald Douglas, illegitimate son of Bruce's foremost knight, on a mission to the French court. Had David lived longer he might have taken even greater advantage of the revival of French power by playing off France against England.

As it was, the king's brinkmanship had been remarkably success-ful: despite the weakness of his diplomatic position he had paid only enough of his ransom to maintain the truce; at the same time he had extended his influence in the Borders, even over areas that the English still occupied; and at his death Scotland remained as independent as ever.

These achievements were accompanied by a striking restoration of royal authority. The council of November 1357 did not look in vain to the king 'to strike terror into wrongdoers'. He had come back to Scotland toughened by years of adversity and soon showed that he could rule with 'radure' (rigour), punishing 'mysdoaris' so that 'nane durst welle wythstand his will'.

First, reliable political support had to be enlisted against the great nobles who were ranged with the Steward in real or potential opposition. This support was forthcoming from talented knights such as Sir Robert Erskine and Sir Archibald Douglas 'the Grim', from churchmen such as William Landallis, bishop of St Andrews from 1342 to 1385 and Walter Wardlaw, archdeacon of Lothian and secretary to the king, who became bishop of Glasgow in 1367 and Scotland's first cardinal in 1383. Nor did David regard merchant burgesses such as John Mercer of Perth, Roger Hogg of Edinburgh and John Crabb of Aberdeen, merely as financial agents: they and their like wielded an economic power that merited political recognition. It was nothing new that the burghs were represented by commissioners in one council at Perth in January 1357, in another at Edinburgh in September, and in a third held by King David at Scone in November. What was new was the phrase *tres communitates* (three estates) which seems then to have been used for the first time in Scotland. The old community of the realm had become a trinity in which the burgesses figured, alongside churchmen and barons, as a political entity, an 'estate' whose approval must be sought for any government measure that relied upon a consensus of opinion.

For a few years the king acted cautiously and showed no sign of antagonising the magnates: in 1357 the Steward was granted the earldom of Strathearn and in 1358 William Douglas was given the new title of Earl of Douglas. A turning point came in 1360 when the king's mistress, Katherine Mortimer, was treacherously stabbed to death. The Earl of Angus, suspected of having arranged the assassination, was imprisoned in Dumbarton castle, where he soon died of a fresh outbreak of plague. During this 'second mortality' of 1362 David moved north to seize Kildrummy Castle, the stronghold of the Earl of Mar, who in 1359 had done homage to Edward III. A few months later, in January 1363, Robert the Steward rose in rebellion with his sons and allies. Complaining that money raised for the ransom was being squandered by 'evil counsel' they demanded that the king follow 'better counsel' – which would naturally be forthcoming from themselves rather than simple knights, churchmen and burgesses. But another issue was involved – the king's liaison with Dame Margaret Logie, daughter of Sir Malcolm Drummond and widow of Sir John Logie. David's queen had tactfully gone to England soon after he returned to Scotland, and her death in 1362 allowed him to contemplate marriage with Dame Margaret. If she bore him a child the Steward would lose his hopes of the crown.

In the crisis of 1363 the king did not waver; and among the rebels only the Earl of Douglas showed fight. By April the 'great conspiracy' was over. At Inchmurdoch, a manor of the bishop of St Andrews, David celebrated his victory by marrying Dame Margaret and extracted from the Steward a sealed undertaking that 'I will be faithful for all the term of my life to . . . the Lord David, illustrious king of Scots.'

Towards the end of his reign David devoted himself to three tasks – improving the efficiency of government, strengthening the crown's economic position and disciplining the great nobles. The Three Estates frequently met, usually at Scone or Perth, either in parliaments or in councils that were described as 'full' or 'general'. Increased use of parliamentary commissions and committees helped to streamline business, particularly the judicial business that came before parliament as the supreme court of law. The exchequer audits, which were held regularly at Perth, were often attended by the king, who used the constant question of the ransom as a pretext for the levying of contributions. These, towards the end of the reign, approximated to an annual income tax – and it was David, rather than the English, who received most of the proceeds. Between May and July 1366 a new assessment of landed rents was made throughout the kingdom. In the following year a parliamentary commission issued a sweeping act of revocation designed to restore to the crown all lands and revenues that had been alienated since 1329. It was not necessarily intended to put this act into full effect; but it gave the king a bargaining position in his dealings with the magnates, particularly Robert the Steward, his brother-in-law William, Earl of Ross, and his son-in-law John, lord of the Isles.

John, greatest of the Gaelic chiefs, who dominated the western isles and had long pursued an independent course, had no desire to be subjected to firm royal control. He and his allies (with the exception of the cautious Steward) were usually 'contumaciously absent' from parliament. The reckoning came in the winter of 1369 when David visited Inverness: the Lord of the Isles humbly begged pardon, delivered hostages and undertook to pay taxes and obey royal officials. About the same time William, Earl of Ross was forced to accept Sir Walter Leslie, one of the king's favourite knights, as son-in-law and eventual heir 'on account of the rigour of the same lord king'. Latterly no noble could offend the king (or queen) with impunity: the Steward and some of his sons were temporarily imprisoned in 1368; in 1369 he was deprived of his earldom of Strathearn for a few months; in 1370 the Earl of Mar was a prisoner on the Bass Rock.

Only in Dame Margaret Logie did David meet his match. It was not her fault that she failed to produce an heir – she already had a son by her first husband while no child had blessed David's various liaisons. By 1369 he had been struck by the attractions and potential fecundity of Agnes Dunbar and assumed that Dame Margaret would be content with a pension of £100 'after the celebration of divorce'. Instead she took ship, made her way to the papal court, and appealed against her divorce; her charms won the kindly eye of pope and cardinals, and there was talk of placing Scotland under interdict. The prospect of wearing a crown was revealed to Agnes Dunbar when she was granted a pension of 1,000 merks; a month later, on 22 February 1371, at the age of forty-six, King David unexpectedly died.

At the exchequer audit held a week before the king's death the chamberlain's account showed receipts of over £15,000, nearly all forthcoming from the great customs and direct taxation. Thanks to the ransom David II ended his reign in a stronger financial position than any other ruler of medieval Scotland. His own prosperity was matched by that of the merchant burgesses, who had brought the export trade to a peak that would not be surpassed until the sixteenth century. Sometimes capricious, but never cruel, David had taught the great nobles to respect royal authority.

These achievements soon withered away. It was symptomatic that at David's death the Earl of Douglas made a bid for the throne and had to be mollified by concessions before the Steward could be crowned as Robert II. Likeable, but mediocre, the first Stewart king failed to rule his own family, let alone his kingdom. He had at least twenty-one offspring. Four, including Walter, Earl of Atholl, were the children of his second marriage (with Euphemia of Ross) and had undoubtedly been born in lawful wedlock. Others, including the heir apparent, John, Earl of Carrick, were the product of a previous marriage (with Elizabeth Mure) for which the necessary papal dispensation had been belatedly obtained. The obvious illegitimacy of the king's remaining sons and daughters did not prevent their expecting advancement. Through the marriages of his 'multitude of offspring' the whole nobility of Scotland was rapidly Stewartised; and those who were 'sib to the king' often stood above the law. Lacking the will to enforce the law Robert II did nothing in

1382 when his nephew, Sir James Lindsay of Crawford, murdered his son-in-law, John Lyon, thane of Glamis. In a general council of 1384 the Three Estates asserted that 'offences and outrageous crimes have been wont to be committed . . . for no short time' and appointed the Earl of Carrick to restore law and order. By 1388 the heir apparent had shown his incapacity, and the king's second son, Robert, Earl of Fife and Menteith, the only member of the royal family who displayed political talent, was appointed guardian of the realm.

Thanks to the lassitude of Robert II the Scots failed to win much profit from the favourable international situation. English reverses in France, together with the death of the redoubtable Edward III, allowed them to stop further payment of David II's ransom. But although the troubles of England during the minority of Richard II invited a Scottish offensive on the Borders this was pursued aimlessly: the initiative came not from the crown but from Border magnates who were inspired less by nationalism than by the quest for booty and chivalric renown. On 2 February 1384, the truce, often broken, was not renewed; the surrender of Lochmaben ended the English occupation of Annandale but was followed by a punitive expedition during which John of Gaunt, Duke of Lancaster, held Edinburgh to ransom. Nor did much result from the renewal of the Franco-Scottish alliance in 1371, even although an ambitious scheme was devised for a joint attack upon England in the summer of 1385: the French would land in the south while the Scots invaded in the north. Jean de Vienne, admiral of France, arrived in Scotland with over a thousand men-at-arms and 50,000 gold francs, which were distributed to the more bellicose Scottish nobles. But there was no French invasion of southern England, and the Franco-Scottish expedition which set out for the Borders in July merely brought another English punitive expedition under Lancaster and the young Richard II. This time Edinburgh was burnt, together with the abbeys of Melrose, Dryburgh and Newbattle.

There followed a number of short truces until the Scots took advantage of fresh English dissensions to mount two simultaneous raids in the summer of 1388. One raid, upon Cumberland, brought booty. The other, upon Northumberland, brought chivalric glory as well. At Otterburn, on 5 August, Henry Hotspur, son and heir of the

Earl of Northumberland, was made prisoner. Although the victor, James, Earl of Douglas, was slain in the fight, he achieved immortality in the dying speech attributed to him by the chronicler Froissart, whose tales made the aristocracy of Europe well aware of the knightly prowess (and barbarous poverty) of the Scots.

The death of the second Earl of Douglas at Otterburn had important consequences within Scotland. The succession to most of his lands was laid down in a tailzie (entail) of 1342, of which Archibald the Grim was the sole surviving beneficiary. In 1369 David II had granted him the lordship of eastern Galloway; in 1372 he had bought western Galloway and reunited the distinctive province that had been divided in the previous century. As principal heir of the victor of Otterburn Archibald now became third earl of Douglas and acquired Douglasdale, Eskdale, Lauderdale, and the lucrative forest of Selkirk. His tower house of Threave established a new and austere fashion in baronial architecture, just as his foundation of collegiate churches at Lincluden and Bothwell established a new fashion in ecclesiastical development. His firmness and justice in administering his lands, together with his prowess in warfare, stood out in sharp contrast to the maladministration and lack of spirit of Stewart kingship. When Robert II died on 19 April 1390 the house of Douglas dominated southern Scotland.

The Earl of Carrick, who now became king at the age of fifty-three, changed his name of John (then thought unlucky) and reigned as Robert III. But fortune was not to be cheated: one of the new king's brothers, Alexander Stewart Earl of Buchan, popularly known as the Wolf of Badenoch, had long been at feud with the aged bishop of Moray; on 17 June 1390, two months before the coronation of Robert III, the Wolf emerged from his fastness at Lochindorb with a band of 'wyld wykkyd Helandmen' and burnt the cathedral of Elgin. His royal blood protected him from undue criticism.

The burning of Elgin was followed by further trouble in the north-east and central Highlands. In 1392 a troop of Highland caterans mauled the chivalry of Angus at Gasklune. In 1396, in an effort to compose the differences between two feuding clans, a trial by battle on the grand scale was held on the North Inch of Perth. The king presided while 'thre score wyld Scottis men', thirty from each clan, fought in mortal combat. When he cast down his baton to end the conflict only a dozen survived. Disorder continued. The chronicler of Moray, inspired by the wording of a statute of 1397 that vainly devised new procedures for the apprehension of criminals, despondently wrote of the state of affairs in 1398:

In those days there was no law in Scotland, but he who was stronger oppressed him who was weaker, and the whole realm was a den of thieves; murders, herschips and fire-raising, and all other misdeeds, remained unpunished; and justice, as if outlawed, lay in exile outwith the bounds of the kingdom.

These were days when Scottish knights were winning renown in English tournaments, attracted by the liberality of Richard II, who had no desire to continue warfare with the Scots. Liberality was also manifested by Robert III, who, since he could not dominate the nobles, tried to quieten them with gifts of cash, remissions of customs duty, life pensions and heritable pensions. The last were sometimes combined with a bond of retinue by which the recipient was contracted to serve the king or his son and heir, David, Earl of Carrick. For their own defensive or offensive purposes the nobles resorted to similar devices: in a general council of 1399 it was hopefully enacted that all the king's lieges were to uphold the authority of his lieutenant notwithstanding 'ony condiciouns of retenewis'.

The person appointed to the new post of king's lieutenant was the heir apparent, who in 1398 had been raised to the dignity of Duke of Rothesay at the same time as his uncle, Robert Stewart, Earl of Fife and Menteith, had been created Duke of Albany. Scotland's first dukes were soon engaged in a power struggle while Robert III stood helplessly aside. In a general council of January 1399 the king had been blamed for the misgovernance of the realm, and it was thought 'expedient' that his son and heir be appointed royal lieutenant for three years. In practice this meant that Albany was ousted from a dominant position in government. He was still powerful enough to see that his nephew's authority was restricted by twenty-one councillors appointed by the Three Estates. The council included only one burgess and was probably divided by the rivalries of the two ducal factions. Nor was the capricious Rothesay the man to compose differences: in 1400 he jilted the daughter of the Earl of March in order to marry the daughter of Archibald the Grim, and the insulted earl absconded to the English court. When Rothesay refused to give up office at the end of his three-year term the king was persuaded to allow his arrest. On 26 March 1402 the heir apparent died in Albany's castle of Falkland of dysentery or of starvation. In a general council held in May lengthy debates and interrogations resulted in the conclusion that Rothesay had 'departed this life by divine providence and not otherwise'. Having won the power struggle Albany succeeded Rothesay as royal lieutenant.

But between Albany and the crown stood the figure of the king's remaining son, James. With some forethought Robert III decided to send the boy to France. He was escorted to North Berwick by Sir David Fleming, who was waylaid and slain on his return journey. For a month James lingered among the gannets of the Bass Rock before the *Maryenknyght* of Danzig called to take him aboard. When the vessel was off Flamborough Head on 22 March 1406 it was seized by English pirates and James was lodged in the Tower of London. On 4 April, a few days after he had received the news of his son's capture, Robert III died. He had once told his queen: 'Bury me, I pray, in a midden, and write for my epitaph "Here lies the worst of kings and the most wretched of men in the whole realm".'

Although the Three Estates recognised Robert III's son as James I, his youth and captivity necessitated the fullest delegation of royal functions. Albany, now heir presumptive, was appointed governor of the realm and assumed most of the trappings of kingship during a period when the relationship between Scotland and England was chaotic, but hardly dangerous. Possession of the person of James I gave the English a diplomatic advantage in their dealings with the Scots. The latter had been shocked by the deposition of Richard II in 1399 and were inclined to regard his successor, Henry IV, as a usurper. Although Henry had led an army to Edinburgh in August 1400 he had behaved with unique restraint, hoping to reach a peace settlement. But since he was not prepared to abandon the pretensions of his predecessors all that could be achieved was a series of truces, often interspersed with piracy at sea and affrays on the Borders. One of these, at Nesbit Muir on 22 June 1402, had ended

28 *North-west tower, Holyrood Palace*

29 The great Michael

30 James V and Mary of Guise

31 *Chapel Royal in Falkland Palace, Fife*

32 *The second Earl of Arran*

33 The Fetternear banner

MARIA
D G
SCOTIÆ
PIISSIMA REGINA
FRANCIÆ DOTARIA
ANNO
ÆTATIS REGNIQ
36
ANGLICÆ CAPTIVIT
IO
S H
.1578

34 *Mary, Queen of Scots*

35 Lochleven Castle, Kinross-shire

IOANNES CNOXVS.

36 John Knox

37 *Hermitage Castle, Roxburghshire*

38 James VI as a child

39 George Buchanan

40 *Linlithgow Palace, West Lothian*

41 *Crichton Castle, Midlothian*

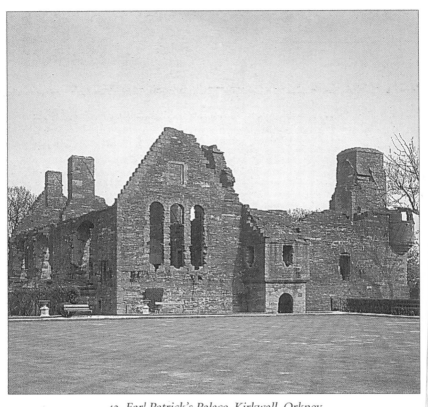

42 *Earl Patrick's Palace, Kirkwall, Orkney*

43 The first Marquis of Montrose

44 The first Marquis of Argyll

45　The execution of Charles I

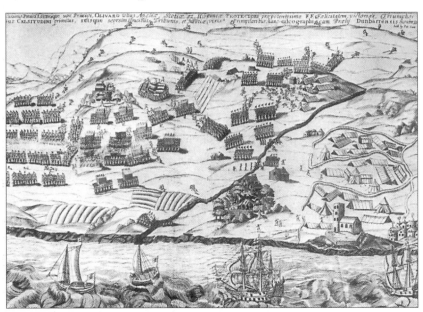

46　The Battle of Dunbar (from a contemporary plan)

47 *Sir William Bruce's Kinross House, Kinross-shire*

48 *The first Duke of Lauderdale*

49 *Crathes Castle, Kincardineshire*

50 *Late seventeenth-century silverware*

Prospectus Civitatis PERTHI . The Prospect of ye Town of PERTH

51 *Slezer's prospect of Perth, 1693*

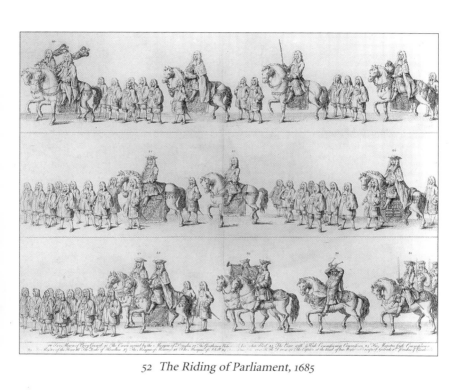

52　*The Riding of Parliament, 1685*

with the capture of 'the flower of the chivalry of a great part of Lothian': in another at Homildon Hill on 14 September 1402 'the flower of chivalry of the whole realm of Scotland was captured and held to ransom'. Among the captives was Albany's son and heir, Murdoch Stewart. For many years there would be abortive negotiations for the ransom and release of Murdoch and James I. The only national advantage that was gained during this period was the recovery of Jedburgh in 1409; and this was the achievement not of Albany, or the nobles, but of 'mediocre persons of Teviotdale'.

Soon Albany's attention was distracted from Border warfare by a crisis in the north. When Alexander Leslie, Earl of Ross, had died in 1402, he left his young daughter, Euphemia, as heiress to his earldom, and Albany (her grandfather) had assumed her wardship. By 1411 he was trying, in devious fashion, to obtain her earldom for his second son, John, already Earl of Buchan. Albany's moves antagonised his nephew, Donald, Lord of the Isles, whose wife, Margaret (or Mary) Leslie, had contingent claims upon Ross.

Although half Stewart by birth, Donald represented the independent traditions of the MacDonalds of Islay, not those of the royal house. He was no mere leader of Highland caterans. His lordship of the Isles, organised partly in feudal fashion, was virtually autonomous – in 1408 there were negotiations for a league of perpetual peace and friendship between the Lord of the Isles, Henry IV, and their subjects. It was a time when there was a growing realisation of the differences between the English-speaking Lowlanders and the Gaelic-speaking Highlanders and islesmen (half the population of Scotland), whom the chronicler John of Fordun described as 'Wild Scots'. Although the latter were no more clannish than their Lowland contemporaries they were more influenced by continued contact with Gaelic Ireland than by the cosmopolitan institutions that in the last three centuries had transformed the Lowlands; their archaic way of life was proudly idealised by the bards; and the Lord of the Isles, descendant of the illustrious Somerled, was the one man who might unite them all.

In 1411, in an attempt to foil Albany's designs upon the earldom of Ross, he seized Inverness and marched towards Aberdeen. His object of assuming control over the lands that belonged to the earldom of Ross was not incompatible with higher ambitions. At

Harlaw, some twenty miles from Aberdeen, he engaged in battle on 24 July with his cousin, Alexander Stewart, Earl of Mar. Then, and for long afterwards, this bloody encounter was regarded as a contest between Highlanders and Lowlanders. Just as the battle was inconclusive so also were the results: the Gaelic regions were no longer likely to be easily assimilated into Lowland Scotland; but the government, increasingly associated with the Lowlands, lacked the strength for an outright attack upon Gaelic culture and the separatist tendencies of the lordship of the Isles.

In any case attention was soon drawn to a renewed conflict between England and France: in 1415 Henry V bid fair to emulate Edward III's exploits by defeating a vast French army at Agincourt. In a bid to secure Scottish neutrality he accepted a ransom of £10,000 for Murdoch Stewart in 1416. But this did not have the desired effect: in October 1419 a Scottish expeditionary force under the Earl of Buchan landed at La Rochelle to aid the Dauphin. On 22 March 1421 the Dauphin's troops and their Scottish allies defeated an English force at Baugé; although the Scots were on the losing side at Cravant on 31 July 1423 they had demonstrated that the English were not invincible.

Meanwhile the octogenarian Albany had died on 3 September 1420. Had he been king, rather than merely the power behind the throne, he might have made a good ruler – there can be no doubt that he was astute enough to win popularity. But he lacked the prestige that kingship would have conferred and was always forced to come to terms with the great nobles, as in 1409 when he concluded a bond of alliance with Archibald the Tyneman, fourth Earl of Douglas. The chronicler Bower significantly remarked that 'if any enormities perchance were committed in the realm by the powerful he [Albany] patiently temporised, knowing how to reform them prudently enough at an opportune time'. The opportune time – his own accession to the throne – never came. But Albany was suspected of having done little to obtain the release of James I, and when the duke died it was his son, Murdoch, who stepped into his shoes as heir presumptive, second Duke of Albany and governor of Scotland. What had eluded the father might not elude the son.

This prospect was distasteful to some nobles. Moreover Duke Murdoch lacked the political talent of his father and failed to keep his own sons under control. During his governorship the waning of central power was complete. This was particularly evident in the finances of government. The direct taxation so prudently introduced under the cover of David II's ransom had long been allowed to lapse. By 1418 the gross receipts from the great customs were scarcely £3,000 – only one-third as much as in 1371. Little enough of the proceeds reached the government: between 1409 and 1420 Archibald the Tyneman seized about £5,000 from the customs officials of Edinburgh; and in 1420 his henchmen had seized their records lest they be produced in audit. The exchequer audit of 1422 showed that arrears of almost £4,000 were owing to the governor. The finances of central government had collapsed and it had been demonstrated that there was no substitute for a masterful king.

While there was a growing demand in Scotland for the return of James I it was also thought in England that his release might be opportune. A move in this direction had been contemplated by the late Henry V, who had induced James to serve him in France in return for the chance of a trip to Scotland on parole. But nothing resulted until James attracted the interest of the powerful family of Beaufort, of royal, but illegitimate, descent. Its members were anxious to obtain royal connections and were well aware that the poet king had detected in the Lady Joan Beaufort 'beautee eneuch to mak a world to dote'. On 4 December 1423 a treaty for James's release was sealed at London. He could not be held to ransom since he was no prisoner of war, but £40,000 (60,000 merks) were to be paid in yearly instalments of 10,000 merks to cover the 'expenses' of his long residence in England. Already it was assumed that 10,000 merks would be remitted as dowry of the Lady Joan, whom James married in February 1424. In the following month the pair were at Durham, where final negotiations included the sealing of an indenture for a seven-year truce. While James and his bride arrived in Scotland at the beginning of April a concourse of Scottish nobles headed southward from Durham to act as hostages.

On his return James faced a sorry state of affairs. Since the accession of the first Stewart king there had been a progressive decline in the authority of central government, in its finances, in the export trade, but most of all in law and order. Although the consequent sufferings of the common people are seldom revealed

in any detail their extent may be inferred from the frequent enact-
ments of the Three Estates which testified to a wholesale collapse in
respect for the law. Occasionally this was demonstrated in some
violent crime that attracted the attention of the chroniclers since it
took place within the ranks of the nobility. In 1402 Sir Malcolm
Drummond, brother-in-law of Robert III, died in the prison of
some assailant, possibly Alexander Stewart, illegitimate son of the
Wolf of Badenoch; it was certainly in curious circumstances that
Alexander married Sir Malcolm's widow and thereby obtained her
earldom of Mar. In 1413 Patrick Graham, Earl of Strathearn, was
slain by Sir John Drummond, with whom he had lately concluded
a bond of alliance.

Disorder of a different type – in the shape of heresy – simultaneously troubled the church. In 1406 or 1407 Master Laurence of
Lindores, inquisitor of heretical pravity, condemned James Resby,
an English Lollard, and consigned him and his writings to the
flames. Nonetheless in 1410 Quintin Folkhyrde, a Scottish esquire,
zealously expressed radical views in the 'News from Scotland' that
he sent to Prague, the centre of continental heresy.

Criticism of the church had been partly inspired by the consequences of the centralisation (sometimes bungling and always
costly) that had taken place during the residence of the papacy at
Avignon between 1309 and 1377. Increasingly the pope controlled
the greater appointments in the church; increasingly they were
hedged about with financial and political considerations. The
situation worsened (and criticism increased) when the return of
the papacy to Rome was followed in 1378 by the disputed papal
election that brought on the Great Schism. Until this was healed
by a general council of the church that met at Constanz from 1414
to 1417 there would be two popes (eventually three) – one at Rome,
a second at Avignon, and a third elected at Pisa in 1409. The troubles
of the Scottish monarchy coincided with those of the papacy just as
the restoration of royal authority by James I would coincide with
the restoration of papal authority by Martin V.

It would be wrong, however, to convey too grim an impression
of early Stewart Scotland. Although there was a withering of central
authority this did not necessarily lead to anarchy within each of the
baronial or clannish communities that bounded the horizons of

most of the population. In contrast to France and England there were no peasant risings in Scotland. On his own lands, among his own kinsmen and dependants, the great noble was a patriarch rather than a robber baron. His devotion to chivalry was no quixotic idiosyncrasy but a way of life that was taken for granted and earned him popularity. Nor was he uninterested in economic matters: he controlled land, by far the chief source of wealth; and in days when the merchant burgesses were hampered by various economic restrictions, sometimes self-imposed, only the chivalric noble was an uninhibited free agent. His 'crusading' ventures with the Teutonic Knights opened the Baltic to Scottish trade; the first Sinclair Earl of Orkney crossed the Atlantic *c.* 1390 (though he found nothing that was considered rewarding); and the exploits of Scottish knights in France won for all classes of their compatriots the opportunities for advancement that were available in that rich land – when Joan of Arc triumphantly entered Orleans in 1429 the bishop who welcomed her was a Scotsman.

Moreover even during the Great Schism there were aspects of ecclesiastical life that were positive as well as those that were negative. Noble birth and financial backing were seldom by themselves a qualification for an important benefice unless they were supplemented by a university degree, especially one in canon or civil law. Benedict XIII, driven from Avignon to a citadel in Aragon, and grateful for the continuing support of the Scots, gave in 1413 the necessary confirmation to Bishop Wardlaw's foundation of Scotland's first university at St Andrews. Also, since England adhered to the Roman popes while Scotland recognised the Avignonese, the ecclesiastical conflict acquired patriotic overtones – Thomas Rossy, Bishop of Galloway, even challenged the Bishop of Norwich to mortal combat.

Patriotism, almost inextricably intermingled with an interest in chivalry, was a prominent characteristic of the literature of the period, most of it the work of ecclesiastics. In 1375 Archdeacon Barbour of Aberdeen produced his epic poem, *The Bruce*, written in the English dialect that had replaced French as the language of the Lowland aristocracy. Some ten years later, John of Fordun, a chantry priest of Aberdeen, composed a Latin chronicle which flatteringly traced the origins of the Scots to Scota, daughter of the pharaoh overwhelmed in the Red Sea, and thus showed that the Scots were not derived from the mythical Trojan heroes whom the English claimed as forebears. Shortly afterwards Thomas Barry, canon of Glasgow, celebrated the Scottish victory at Otterburn in spirited Latin verse. The *Orygenale Cronykil*, compiled sometime between 1420 and 1424 by Andrew of Wyntoun, prior of Lochleven, was equally bad both as poetry and history but deliberately sought to inculcate loyalty, patriotism and virtue. If patriotism had found little practical expression in the Scotland of the early Stewarts, and had not been harnessed to national advantage, it had at least matured as a prevailing sentiment in the minds of the Scots.

CHAPTER 11

TAMING THE MAGNATES?

Jenny Wormald

THE period 1424–88 is not a particularly well-known one. Traditionally it has been written off as one of the most lawless in Scottish history, and for that reason one of the least interesting. Only a few incidents stand out as familiar, and these are, without exception, cases of conflict between king and magnates: the murder of James I, the struggle between James II and the Black Douglases, the crises at Lauder where James III's favourites were hanged by a dissident nobility, and Sauchieburn, where James was killed. The traditional interpretation is that this was a period which saw a power struggle in which one or other side sometimes gained the upper hand, but which neither side actually won. The puzzle is why this should have been so. Why should the magnates of the fifteenth century, unlike their predecessors of, say, the twelfth and thirteenth centuries, have apparently moved into direct and open opposition to the monarchy? A possible explanation, which has been put forward for the whole of northern Europe, is that this century saw the decline of 'medieval' ideas in both church and state, that this was a society in its last decadent stages, about to give way to the new ideas of the modern world. Applied to Scotland, this would explain the traditional idea that the overmighty nobility who fought and killed James III in 1488 became the rather more civilised and co-operative magnates under the Renaissance King James IV. Another possibility, however, is that there is no good answer to the question of why there was conflict between crown and nobility because there was no such conflict. Rather, there were two ruthless, tough and unscrupulous kings who were very powerful indeed, and who hounded out the two greatest magnate families of the early fifteenth century; and a third king who failed to govern effectively, and who provoked a minor and limited rebellion which, remarkably, succeeded.

One major problem about the fifteenth century is the serious lack of reliable contemporary sources, both record and chronicle. Historians turn with relief to the reign of James IV simply because so much more information is available; the daily life of the king, for example, can be described in a way which is not possible for earlier monarchs because the Treasurer's Accounts, which give a wealth of detail, have survived continuously after 1488 but for only one year before that date. Much of our information about the fifteenth century, and in particular its crises, has therefore been drawn from the writings of sixteenth-century chroniclers, the best known of which is the racy, entertaining and almost wholly unreliable history by Robert Lindsay of Pitscottie, produced in 1579. Recent research has shown that the traditional and previously accepted account of James III as the king who antagonised his nobility because of his dependence on lowborn favourites – the mason, the tailor, the musician – is a legend developed by sixteenth-century writers without any contemporary justification. Likewise the Black Douglases, who dominated the early years of James II's personal rule, emerge as opponents of royal authority on the grand scale in Pitscottie's story; but one of his main examples of their over-mighty defiance is as much invention as his account of James III, for it turns on their illegal execution of one Thomas Maclellan, tutor of Bombie, a man for whose existence there is no evidence at all.

If the details which have gone into the building up of the idea of the overmighty nobility are suspect, the idea itself contains inexplicable paradoxes. While two of the kings of this period died violent deaths at the hands of their subjects, there remains the impressive fact that the ruling house survived unchallenged in spite of its problems and misfortunes. This in itself may seem a weak enough statement. But it is put into context when it is contrasted with the situation in England where the crown changed hands by violence six times between 1399 and 1485. In Scotland, the possibility that the legitimacy of the descendants of the first marriage of Robert II might be disputed has been used as the basis of the idea that the descendants of the second marriage entertained dynastic ambitions; it has been suggested that these ambitions lay behind the murder of James I, and also had their part in the Douglases' opposition to James II. Such an interpretation seems highly dubious, however, because it rests on the assumption that the descendants of the second marriage let their claim lie between 1390 and 1424 when the government was at its most vulnerable, and chose to press it in 1437 against a strong and effective king, having failed to take the elementary step of securing the person of the heir to the throne; and the actions of the Douglases after the murder of the eighth earl in 1452, while provocative enough, do not bear out the idea of a genuine dynastic attempt. In fact there was only one undoubted usurpation attempt in fifteenth-century Scotland, that of James III's ambitious and totally irresponsible brother Alexander Duke of Albany; and the most significant feature of that attempt was that Alexander found no support in Scotland, in spite of the obvious deficiencies of the king, a situation very different from that in England, where men were amazingly willing to support rebellions, however slight their chances of success. Moreover, as English experience showed, support for a usurper might bring appreciable reward if the rebellion was successful. Here was an opportunity for self-interested advancement for the 'overmighty' Scottish magnates. Yet they made no use of it.

There were also the opportunities offered by the appalling problem of the recurrent royal minorities, a problem which, while bad enough in the intermittent form in which it appeared in other countries, amounted to staggering proportions in Scotland where in the period 1406–88 there was no adult ruler for thirty-eight years. Yet with a few exceptions, these opportunities were not exploited; only four families – the Douglases, Livingstones and Crichtons in the 1440s, the Boyds of Kilmarnock in the 1460s – turned the situation to their advantage. In this century, the nobility had an unparalleled chance of self-aggrandisement at the expense of the crown. That they let it go is strong evidence of the position of prestige and respect which the fifteenth-century monarchy enjoyed, a position which is completely at odds with the idea of the 'overmighty nobility'. Indeed, so self-confident were these kings that they felt it unnecessary to resort to the usual pursuit of monarchs of surrounding themselves with a mystique based on a mythical line of ancestors, bolstered up by signs of unusual saintly or divine favour; the use of the name 'Jacobus Seneschallus' – James the Steward – shows how unconcerned they were to obscure the fact that their origins were neither mythical nor divine.

In terms of the traditional concept, it is curious that 'the nobility' did not challenge the crown; it is also curious that the crown did not challenge 'the nobility'. One problem about the traditional view is in fact a problem of terminology. There is an obvious convenience in referring to 'the nobility' rather than to 'a few of . . .' or 'some of the nobility'; the trouble is that one begins to believe it. But the phrase is seriously misleading in two ways. It suggests that the nobility as a class was regarded by the crown as a threat and a danger; and this is manifestly untrue. It also suggests a static group, and obscures the fact that there was a major change in both personnel and titles by the mid-fifteenth century; the paradox here is that the crown which was apparently threatened by the nobility managed to rid itself, partly by its own efforts, of many of them, and then proceeded to create the problem anew by replenishing the ranks.

The factors which produced this change show the idea of 'taming the magnates' to be an oversimplification, indeed a gross understatement when applied to the policy of James I; annihilating might be a better word. In 1424 there were fifteen earldoms (excluding the earldom of Orkney) and one dukedom. In 1437 when James died the dukedom had gone, and the earldoms were reduced to eight. The revenues of one of these was in the hands of the crown; one was held by a woman, the daughter of James I; two earls were in England as hostages; and only four remained with the families who had held them in 1424. The other seven had all fallen to the crown, either because of forfeiture or because of the failure of direct heirs, that situation which was potentially dangerous for any medieval landowning family and which became actually disastrous with a king as acquisitive and unscrupulous as James I.

James returned from England in 1424. He was a complex personality, an accomplished poet and good family man, vigorous, extremely efficient and vindictive. The vigour and efficiency at once showed themselves in the flood of legislation poured out by his first three parliaments, the first of which was held in the minimum possible time after his return; in his attempts to reform parliament on English lines, which were unsuccessful; and in his rather more successful attempts to make administration more effective. His vindictiveness, which was understandable enough after eighteen years' enforced absence in England, but at the same time repellent in its cold and calculating quality, was less immediately apparent. James waited for a year, during which he seems to have been on good enough terms with the former governor, Murdoch Duke of Albany, who had negotiated James' return and created no problems for the king when relinquishing his office. Then, entirely unexpectedly, James turned with great savagery on Murdoch, the two sons of Murdoch on whom he could get his hands, and, worst of all, Duncan Earl of Lennox, an old man of about eighty whose only crime, apparently, was that of being Murdoch's father-in-law; in May 1425, they were all tried and executed at Stirling. James' delay of a year may be explained on the grounds that he was consolidating his position before taking such drastic action; the action itself is much more difficult to explain in any terms other than those of personal and unrelenting animosity reinforced by greed – because the windfall from the wholesale destruction of the Albany family, the earldoms of Fife and Menteith and the revenues of Lennox, was of course considerable.

The same personal vindictiveness showed itself again in the treatment of Malise Graham, Earl of Strathearn. Graham, a descendant of Robert II's second marriage, not only lost his earldom, but was sent to England in 1427 as a hostage and remained there until 1453, with only the less valuable earldom of Menteith as compensation. The sending of hostages to England, as security for his unpaid ransom, was used by James on other occasions as a convenient device. Most hostages remained in England for short periods, of one, three or five years. Graham was a notable exception; David, master of Atholl, son of the last surviving son of Robert II, was sent south in 1424 and died there in 1434; John, Earl of Sutherland was in England from 1427 until 1444, or possibly 1448. Acquisitiveness lay behind the king's contention that the earldom of Ross had lapsed to the crown after the death of John Stewart, Earl of Buchan and Ross, in 1424, and the exclusion of the Erskine claimant to the earldom of Mar after the death of Alexander Stewart, Earl of Mar, in 1435.

The greed and vindictiveness of James I can be amply demonstrated. The question remains whether his treatment of these magnates can be explained simply in these terms, or whether, as with his reorganisation of financial administration, greed and a genuine desire for more effective royal government intermingled to produce a consistent policy. Did James, in other words, regard it as essential to 'tame' the magnates? That such was his intention has been suggested as the motive behind the act of 1428 which attempted to bring the lairds as shire representatives to parliament, thus introducing an equivalent to the English House of Commons. Here is a clear example of the influence of his English experience. Yes – but one cannot be selective about the English influence, and argue that James saw the introduction of a lower house as a means of counteracting magnate power when his English experience must have shown him not only the advantages, as he saw them, of the English parliament, but also the fact that the Commons in England were by no means consistent supporters of the monarchy against the lords, and indeed sometimes acted in the reverse role. In any case, the lairds depended on the magnates, and this was not necessarily an anti-social force, but one which medieval kings used to their advantage. What James wanted in his attempted reforms can be seen in his legislation of 1426 which demanded that acts of parliament should be registered and circulated throughout the country that all might know his laws; in that year, he himself complained about and tried to legislate against absenteeism on the part of the magnates. The legislation of 1428 was an extension of his desire to ensure that parliament was more representative, and that its legislation was everywhere known; hence the lairds should be brought in, both to take part in the work of parliament, and to transmit it back to the localities.

The legislation of James' first three parliaments has similarly been seen as a reaction to a special situation in which, freed from control by the king, the irresponsible and overmighty magnates had increased the extent of lawlessness in Scotland. To a limited degree, this was true, but only in respect of certain individual nobles, and for the period before 1400 rather than after. The great theme of the first years of James' reign, justice for rich and poor alike, is not peculiar to this period. 'The pur comownis' appear time and again in parliamentary legislation of the fifteenth and sixteenth centuries. Concern for the lower classes had no doubt a certain propaganda value; but it was a genuine enough reflection of a fundamental social tenet of medieval society, the protection by the great of the lesser men who depended on them. James' legislation, therefore, did not consist of exceptional measures for an exceptional situation.

What was exceptional was the nature of the nobility; and it is this, along with his own unpleasant characteristics, which explains James' actions. In the period 1371–1424, the extensive family of Robert II had so successfully cornered the market that in 1424 eight of the fifteen earldoms were held by Stewarts. What James quite clearly embarked on was a family vendetta. Thus the Albany family were exterminated; Malise Graham lost his earldom and his freedom. But the Lord of the Isles, a greater trouble-maker than any Stewart in this reign, was merely temporarily imprisoned, and the most notable example of all was the Earl of Douglas. The greatest heights of Douglas power were not reached until the minority of James II. But the Earl of Douglas under James I was nonetheless a man of great power and influence; and if James indeed had a policy of 'taming the magnates' as a class, then his inaction against Douglas, apart from imprisoning him briefly in 1431, apparently because of suspected dealings with England, was an aberration totally unbelievable in a man of James' ruthless intelligence and efficiency. There are exceptions to this general view; to one Stewart, Walter Earl of Atholl, James showed no animosity, though in 1437 this did not pay off. But on the whole, the most consistent explanation of James' attitude is that he was determined to 'tame' not the nobility but the Stewart nobility; and so successfully did he do so that in the minority of James II the only Stewart earl left was Malise Graham, in England.

It has already been said that there is no evidence that any of the Stewarts had dynastic ambitions. But James clearly felt hemmed in by too many magnates close in blood to the crown, and regarded attack as the best form of defence. Why should he have felt this? In general, such a concentration of power in the state was a potential danger. And possibly James' English experience, which influenced his ideas on government, and his ideas on the burning of heretics, also influenced him here and heightened his concern; he had seen that English rebels readily found support, and he may not have felt inclined to wait for the situation to arise in Scotland. In the event, the family vendetta which he had begun was taken up by the other side, not to overthrow his line, but to remove a tyrant. When the final crisis came, even Atholl, the one Stewart who had not suffered under James, joined those who had, and James was murdered by a small and unrepresentative group of people, engaged not in a power struggle between crown and nobility, but in a family feud.

The depletion of the magnate class by 1437 cleared the way for the spectacular rise to power in the minority of James II of the lesser families of Livingstone and Crichton. It also threw into sharp relief the growing power of the Douglases. By 1449 there were eight earls in Scotland: three of them – Douglas, Ormond and Moray – were Douglas brothers, whose lands gave them powerful areas of influence both in the south-west, centred round their massive stronghold of Threave near Castle Douglas, and in the north. Again there was a concentration of power which the crown might well view with alarm. Beyond that, it is impossible to show any real threat by the Douglases. Only in the rationalisation of events found in later accounts is there any real suggestion that they were abusing the power they had. And the idea that James II brought them down because of their treasonable dealings with England can be demonstrated only after James' murder of Earl William in 1452. It cannot be substantiated before then, for the evidence is simply not available; indeed, apart from the episode in the reign of James I, the Douglases had a long tradition of friendship with France, to the extent that the fourth and fifth earls had held French titles, the fourth being killed at Verneuil in 1424 while fighting for the French against the English. Open provocation first came not from the Douglases but from the king. In 1450–1, while the earl was abroad, James took over his lands of the earldom of Wigtown, and built up as a rival family in the south-west the Kennedies of Dunure. What the Douglases apparently wanted was to be left to enjoy their vast possessions. The crown's inroads into these possessions sparked off the chain of events and worsening relations which led to the famous murder of February 1452. This murder left James in a highly vulnerable position; and he survived only because most of the magnates, once again failing to take advantage of an opportunity to fulfil the role ascribed to them of opposing the crown, supported the king against the Douglases, to the extent that when the final conflict came in 1455, the Douglases were left entirely without allies, and easily defeated. It was a curious, dangerous affair. It is impossible to prove that the king's actions were justified, to be sure that the Douglases were an actual rather than a potential threat. But the parallel between James II and his father, the ruthlessness with which they reacted to a potential threat seems fairly close. And not only ruthlessness. The acquisitiveness of James I is seen again in James II's unscrupulous annexation of the earldom of Moray when direct male heirs had failed, and his exclusion of the Erskine claimant to the earldom of Mar; and it may well have been a large part of his attitude to the Douglases.

The crisis which resulted in the crushing of the Black Douglases has overshadowed by its drama the other events of the reign. The other side of the story of James II's relations with his nobles is much more prosaic, but also much more important. In 1444–5, during his minority, the earldom of Huntly had been created. After the Douglas murder, in 1452, the crown used its patronage to attract or reward support, and created three further earls and a number of lords of parliament; two of these earldoms were short lived, but the third, the earldom of Erroll, was another creation of major significance. Finally in 1457–8 came four more: the earldoms of Argyll, Morton, Rothes and Marischal. The reign of James II in fact saw the first group of creations which brought to the top families who dominated Scottish politics in the sixteenth century; the second group came with James IV. What had happened was that the peerage had been changed beyond recognition; the old Stewart dominance had gone, and the crown now gave influence and high position to families who had served it well, and who were to continue to do so with a remarkable degree of consistency. The Gordons, earls of Huntly, and the Campbells, earls of Argyll, for example, both had a record of crown service which was interrupted in the first case only in the late sixteenth century, and in the second not until the seventeenth, apart from a temporary break in the pattern, for reasons which were understandable, in 1488. Their position as the representatives of royal authority in the north and the west is better known in the sixteenth century, but both James II and James III used them in this role; and if it was a gamble to give men power in fifteenth-century Scotland, then the gamble paid off handsomely, for these magnates, while naturally intent on building up their own prestige and dominance, at the same time served the crown both in the central government and in the localities. A striking example of this is seen in the reign of James IV, when the king first instructed the Earl of Huntly to take bonds of allegiance to the earl from all the landowners north of the Mounth as a means of giving him formal control; then ordered him to build a tower at Inverlochy as a focal point for royal authority, as exercised by the earl; and finally forgave him for failing to complete it, because his presence had been required at court. This was the busy – and typical – life of a Scottish magnate.

The magnate problem of the early fifteenth century was one of two families, Stewart and Douglas, who had built up too great a concentration of power and wealth. Greed and fear of this power on the part of two strong and ruthless kings had brought them down. After 1455, the issue changes completely. The last years of James II's reign were years of good relations between the crown and all its magnates; years when the power of the crown was seen at its height, when the king, far from feeling that he was the insecure head of a state which was backward by European standards and wracked by an internal power struggle, pursued active and effective policies both abroad and at home. His foreign policy was aggressive and high-handed to the point of making the amazingly arrogant offer of arbitrating in a dispute between the French king and the Dauphin. At home, he showed the same interest in justice as had his father; and so successful was he that in 1458 the parliament, which, as it happened, was his last, paid him a fitting and impressive tribute:

God of his grace has send our soverane lorde sik progress and prosperite that all his rebellys and brekaris of his justice ar removit out of his realme, and na maisterfull party remanande that may caus ony breking in his realme;

a comment which incidentally suggests that the king and his most powerful subjects were at one in disliking the potential threat of one family who had too much power and who therefore 'may caus ony breking'.

This period anticipates the reign of James IV, which has always been regarded as one in which the power struggle had abated. It was interrupted by James II's death in 1460, and the problem of another minority, in which the Boyds of Kilmarnock seized temporary control. More serious, however – for the new king had no difficulty in taking over government and bringing down this family in 1468–9 – was the personality of James III himself. In this reign, the problem was not that of the crown taming the magnates; it was the magnates who were trying to tame the crown. The traditional account of James III's downfall, brought about by widespread resentment by the nobles of the king's reliance on lowborn favourites, is legend. James, like many other kings, did have favourites, but they were neither numerous nor lowborn; and the explanation of his failure lies elsewhere. James was a man of grandiose and exalted ideas of kingship, and at the same time a man who was lazy in the business of government and who acted on arbitrary whim. He indulged in wild schemes of continental expansionist campaigns to the extent of giving the impression that all he wanted was to get out of Scotland. He completely failed to understand how to use and gain the trust of his most powerful servants, failing to reward Huntly, for example, for his service against the Lord of the Isles in 1476, and giving and taking away lands and offices without reason or justification, thus producing a state of tension and uncertainty among the nobles which prevented any hope of co-operation and good relations. He tried to centralise government in Edinburgh, rarely moving from the capital except on hunting holidays to Falkland. This was an age when Scottish kings were expected to travel throughout their kingdom, being seen by their subjects and taking a personal part in the exercise of justice and the control of the troubled areas of the country, and James' failure to do this increased the idea that this king was remote, uninterested and ineffective. Time and again parliament begged him to do his job properly, pointing out, for example, in 1473 that the business of a king was to govern his country and not to rush off on foreign expeditions. Here it would appear that the magnates were more politically responsible than the crown.

Yet for all this, respect for the monarchy outweighed, for the great majority of the magnates, the fact that James III was personally disastrous. In June 1488, the rebel army at Sauchieburn contained only two earls, Angus, a chronic and individualistic trouble-maker, and Argyll, who had been arbitrarily removed, in February 1488, from the chancellorship which he had held since 1483; and there was also a small number of lords who had suffered from James' high-handed and whimsical actions. Some of the nobility who had given the king active support up to the point where he broke the agreements made with his opponents in April and May, at Aberdeen and Blackness, did not turn up to fight for him at Sauchieburn; possibly after this double-dealing they preferred to solve the problem of the conflict between loyalty to the crown and the feeling that James had finally shown himself impossible to serve by remaining neutral. Others – the majority – continued to support the crown.

The rebels of 1488 – surprisingly – won because James was killed, though it is by no means certain that they had wanted a solution as extreme as this. Whatever their aims, however, the nobles who in the reign of James III apparently fitted into the concept of 'over-mighty magnates' now became, after 1488, the co-operative nobility of James IV; the same people, not a new and better generation. Angus continued to cause trouble; Huntly, Argyll and others like them to serve the crown. The fifteenth century had been a time of intermittent conflict James I and the Stewarts, James II and the Douglases, a minority group of the harassed nobility against James III. None of this adds up to a power struggle between 'crown and nobility', with an underlying ideology which caused the crown to regard the magnates as a social and political class as a threat. The situation was very different. King and nobles were recognised, and regarded themselves as the highest ranks in a hierarchical society, a society in which the king, the motivating force in government, relied primarily on the greatest men in his kingdom for counsel and advice and for co-operation in the practical business of running his country. These were the men close to the king; many were his friends, the men who shared his interests and pursuits. In parliament and on the council, while few of them were interested in the minutiae of government, who better to fulfil the traditional role of the king's principal councillors than the magnates, those nearest to him in rank and outlook? And in the localities, who better – indeed, who other? – to maintain royal authority than the nobles with their pre-eminent position based on their widespread alliances with their kindreds, the lairds and their tenants and servants, alliances based on protection by the magnates in return for the service and loyalty of their dependants? Fifteenth-century Scotland was a unified nation. It was also a network of local societies – and for many, the locality was still more meaningful than the country – in which chances of survival, of safety of life, land and goods, depended on the fulfilling of the contract by which lesser men gave service to the great in return for the very real benefit of their protection and maintenance.

In any case, life for the magnates of fifteenth-century Scotland was not always a matter of high politics and feuding. Their interests lay not in opposition to the crown, but in enriching themselves by extending their lands, and the best way to do this was through crown service or by advantageous marriage. They were intensely conscious not simply of their position in the political state, but also of their place in society. To some extent they may have been threatened, as were the nobility in other European countries, by economic pressures; the great were no longer so distinguished by wealth from lesser men as they had formerly been. And the very fact that many of them had been raised from laird to earl or lord also produced pressure to ensure recognition of rank from those who had formerly been their social equals. Thus, for example, the written bond of manrent and service, given by lairds to earls and lords, became a commonplace document in Scotland from the mid-fifteenth century; here was a means of securing formal recognition. And in this century and the next, the government gave its blessing to the increased awareness of social status and desire to define that status in repeated legislation on the dress, the food, the size of retinue which only the great could enjoy; the lesser one's rank, the less elaborate one's style of life. Their self-consciousness in this, their desire to make a splash, is exemplified by the magnificence of the retinue of William, Earl of Douglas, on his visit to Rome in 1450; the impression this made on the pope was not apparently tinged by any cynicism about the provincial come to town. And if they could not emulate the crown in its acquisition of artillery, that most expensive and supreme status symbol whatever its defects as an effective weapon, they could and did emulate it on a smaller scale in both secular and ecclesiastical building, of which William Sinclair's collegiate church at Roslin is the most striking example. And both Sinclair and Archibald Douglas, Earl of Moray, were literary patrons. Some of them sought fortune abroad. This was an obvious outlet for younger sons, many of whom found a profitable career fighting in France, where their value can be seen in the formation by the French monarchy of a Scots Guard in 1445, and where at least one 'soldier of fortune', Bernard Stewart Lord d'Aubigny, gained an international reputation. But it was not only younger sons; the earls of Douglas and Buchan both fought in France and were rewarded with French titles before being killed at Verneuil.

The fifteenth century was a time of political upheaval, of redistribution of power and wealth from the hands of two families to a wider, non-royal group. But it was not a time when existing concepts of society, of the place of the crown and the place of the magnates and their close and co-operative relationship to one another was in any way challenged. The early sixteenth-century *Porteous of Nobenes*, a work which described the twelve virtues of a nobleman, put second on the list loyalty; the nobles:

> ar nocht sa hie set nor ordanit for to reif or tak be force in ony way bot thai ar haldin in werray richt and resoun for to serf thair king and defend there subjectis.

This was not mere literary piety. Many nobles of the fifteenth century did indeed 'serf thair king and defend there subjectis'. At no time did they regard themselves as involved in a power struggle with the monarchy; nor did the crown, which smashed them when they became too powerful, as two families did, and built them up and rewarded them when they served their king. Two magnate families and one king threatened the ideal. But for the rest, they saw themselves, on the whole, as allies.

CHAPTER 12

NATIONAL SPIRIT AND
NATIVE CULTURE

John MacQueen

SCOTTISH literature, the arts and scholarship in general are often thought to have reached their peak at the court of James IV. The protean character of the king himself – linguist, lover, doctor, builder, alchemist, crusader and rash commander of forlorn hopes – has strengthened the impression that he presided over a great Renaissance court. No fair-minded historian can belittle the accomplishment of the reign, but it must always be made clear that James' reputation has been gained partly at the expense of his father, James III, partly at that of his son, James V. It is virtually certain, for instance, that the greatest Scottish poet, Robert Henryson, wrote his most important works, the *Testament of Cresseid* and the *Morall Fabillis*, during the reign of James III. Henryson was not, it is true, a court poet in quite the same restricted sense as Dunbar and Lindsay, but he was very much in touch with the major issues of his day, and several of his poems (the *Testament* and *Orpheus and Eurydice* in particular) must have been written with a court audience in mind. Henryson too was essentially a man of the early Northern Renaissance – a Christian humanist, widely interested in the classical inheritance. It is not difficult to see in the *Fabillis* 'the combination of levity with seriousness', which has been described as the common humanistic characteristic of Erasmus and Thomas More. The social satire of the *Fabillis* comes close to that of Book I of More's *Utopia*; indeed one almost establishes that Henryson belonged to the company of the humanists by saying that the social condition of Scotland is one of the main concerns of the *Fabillis*. Henryson pretty certainly was a graduate both in arts and law; a marked concern with legal matters is evident both in the *Testament* and in the *Fabillis*. He probably lectured in law at Glasgow

University, where he was incorporated in 1462, although it is with Dunfermline that he is chiefly associated as schoolmaster (that is, headmaster) of the ancient grammar school attached to the Benedictine monastery of the town. One may conjecture that he found the humanistic studies of the grammar school more congenial than the often sordid realities of legal pursuits. His poems are based on experience in terms of a wide reading in Latin, French, Scots and English. One may perhaps single out for special mention the use he made of Boccaccio's *Concerning the Genealogy of the Gods*, the universal handbook of the humanist in Italy and elsewhere; a book too which was to have an important influence on Scottish poetry, notably that of Douglas and Lindsay, through much of the following century. During the 1480s Henryson obtained books from the press of William Caxton at Westminster. But his humanism is perhaps most immediately apparent in the additions which he made, or seems likely to have made, to the vocabulary of the English language; they include such words as invention (used of literary creation), capacity, generable, participant, idol, degenerate, rusticate, brutal, diminute, figural, spoliate, irrational, type, toxicate, intricate and vilipend.

It is in fact during the reign of James III that the existence of a literary and artistic Scottish Renaissance begins to be self-evident. The character of the king is difficult to assess, but it is clear that, partly because of his aesthetic and scholarly interests, he was out of sympathy with the general run of the nobility, and much more to the liking of some at least of the artists, craftsmen and writers among his subjects. The most celebrated of his so-called favourites, eventually hanged at Lauder Bridge by the outraged nobility, was Robert Cochrane, the architect of the Great Hall at Stirling Castle, one of the earliest buildings in Great Britain to which the adjective 'Renaissance' may with some fitness be applied. In the full tradition of European royalty, James was himself a collector of fine classical manuscripts. In this, as in other respects, he probably owed a great deal to his former tutor, Archibald Whitelaw, archdeacon of Lothian and sub-dean of Glasgow, who held the office of royal Secretary for the greater part of the reign. Whitelaw was a university man, who had graduated in arts from St Andrews in 1439, and taught at St Andrews and Cologne before he entered the king's service. The

Secretary's office was probably already to some extent a centre of humanistic influence; in James II's reign it had been occupied by William Turnbull, who afterwards, as bishop of Glasgow, became the founder of Glasgow University, and who had also been one of Whitelaw's predecessors as archdeacon of Lothian. Whitelaw belonged to, and expanded, the tradition of Turnbull. Several classical works from his personal library have survived; they include a Lucan, printed at Venice in 1478; a Sallust, printed at Venice in 1481, and Asconius' *Commentaries* on the speeches of Cicero, printed at Venice in 1477. As Secretary, Whitelaw composed a Latin oration, delivered in 1484 at Nottingham to Richard III, which seems to be the earliest extant piece of extended humanistic prose composed by a Scot. It is carefully modelled on Cicero, and in one or two places there are hints that Whitelaw had at least a minimum acquaintance with Greek. Whitelaw survived James III to die in 1498.

Among civil servants and court officials, this humanistic interest continued throughout James IV's reign. The most eminent figure who spans both reigns is William Elphinstone (1431–1514), Keeper of the Privy Seal under James IV, bishop of Aberdeen from 1483 onwards, and probably acting archbishop of St Andrews for a brief period after Flodden. Elphinstone was a Glasgow graduate who continued his studies in Paris and lectured at Orleans before his return to Scotland in the early 1470s. His most celebrated achievement was to found the University of Aberdeen in 1495; in addition, he was probably responsible for the Education Act of 1496; for the establishment of Scottish printing in 1507, and for the compilation of the *Breviary of Aberdeen*, printed in two volumes which appeared in 1509 and 1510. The books from his library which survive are mostly legal treatises, but he did possess a manuscript copy of Valla's *Elegantiae*.

Another well-known colleague of Whitelaw was John Reid of Stobo, the 'gud gentill Stobo' of Dunbar's 'Lament for the Makaris', who is thus established as a vernacular poet, once of some reputation. No surviving work, unfortunately, can be attributed to him with any certainty. Stobo, however, was also described by James III as his 'familiar servant and scribe' when in 1478 he was awarded a pension for life in return for services to the king and his predecessors as a writer of letters to the Pope and diverse kings, princes and magnates outwith the kingdom. In 1497, under James IV, there is record of a payment to Stobo and Walter Chepman 'for thare lawboris in lettrez writing the tyme the King past in Ingland'. (The reference is to the invasion of northern England by James in support of Perkin Warbeck.) It is significant that Stobo's colleague in letter writing was the same Chepman afterwards associated with Andrew Myllar in one of the most notable cultural achievements of James IV's reign, the establishment in 1507 of the first known Scottish printing house. All this at least suggests that Stobo played some part in the fifteenth-century movement towards a practical humanism. He died in 1505.

Patrick Paniter (c. 1470–c. 1520) became James IV's Secretary in 1507. He was tutor to James' illegitimate and able son, Alexander Stewart, archbishop of St Andrews (1493–1513), who in 1508, perhaps at Paniter's suggestion, became a pupil of Paniter's old contemporary at the College of Montaigu in Paris, the great Erasmus. Stewart and Paniter exchanged a number of affectionate Latin letters. Disappointingly, the surviving volumes of Paniter's library are limited to legal works. Proof of his versatility, and perhaps also of the inefficiency which versatility sometimes entails, is to be found in the fact that he helped to direct the fire of the Scottish artillery at Flodden, the battle in which Stewart, like the king and many others, met his death. Paniter, however, was so fortunate as to escape.

More distinguished still, at least as a writer of humanistic Latin, was Walter Ogilvie, another St Andrews graduate who continued his studies in Paris. Hector Boece, the first Principal of the University of Aberdeen, founded in 1495, and himself a humanist of repute, whose *History of Scotland* was published in 1527, speaks with enthusiasm of the copiousness, the charm and the pithiness of Ogilvie's Latin style. The description may be tested by a long panegyric on Henry VII of England, composed by Ogilvie between 24 January and 2 April 1502, and preserved in the National Library of Scotland in what may be an autograph manuscript. The immediate occasion of the speech is probably the betrothal of Henry VII's daughter Margaret to James IV on 24 January 1502. (The subsequent marriage led, a century later, to the accession of James VI to the throne of England.) The panegyric thus offers an interesting Latin parallel to Dunbar's vernacular, *The Thistle and the Rose*. But much of the speech is devoted to Henry's eldest son, Arthur; the latter part consists solely of a description of the ceremonies at the unlucky marriage between Arthur and Catherine of Aragon on 14 November 1501. Ogilvie, it may be, wrote his panegyric because he desired a position at the English court, perhaps as tutor to the young prince, whose death on 2 April 1502 put an end to such ambitions. The panegyric is floridly Ciceronian in style, and answers well enough to Boece's description.

These men, and others like them, were central to the life and activities of James IV's court, and it is no accident that a summary of their careers has involved references to most of the great events of the reign – the foundation of the University of Aberdeen; the Education Act of 1496, which, in theory at least, obliged the eldest sons of barons and freeholders to obtain perfect Latin at grammar school, and then proceed to three years of arts and law at university; James' military (and naval) ambitions; the European connections of his court; the 'marriage of the thistle and the rose'; the establishment of printing; and the battle of Flodden. In the same general tradition is the foundation of the Royal College of Surgeons in 1506. The only matter of importance which lies somewhat outside the orbit of the humanists is James' attempt to bring the Highlands, and more particularly the Islands, under direct central administration. The attempt was at least partially successful. In 1493 the semi-independent MacDonald lordship of the Isles came to an end, and in subsequent campaigns James substantially altered the balance of Highland power by establishing the dominance of the Campbells in the west and the Gordons in the north. This process too had a literary monument, the origins at least of which may be traced to James' reign. The oldest considerable body of Scottish Gaelic poetry is preserved in the manuscript *Book of the Dean of Lismore*, compiled between 1512 and 1526 by Sir James MacGregor, Dean of Lismore in Argyll and vicar of Fortingall in Perthshire. The Scottish poems in the collection belong for the most part to the middle and late fifteenth and early sixteenth centuries, and the great majority are court poems, composed not for the royal court (although James did have a command of Gaelic), but for those of the major Highland chiefs, notably the houses owing allegiance to the lords of the Isles, the earls of Argyll, and to the chiefs of clan Gregor. Panegyric, lament and satire are the dominant modes, and there are many references to contemporary events. Here, for instance, is a poem composed by a churchman, the Dean of Knoydart, after the murder (c. 1490) of Angus, son of the Lord of the Isles, by Diarmid Ua Cairbre, an Irish harper:

> Thou head of Diarmaid O'Cairbre, though great enough are thy spoils and thy pride, not too great I deem the amount of thy distress though thou hangest from a stake.
>
> I pity not thy shaggy main, nor that it is tossed by the wind of the glens however rough; I pity thee not that a withy is in thy jaws, thou head of Diarmaid O'Cairbre.
>
> Woe to him who hath noted thy throat-stroke, and would not be a foe to thine alliance; woe, alas, to him who rejected not thy shrieks, thou head of Diarmaid O'Cairbre.
>
> By thee was destroyed the king of Islay, a man who dealt wine and silver; whose locks were fresh and crisp, thou head of Diarmaid O'Cairbre.
>
> Islay's king of festive goblets, who raised his friends to honour; woe to him who wounded his bright white skin, thou head of Diarmaid O'Cairbre.
>
> Dear to me was his noble palm, ungrudging of gold or silver; who joyed in feast and hunting, thou head of Diarmaid O'Cairbre.

For Gaelic, the *Book of the Dean* has the same importance as the other great sixteenth-century manuscripts – the Asloan, the Bannatyne, the Maitland – have for the vernacular poetry of the Lowlands. Every major aspect of James' reign, and many minor ones, finds expression in this verse, especially in that of the royal court. James, for instance, established a powerful Scottish fleet, the flagship of which was the great *Michael*, the largest warship in Europe, for the construction of which all the woods in Fife are said to have been cut down. A surprising moment in Dunbar's ornate pageant, *The Goldyn Targe*, is the realistic departure of the followers of Venus on board a warship, which fires a salute as they depart:

In twynkling of ane eye to schip thai went,
And swyth up saile unto the top thai stent,
And with swift course atour the flude thay frak;
Thay fyrit gunnis wyth powder violent,
Till that the reke raise to the firmament,
The rochis all resownyt wyth the rak,
For rede it semyt that the raynbow brak;
Wyth spirit affrayde apon my fete I sprent
Amang the clewis, so carefull was the crak.

swyth: *quickly* stent: *stretch* atour: *over* frak: *move swiftly*
rack: *crack* rede: *fear* sprent: *sprang* clewis: *cliffs*

It is fairly obvious that in this poem Dunbar incidentally reflects some of the enthusiasm for naval achievement to be found among his audience at James' court, an enthusiasm fanned by the achievements of commanders like Sir Andrew Wood and the brothers John, Robert and Andrew Barton.

The importance of the burghs steadily increased in the fifteenth and sixteenth centuries. Henryson in the *Taill of the Uponlandis Mous, and the Burges Mous* had already drawn a picture of the slippery prosperity of the rich merchant class. Dunbar continued the tradition in complimentary terms when he celebrated the welcome given by Aberdeen to the new queen, more critically when he addressed the Merchants of Edinburgh:

> Your proffeit daylie dois incres,
> Your godlie workis les and les;
> Through streittis nane may mak progres
> For cry of cruikit, blind, and lame –

For candid portrayal of the rural life led by the majority, however, it is still better either to turn back to Henryson's *Fabillis*, or forward to Lindsay with his John the Commonweal and Pauper, the poor man.

Again, the reference to Alexander Stewart has shown that James did not confine his activities to politics, humanism and war. The most celebrated of his mistresses was Lady Margaret Drummond, the eldest daughter of John Drummond, lord of that ilk and of Stobhall in Perthshire. In 1496 she became James' mistress, and in 1502, some nine months before the king's marriage to Margaret Tudor, she and her two sisters were poisoned. Three blue stones mark their grave in the choir of Dunblane Cathedral. James ordered dirges to be sung in Edinburgh, and for years he feed two priests to say masses in the cathedral for the repose of her soul.

The love affair is celebrated in the anonymous *Tayis Bank*, a dream poem, composed perhaps after the lady's death, in which she becomes the central visionary figure in the landscape of the Tay Valley:

> To creatur that wes in cair,
> Or cauld of crewelty,
> A blicht blenk of hir vesage bair
> Of baill his bute mycht be.
> Hir hyd, hir hew, hir hevinly hair
> Mycht havy hairtis uphie.
> So angelik under the air
> Never wicht I saw with e.

blicht: *blythe* blenk: *glance* bute: *remedy* hyd: *skin* uphie: *uplift*

The poem ends with the departure of the lady, and the return of the dreamer to the riverside landscape:

> The rever throw the rise couth rowt,
> And roseris rais on raw.
> The schene birdis full schill couth schowt
> Into that semly schaw.
> Joy wes within and joy without
> Under that wlonkest waw,
> Quhair Tay ran doun with stremis stout
> Full efrecht under Stobschaw.

rise: *boughs* rowt: *roar* roseris: *rose-bushes* ('*and rose-bushes rose in a row*') schene: *bright, beautiful* schill: *sweet* schaw: *grove* wlonkest: *fairest* waw: *wall*

Dunbar in his more direct fashion deals with James and a different mistress in *The Wowing of the King quhen he wes in Dunfermeling*. The tod (fox) represents the king:

> The tod wes nowder lene nor skowry,
> He wes ane lusty reid haird lowry,
> Ane lang taild beist and grit with all;
> The silly lame wes all to small
> To sic ane tribbill to hald ane bace;
> Scho fled him nocht; fair mot hir fall!
> And that me thocht ane ferly cace.

skowry: *wasted, withered* lowry: *fox* tribbill: *treble* bace: *bass*
fair mot hir fall: *good luck to her* ferly: *wonderful*

Characteristically, even in the marriage pageant of *The Thistle and the Rose*, Dunbar takes James to task on the subject of his mistresses. Dame Nature is addressing the Thistle, king of all plant life, who symbolises certain aspects of the Scottish crown, and thus of the king:

> And sen thow art a king, thow be discreit;
> Herb without vertew thow hald nocht of sic pryce
> As herb of vertew and of odor sueit;
> And lat no nettill vyle, and full of vyce,
> Hir fallow to the gudly flour delyce;
> Nor latt no wyld weid, full of churlichenes,
> Compair hir till the lilleis nobilnes.
>
> Nor half non udir flour in sic denty
> As the fresche Ros of cullour reid and quhyt;
> For gife thow dois, hurt is thyne honesty,
> Conciddering that no flour is so perfyt,
> So full of vertew, pleasans, and delyt,
> So full of blisfull angeilik bewty,
> Imperiall birth, honour and dignite.

pryce: *value* hir fallow to: *match herself with* denty: *esteem*

These poems stand well apart from the general achievement of the humanists. To a considerable extent, however, poets and humanists belonged to the same company, and emerged from the same background of university education. Dunbar and Douglas were both St Andrews graduates, and John Reid of Stobo achieved distinction both as vernacular poet and as humanist writer of official Latin epistles. The stylistic brilliance of the makars corresponds to the Ciceronian eloquence of the humanists, and mirrors the same careful training in rhetoric. Stobo, Paniter and Ogilvie have a natural place among the honourable servants of the king, as described by Dunbar in *Remonstrance to the King*:

> Schir, ye have mony servitouris
> And officiaris of dyvers curis;
> Kirkmen, courtmen, and craftismen fyne;
> Doctouris in jure, and medicyne;
> Divinouris, rethoris, and philosophouris,
> Astrologis, artistis, and oratouris –

curis: *callings, occupations* jure: *law, jurisprudence*

Correspondingly, for himself Dunbar makes the classical claim of immortality through his verse, and it is notable that when Gavin Douglas in *The Palice of Honour* (1501) lists the eternally famous poets, he includes not merely such names as Homer, Virgil, Ovid, Petrarch and Chaucer, but also, to represent Scotland,

> Greit Kennedie and Dunbar yit undeid
> And Quintine with ane Huttok on his heid.

Huttok: *some kind of hat*

Even in his lifetime, that is to say, Dunbar was regarded by his contemporaries as a classic. It is worth noting too that by implication Douglas places himself in the same high company.

Douglas in fact, by his life as by his poetry, stands most obviously in the tradition of the court humanists. *The Palice of Honour* with its emphasis on the nine classical Muses, and a concept of honour which is subsumed finally in the person of the God of *Revelation*, is essentially a manifesto of the movement. Douglas included among the scholars and poets admitted to the palace the founders of the Italian Renaissance, Petrarch, Boccaccio, Poggio, Valla and Pomponius Laetus. He refers to Valla and Boccaccio in the prologue to the first book of his translation of Virgil's *Aeneid*, completed in 1513, the year of Flodden. In the prologue to the sixth book he mentions the Dutch humanist, Jodocus Badius Ascensius, whose commentary he used extensively. But of course the mere existence of Douglas' *Aeneid*, the first and best of the great Renaissance translations of the British Isles, is the clearest proof of the European accomplishment and classical scholarship of James' court:

> The batalis and the man I wil discrive
> Fra Troyis boundis first that fugitive
> By fait to Ytail come and cost Lavyne,
> Our land and sey katchit with mekil pyne
> By fors of goddis abufe, from euery steid,
> Of cruell Iuno throu ald remembrit fede.
> Gret pane in batail sufferit he alsso
> Or his goddis brocht in Latio
> And belt the cite fra quham, of nobill fame,
> The Latyne pepill takyn heth thar name,
> And eik the faderis, princis of Alba,
> Cam, and the wallaris of gret Rome alswa.

discrive: *describe, record* katchit: *driven, tossed* mekil: *great* pyne: *distress, suffering* steid: *place* fede: *enmity, hatred* or: *before* belt: *built* wallaris: *wall builders* alswa: *also, as well*

Dunbar and Douglas are the greatest individual poets of James' reign. In many ways, however, a lesser figure – John Major (1470–1550), theologian and historian, student of Cambridge and Paris, professor at Paris, Glasgow and St Andrews, commonly called 'the last of the schoolmen' – is more representative of the general style of the era. It may seem almost paradoxical to include such a man in an account, the primary emphasis of which lies on the Renaissance. In fact the paradox is more apparent than real. Admittedly, Major's immediate intellectual concerns were those which had occupied the theologians of the twelfth, thirteenth and fourteenth centuries; his way of thought and expression lies deliberately close to theirs. In this, however, he differs scarcely at all from the majority of his immediate contemporaries – from Dunbar, for instance, at least under the aspect of priest and writer of magnificent vernacular hymns in the full medieval tradition:

> Syng hevin imperiall, most of hicht,
> Regions of air make armony;
> All fishe in flud and foull of flicht
> Be myrthfull and mak melody:
> All *Gloria in excelsis* cry,
> Hevin, erd, se, man, bird, and best,
> He that is crownit abone the sky
> *Pro nobis Puer natus est.*

hevin imperiall: *empyreal heaven, the dweling of God and his angels*

But Major was well aware that the world for which he wrote had changed vastly over the centuries, and the changes have left traces in his works. For instance, in the dedication of the *Quartus Sententiarum* to Alexander Stewart, he defends the theological Latin which Stewart, as we have seen, had been trained to regard as barbarous. And of course the mere fact that Major, a theologian, wrote history, is significant – in the context of his times one might almost say revolutionary. The logical methods which he used sometimes led to important advances. One may illustrate by a story which links Major with his friend Gavin Douglas, and which is preserved by the Italian historian and humanist, Polydore Vergil, who sought information on the early Scottish kings from Douglas, while the latter was in London during the last months of his life.

Of late one Gawine Dowglas, Bishop of Dunchell, a Scottishe man, a manne as well noble in ligniage as vertewe, when he understoode that I was purposed to write this historie, hee camme to commune with me; in forthe with, we fell into friendshippe, and after he vehementlie requiered mee, that in relation of the Scottishe affaires, I showlde in no wise follow the president of an historie of a certaine contriman of his . . .

The countryman was Major who in his *History* (1521) had dismissed much of the traditional history of Scotland as fable. Douglas provided Polydore as an alternative with the usual story of Gathelus and Scota, daughter of Pharaoh. Polydore was not convinced.

> As soon as I hadde redde these thinges, accordinge to the olde proverbe, I seemed to see the beare bringe foorthe her younglinges.... Wherefore I towlde him, even as frindlie as trewlie, that as concerninge the Scottes and Pictes beefore there comminge into Brittaine (which Bedas in his time hadd well assigned), it showlde not bee lawful for me to intermeddell, bie reason of the prescrit which is incident to an historien, which is that hee showld nether abhorre the discooveringe of falsehoode, nether in anie case alowe the underminge of veritee, nether to gyve suspition of favor nor yeat of envy. This Gawine, noe doubte a sincere manne, didd the lesse dissent from this sentence, in that it plainlie appeared to him that reason and trewthe herin well agreaed, so easilie is trewthe allwaise discovowred from feyned phansies.

Schoolman and man of all the full Renaissance are here momentarily at one (Polydore, however, carried his doubts further than Major), and Douglas at least begins by adhering to older superstitions – although it is notable that he was open to rational conviction by Polydore. Major too is well aware that the style and method of his history is unusual, but he is prepared to defend himself. For him, as for the earlier Whitelaw and Ogilvie, the most distinguished historians are the humanist idols, Sallust and Livy – interestingly he adds Bede to the company – but he pleads the passage of time, that sixteenth-century Scotland differs significantly from pagan Rome. He adds that theology is a training peculiarly appropriate for the writer of history, who must make distinctions. 'And, indeed, I have given my utmost endeavour to follow this course in all cases, and most of all where the question was ambiguous, to the end that from the reading of this history you may learn not only the thing that was done, but also how it ought to have been done, and that you may by this means and at the cost of little reading come to know what the experience of centuries, if it were granted to you to live so long, could scarcely teach.' Such an idea of history reaches back beyond Sallust or Livy to the greatest Greek historian, Thucydides.

Major thus provides much interesting material on the intellectual climate in which he lived, and it is all the more interesting because he himself appears to have been singularly broadminded and tolerant in his treatment of ideas and the effects which they had on his contemporaries. Thus he is an advocate of political union between Scotland and England. He nowhere directly attacks the views of Erasmus, who had been a student in the same college as himself in Paris. He is acquainted with the Latin works of Petrarch and Pico della Mirandola. He was clearly aware that Gavin Douglas, then Provost of St Giles in Edinburgh, held views on theological method very different from his own, but he made no direct attack on Douglas; instead he prefixed to his *In primum Sententiarum* a Latin *Dialogue concerning the material appropriate to the Theologian*, in which the speakers are Gavin Douglas himself and David Cranston, one of the most distinguished of Major's pupils, who like Major himself had some knowledge of Greek. Douglas is given a full and friendly opportunity to state his views, which are very much those of the Renaissance. Theologians are too much concerned with Aristotelian subtleties, not enough with the fathers of the church and with scripture; they write too much and too little to the purpose; they are arrogant. He quotes Laurentius Valla to support his position. Cranston replies that theological methods have more value for some than for others, that Major himself has always been opposed to needless verbosity, and that Douglas is attacking not theological method itself, but the inappropriate use of theological method. He dismisses the views of Valla as those of a lunatic; Valla made more mistakes in his dialectic than there are spots on a leopard. Douglas parts amicably from Cranston reminding him that Major's birthplace at Gleghornie is only 'a sabbath journey in the law of Moses' from his own at Tantallon. Douglas and Major, incidentally, held identical opinions on at least one matter, the scholarly achievement of the first English printer, William Caxton. Douglas justifiably has no good word for Caxton's *Aeneid*; rather less justifiably Major despises Caxton's edition of Trevisa's translation of the historian Higden's *Polychronicon*, which he probably believed was the printer's own composition. But at least Major made some attempt to be judicious, even about Caxton. 'Now in a measure, if not altogether,' he says, 'we may make allowance for an unlettered man: he followed simply the fashion of speech that was common amongst the English about their enemies, the Scots.'

In conclusion, two points must be emphasised. In James' reign, the Scottish Reformation was still a matter of the far future. At the same time, many of the characteristics of the reformers were already visible in isolation among individuals, and the society in which these individuals lived was particularly open to reformation influences. Dunbar combines an intense imaginative experience of Catholicism with disillusion about the state of the society and the position of the church within that society:

> Kirkmen so halie ar and gude,
> That on thair conscience, rowme and rude,
> May turn aucht oxin and ane wane.

rowme: *broad* rude: *rough* aucht: *eight* wane: *wagon, cart* (*the eight-ox team was the usual haulage unit*)

or:

> Quhat help is thair in lordschips sevin,
> Quhone na hous is bot hell and hevin,
> Palice of lycht, or pit obscure?

The extraordinary appointment of a gifted boy, a royal bastard, to the primatial see of St Andrews cannot have strengthened the church, any more than did the excommunication of James at the end of his reign by Pope Julius and his successor Pope Leo, whose main intention was to keep France in political isolation, and who found an excuse when James, in violation of the treaty of peace which he had signed in 1502, at last invaded England. The abstract and courteous debate between Major and Douglas held the potential of the very different style later adopted by John Knox and George Buchanan.

Second, the idea that Flodden was the crowning disaster of

Scottish history, and that the achievements of national spirit and native culture which had preceded it came to an end with the death of James IV will not bear close examination. The supreme tragedy of Flodden is a romantic myth. The careers of several of the men discussed in this chapter continued as if the battle had never taken place. Culturally, the achievement of James V's reign compares very favourably with what had gone before. In literature, in architecture and in music, pre-Reformation Scotland still had much to accomplish when the infant James V succeeded his brilliant father.

CHAPTER 13

FLODDEN AND ITS
AFTERMATH

Caroline Bingham

'INEVITABLE' is a word too much beloved of historians; the appearance of inevitability derives most often from the advantage of hindsight. Yet this said, there is an appearance at least of inexorability in the chain of events which led from the marriage of James IV and Margaret Tudor in 1503 to the fatal battlefield of Flodden in 1513.

The marriage had been discussed as early as 1495, when Margaret was aged about seven. The marriage negotiations, however, were preceded by negotiations for a treaty of perpetual peace between Scotland and England. The treaty, concluded in 1502, was made under papal confirmation, with automatic excommunication laid upon which ever party should break the peace. The marriage took place in August of the following year.

James IV, desirous of maintaining peace on all fronts, and at the same time of safeguarding himself against political domination by England, declined specifically to repudiate Scotland's traditional alliance with France. Peace with both England and France remained feasible as long as Henry VII reigned. The delicacy of James' position was revealed soon after Henry VIII succeeded in 1509.

Henry VII had been too concerned in consolidating his hold upon the English throne to indulge in military adventures abroad, besides which he had been restrained by his essential parsimony from indulging in the vast expense of warfare. Neither consideration applied with Henry VIII. He was young and hot-headed, and ambitious for military glory, which he hoped to gain by recovering some of England's lost territories in France, emulating Henry V.

The involvement of France in the Italian Wars provided his opportunity. In 1511 Pope Julius II formed his mis-named 'Holy

League' to expel the French from Italy, and the following year Henry allied himself with the Papacy, Spain, Venice and the Emperor Maximilian, and prepared to invade France in the name of the Holy League. In 1513 his invasion culminated in a pointless but satisfyingly 'glorious' victory at Guinegate.

James IV had watched these events with mounting anxiety. Henry VIII, from the beginning of his reign, had shown a high-handed and bellicose attitude towards Scotland, and James had soon begun to doubt the permanency of the perpetual peace. In 1512, at the urgent request of Louis XII of France, James agreed to a formal renewal of the auld alliance. He was thus in the unhappy position of being committed to both France and England when Henry VIII invaded France.

James IV has often been condemned as quixotically chivalrous for launching a counter-invasion in response to the pleas of his French ally; but in fact the deterioration of relations between Scotland and England left him little choice but to revert to the traditional policy of the auld alliance. On 22 August 1513 he invaded England and proceeded to reduce three fortresses, Norham, Etal and Ford, which served the double purpose of safeguarding his line of retreat, and drawing northward the English army, commanded by the Earl of Surrey. The two armies met near Flodden Edge in Northumberland where, on 9 September, James IV was defeated and slain.

It was said by a contemporary that James' principal fault as a general was that 'he begins to fight even before he has given his orders'. No doubt it was his primitive heroism that cost him his life, but what in fact cost the Scots the battle was the effectiveness of the English artillery and the technological superiority of the English in other weapons. The Scots were armed with fifteen-foot wooden spears, the English with bills, which had an eight-foot shaft and a long, axe-like blade terminating in a spike. The Scottish spearmen, with the king, charged downhill, irresistible as long as they kept moving. When their impetus was halted, in muddy ground at the foot of Flodden Edge, they found their long weapons useless against the bills of the English. The shafts of their spears were sliced through by the blades of the bills, and spearmen who managed to draw their swords were still defenceless against the longer reach of their adversaries. It was in this *mêlée* that the king died, not at the last, surrounded by a 'dark, impenetrable wood' of spears.

Traditionally, Flodden has always been regarded as one of the great disasters of Scottish history, and small wonder since the king himself died, and with him the archbishop of St Andrews (the king's illegitimate son), two other bishops, three abbots, one dean, fourteen earls, about the same number of lords, three Highland chiefs, and a great number of lairds, variously estimated. However, recent research has tended to reduce earlier estimates of the number of the nameless dead, especially among the Borderers, those very 'Flowers of the Forest' whom the romanticism of later generations particularly lamented. And, as Professor Donaldson has rightly remarked, there was 'nothing novel about a heavy defeat at the hands of the English, and Flodden was neither the first nor the last in a long series'.

Flodden was a disaster principally in that it occasioned the loss of a king who was the guiding spirit of the nation. It brought to an end an epoch of growing prosperity and creativity which might have continued and developed even more remarkably had James IV lived longer.

In historical perspective, however, the significance of Flodden was not merely that of a massive defeat which caused the loss of an able king and the end of a period of stability, its significance was rather that of an event which reshaped Scotland's future through the changing political attitudes which resulted from it. The history of the aftermath of Flodden is the history of Scotland's growing disillusionment with the auld alliance, and in consequence of that disillusionment, the painfully reluctant drawing together of Scotland and England, especially under the influence of developing Protestantism.

Immediately after Flodden the seventeen-month-old James V was crowned king, and in accordance with the will of James IV Margaret Tudor was appointed tutrix or guardian of her son, which made her in effect the head of state, although she did not enjoy the title of regent.

Her position as head of state was not in itself acceptable to the most powerful of the men associated with her in the government. James Hamilton, first Earl of Arran, James Beaton, archbishop of

Glasgow, and Alexander third Lord Home, the High Chamberlain, opposed Margaret largely because she was the sister of the king who had not only inflicted upon Scotland a disastrous defeat, but had also made clear his basic attitude towards Scotland to the herald of James IV who visited him in France immediately before the Flodden campaign. 'I am the very owner of Scotland,' Henry had said, 'and he (James IV) holdeth it of me by homage.' This clear statement of Henry's renewal of the medieval English kings' claim to overlordship of Scotland naturally made the more nationally conscious members of the Scottish government unwilling to accept a Tudor as head of state.

The most obvious alternative to Margaret, and the most accept-able candidate in accordance with Scottish theory, was the heir presumptive, John, Duke of Albany. He was the son of James III's treacherous brother, Alexander, Duke of Albany, by his French wife, Agnès de la Tour d'Auvergne. Born and brought up in France, the country to which Alexander had been banished, John, Duke of Albany was a veritable personification of the auld alliance.

Margaret played into the hands of the pro-Albany party by her marriage to Archibald Douglas, sixth Earl of Angus, in 1514 since under the terms of James IV's will she was to be tutrix of the king only so long as she should remain a widow. Upon her remarriage she was forced to resign her position and consent to the appointment of Albany as regent.

Albany, who spent three periods of residence in Scotland between 1515 and 1524, was an able and conscientious man who attempted to balance the duty which he felt towards the French King Francis I with the duty which he owed as regent to James V. This proved a thankless task since the Scots felt keenly that at Flodden they had fought and sustained a heavy defeat on behalf of an ungrateful ally. Indeed, the appointment of Albany as regent was very much more a device to exclude Margaret Tudor than a pro-French appointment. This was made clear by two recurrences of enmity with England in 1522 and 1523, both consequent upon hostilities between Francis I and Henry VIII. On both occasions Albany attempted to lead a Scottish army into England, on the latter occasion an army reinforced with French troops and artillery. But on both occasions the army advanced as far as the Border, only to refuse actual invasion. These two manifestations of the so-called 'Flodden complex' did not illustrate that the Scots shrank from facing the English in the field, but that they were unwilling to sustain further loss on behalf of France. They were firm in insisting that defence and not attack was all that could be asked of them.

When Albany left Scotland in the spring of 1524, his influence weakened by two inglorious and unpopular military expeditions, his political opponents had an opportunity to seize power and reverse his policy. The Scots did not appreciate that Albany's regency had probably saved the country from English domination. They were aware only that Francis I had attempted to manipulate Scotland in his own interests, and that the auld alliance had been too frequently invoked to make Scotland the tool of French policy. However, the alternative was that Henry VIII would attempt to make Scotland an English satellite through the influence of Margaret and her husband Angus.

Had there been any reasonable degree of concord between Margaret and Angus, it is possible that Henry could have developed a strong enough pro-English party to have achieved his objective. But between them there was not only marital disharmony but conflicting ambition. Margaret, usually a staunch supporter of her brother, was temporarily estranged from him when he refused to assist her in obtaining a divorce from Angus; indeed, it was by cultivating Albany, who was related by marriage to the Medici, the family of Pope Clement VII, that she finally gained her divorce. After that it was remarked that Henry 'never carried such respect to his sister as he had done before'.

In 1524, after Albany's departure, Margaret briefly regained control of the king, and supported by Arran, her position as head of state. But a year later Angus secured the person of the king by a coup d'état. James V remained a virtual prisoner of the Douglas faction, which enjoyed the support of Henry VIII, until 1528.

James therefore spent some of his most influential formative years in the hands of the Douglases. His education had been abandoned before he was thirteen, leaving him with a somewhat inadequate grounding in French and Latin, a poor standard of education by comparison with that of most Renaissance princes. By the time he was fifteen or so the Douglases, according to George

Buchanan, with a cynical disregard for the king's welfare 'made him more inclinable to women, because by that means they hoped to have him longer under their tuition'. However, a course of systematic spoiling and incitement to immorality did nothing to blunt the king's intelligence. During his unwilling sojourn with the Douglases James developed into a shrewd and observant young man, with strong ideas of his own, which he was capable of keeping to himself until he was free to act upon them. He became, therefore, mentally somewhat isolated and, again according to Buchanan, 'naturally suspicious'.

James had learnt from his mother to dislike and distrust Angus. His own experience at Angus' hands turned those feelings into a lasting detestation which he extended from Angus himself to almost every other member of the house of Douglas. Furthermore, since Angus was the principal agent of English influence in Scotland, the English alliance became repugnant to James V, together with the faction which supported it.

In 1528, at the age of sixteen, James escaped from the Douglases, and within a few months was able to assert his authority and banish his former gaolers. Angus and his principal kinsmen, forfeited and under sentence of death, fled the country and placed themselves under the protection of Henry VIII.

In the interstices of Albany's regency and following his departure the strife of factions in Scotland had been largely a matter of family ambition. Arran and his Hamilton kindred had been pro-French in that they opposed the Douglases. But both groups were principally concerned to use the influence of foreign powers for their own aggrandisement. The Douglases were always for the Douglases; the Hamiltons were interested basically in their reversionary rights to the Scottish throne. With the emergence of the king, factionary attitudes were submerged in a national policy once more.

James V, concerned to maintain his freedom of action against England, was obliged to turn to the auld alliance. As an eighteenth-century historian expressed it, Henry 'in supporting the infamous Douglases against their sovereign . . . in a manner forced James to fix a connexion with France'. But there were certain advantages to be looked for from France: for instance, the Treaty of Rouen, negotiated by Albany in 1517 and ratified in 1521, promised James marriage with a daughter of Francis I, and a mutual offensive and defensive alliance against England.

Francis I, whose policy throughout his reign was shaped by his rivalry with the Emperor Charles V, long remained reluctant to take up a definitely anti-English standpoint by honouring the Treaty of Rouen. James V, however, responded with patience and astuteness. Though eager to bring Francis to a decision – not only for political but for financial reasons, since he stood in great need of a French princess' dowry – James played skilfully upon Francis' basic unwillingness to see him marry elsewhere by inviting counter-proposals. After prolonged negotiations with the emperor, with the deposed King of Denmark, with the pope, for the hand of his ward Catherine de Medici, and even with Henry VIII, James at last persuaded Francis I to part with his daughter Madeleine, and a dowry of 100,000 livres. The marriage took place in Paris on 1 January 1537. Madeleine died within the year, but James reaffirmed his fidelity to the auld alliance by marrying a second French bride, Mary of Guise-Lorraine, in 1538.

James was able to follow a pro-French policy as long as it did not involve him in military action on behalf of France; but when enmity with England was renewed at the end of the reign the latent unpopularity of his policy was quickly revealed. And throughout the reign the unpopularity of his foreign policy was enhanced by that of a domestic policy equally ill-calculated to commend itself to the most influential class of his subjects.

The natural result of a minority in which he had been the prisoner of a turbulent subject was that James reached adulthood with a particular determination to impose a strong discipline upon the nobility. At the same time, the authoritarianism of James V should be seen not only in its Scottish but also its European context, for James shared the preoccupations common to Renaissance sovereigns. Like Francis I and Henry VIII, James V was absolutist in his aims, concerned to increase the power of the crown, to reduce the nobility as far as possible to a condition of dependence, and to develop an administration served by men who were not of noble family and therefore had no inherent belief in their own independence. Much of this remained greatly beyond his scope, but his aims were clear enough.

James' determination to discipline his nobility accompanied a desire to impose law and order throughout his realm. He began with those perennial problem areas, the Borders, the Highlands and the Isles.

His first expedition to the Borders took place in the spring of 1529 and resulted in the execution of two notorious reivers, Scott of Tushielaw and Cockburn of Henderland. The following spring he made his famous raid upon the Armstrongs of Liddesdale, who had boasted that they acknowledged the authority neither of the King of England nor the King of Scots. The result was the execution of Armstrong of Mangerton, the head of the family, and his brother Armstrong of Gilnockie, the 'Johnie Armestrong' of the well-known ballad. As a result of this rough justice, and of spells of imprisonment endured by various Border magnates, including the Earl of Bothwell, Lords Home and Maxwell, and the lairds of Johnston, Polwarth, Ferniherst and Buccleuch, the Borders were quietened, and remained so for the rest of the reign.

The western Highlands and the Isles presented a conjoint problem. During the king's minority and under Angus' regime the keeping of order in the whole area had been entrusted to the third Earl of Argyll, who died in 1529. James, deeply suspicious of the immense influence wielded by his family, the Campbells, took the opportunity to reduce the official powers of the fourth Earl by refusing him the commission of lieutenancy of the Isles which had been held by his father, and granting it instead to his enemy MacDonald of Islay, who had informed the king that the Campbell policy had been to foment disorder in the Isles and then gain credit and profit by stamping it out. Argyll spent a short spell in prison in 1531, and thereafter remained out of favour for several years. The Isles remained quiet until 1539, when a rebellion broke out led by Donald Gorm of Sleat, who laid claim to the lordship of the Isles which had so long maintained an existence almost independent of the crown of Scots. The rebellion was abortive, but no doubt its occurrence influenced the king in his decision to make a circumnavigation of the north in 1540.

The king's voyage was conceived partly as a royal progress, to illustrate the splendour and authority of the sovereign, and partly as a naval expedition, to overawe unruly and potentially rebellious subjects. Twelve ships, heavily equipped with artillery, carried the king and his entourage from Leith, up the east coast and across the Pentland Firth to Orkney, thence around Cape Wrath to the Isles of Lewis, Harris, North and South Uist and to Skye. James landed also upon Coll, Tiree and Mull, Arran and Bute, and ended his voyage at Dumbarton.

The voyage had taken him to some outlying parts of his kingdom previously unvisited by any kings of his house. It had enabled him to pursue his policy of placing lesser men dependent upon himself in positions customarily occupied by members of the greater nobility, by appointing his favourite Oliver Sinclair as sheriff of Orkney – no bad choice since Oliver Sinclair was a cadet of the family of the earls of Caithness and Orkney, yet nonetheless dependent upon the king for his advancement. More importantly the voyage enabled James to take prisoners and hostages from several clans whose loyalty he doubted. His prisoners included John Mackenzie, chief of the Clan Mackenzie, Hector Maclean of Duart and James Macconel of Islay. He also brought home with him a number of chieftains' sons, for education at court, with the hope, no doubt, of producing a more tractable generation to succeed to estates in a notoriously turbulent part of his kingdom. Finally, the voyage enabled the king to annexe the lordship of the Isles to the crown. The annexation was enacted by the parliament which met in the winter of 1540, following the king's return. James' companions on his voyage were Oliver Sinclair, the fourth Earl of Huntly, and Cardinal Beaton.

Huntly, James' cousin and his only friend among the greater nobility, had been responsible for keeping law and order in the north throughout the reign. The power of his family, the Gordons, in the north equalled that of the Campbells in the west; but James made no inroads upon it, and he seems to have been justified in his confidence that Huntly would use his power in the interest of the crown. Huntly was to emerge as a turbulent subject in the reign of James' daughter.

James' unpopularity with the nobility arose from two causes: the harshness of his disciplinary measures, and the acquisitiveness he showed in attempting to build up the finances of the crown. From their own viewpoint the nobles had cause for complaint: Angus was in exile throughout the reign, Argyll, Bothwell, Moray, Home and Maxwell were all imprisoned at one time and another; the eighth Earl of Crawford was mulcted of large sums of money and his son was compelled to resign his succession to the earldom; the third Earl of Morton was forced to resign his lands to his kinsman Douglas of Lochleven, who made them over to the king; and Hamilton of Finnart, the illegitimate son of Arran and at one time a favourite of the king, was suddenly put on trial for treason and executed, according to contemporary opinion chiefly because James coveted his wealth. It was little wonder that, as Norfolk informed Henry VIII, 'so sore a dread king, and so ill-beloved of his subjects was never in that land'.

It must be remarked that James' unpopularity with his nobility contrasted sharply with his popularity with the common people. The king's desire to see law and order imposed throughout the kingdom, and the severity with which he pursued and punished malefactors, made him in the eyes of the defenceless mass of his subjects their champion and protector. In this his popularity was well enough deserved. It was further enhanced by his fondness for slipping away from the ceremonial of his court and wandering about the countryside disguised, perhaps rather ineffectually, as a farmer. The adventures which he encountered in the guise of the 'Gudeman of Ballengeich' belong rather to folklore than to history.

The Gudeman of Ballengeich is a pleasanter aspect of James V than that of the covetous oppressor of the nobility. But perhaps it is a somewhat extenuating circumstance that James' acquisitiveness did not arise from mere avarice. Though it was truly observed that he 'marvellously enriched' himself, he also spent lavishly on patronage of the arts, especially architecture. A lavish building programme, mostly of decorative schemes completing works begun in his father's reign, was undertaken in the later years of James V. The grandest surviving examples of the patronage of James V are at Stirling and Falkland.

When James went to France to marry the Princess Madeleine, he spent some months as the guest of Francis I, at Blois, Chambord and Fontainbleau among other places. With the evident wish of making his own royal palaces worthy of comparison with those of France, he set about superimposing upon his still basically medieval residences the appearance of Renaissance châteaux. At Stirling James V's 'Palace' displays a riot of Renaissance sculpture, reminiscent of Blois, which covers a building begun in the reign of James IV. Similarly, the courtyard façade of the south wing at Falkland shows the Renaissance embellishment of a late Gothic structure. At Holyrood James V added an imposing main façade to the existing James IV Tower. But his buildings were damaged in the Earl of Hertford's invasion of 1544, and were finally demolished to make way for Charles II's complete scheme of reconstruction. Linlithgow is a palimpsest of all architectural styles from the reign of James III to that of James VI; but the gatehouse complete belongs to that of James V.

Upon these works, and their commensurably rich interiors, of which little survives but the series of oak medallions known as the 'Stirling Heads' now on display at Stirling Castle, James V spent much of the money which his nobles were forced to disgorge. Posterity may be grateful to him, though they were not.

James' unpopularity with the nobility led him to rely disproportionately upon the support of the church. Gavin Dunbar, archbishop of Glasgow, was chancellor from 1528 onwards, and Cardinal Beaton was James' chief adviser from 1538 to the end of the reign. Furthermore, the church provided James with two important sources of finance: commendams and taxation. James V secured the appointment of several of his illegitimate sons as commendators or titular abbots of the richest abbeys in Scotland: Kelso, Melrose, St Andrews, Coldingham, the Abbey of Holyrood and the Charterhouse of Perth. He was able to extract even larger sums in taxation. The most impressive instance was the foundation of the College of Justice in 1532 which provided an excuse for imposing upon the church a tax of £10,000 a year, ostensibly for the payment of judicial salaries, in reality almost exclusively for the benefit of the crown. Ultimately the Scottish prelates compounded for the sum of £72,000 to be paid in four instalments. Much of the money James gained from the church contributed to his building programme. The pope sanctioned and the church endured taxation on this scale as the price of James V's refusal to follow Henry VIII's example in repudiating papal supremacy and participating in the Reformation.

James V was a Catholic by personal conviction and by policy. He supported the church in attempting to prevent the spread of Reformation ideas in Scotland, and he countenanced a limited amount of persecution to this end. Attempts to stem the spread of the Reformation to Scotland had begun as early as 1525, when an act of parliament forbade the import of Lutheran books. Nonetheless, they continued to arrive, mostly coming in through the east-coast ports, especially St Andrews, where the university became a nursery of Lutheran ideas. At St Andrews occurred the first Protestant martyrdom, that of Patrick Hamilton, who was burnt in 1528. He was the author of a widely read religious treatise setting forth Lutheran opinions. His fame, together with the fact that he was a relative of the king and a martyr who died with the most exemplary courage, served to spread his opinions with a speed which was intensely alarming to the church. A second martyrdom took place in 1532 or 1533 also at St Andrews, and in 1534 the king himself presided at the trial of two men named Straiton and Gourlay, who were duly burnt. In 1532 an act of parliament had recorded his resolution to 'defend the authority, liberty and freedom of the seat of Rome and halikirk'. But from 1534 onwards James came under considerable diplomatic pressure to imitate the religious policy of Henry VIII. It was in the matter of religion that James' domestic and foreign policy interacted, ultimately to his detriment, for his Catholicism was integrally related to his determination to maintain alliance with France.

Henry did all he could to prevent the marriage of James and Madeleine, and after Madeleine's death he attempted to prevent James from marrying Mary of Guise by negotiating to marry her himself. Even after James had affirmed his fidelity to the auld alliance by his second French marriage, Henry sent Sir Ralph Sadler to Scotland in 1540, with instructions to attempt to undermine the influence of Cardinal Beaton, and to point out to James the financial advantages of imitating Henry's policy in dissolving religious foundations and annexing church property. James, however, stoutly affirmed his confidence in Cardinal Beaton, and on the subject of the Scottish abbeys pointedly demanded of Sadler 'What need I to take them to increase my livelihood, when I may have anything that I can require of them?'

In their relations with each other James and Henry were principally motivated by fear. James, not without reason, feared Henry's ultimate intention in seeking to extend the Henrician Reformation to Scotland; he feared in the background the old claim to overlordship which Henry had overtly voiced in 1513 and covertly sought to make good during James' own minority. Henry on his side feared the auld alliance, since a rapprochement between Francis I and the emperor led him to fear the formation of a Franco-Imperial alliance against heretical England; and since the league between France and Scotland had become so close he felt intensely vulnerable to a tripartite league and to the possibility of invasion from the north.

In an atmosphere of mutual fear and mistrust relations between the two sovereigns deteriorated during 1541, and by the following year the outbreak of war seemed unavoidable. In 1542 the triangular relationship of Scotland, England and France was not unlike that of 1513, but the old configuration was altered by a new element – the influence of Protestantism. It was as the ally of both France and the Papacy that James V faced enmity with England in the last year of his reign. In addition to the post-Flodden unpopularity of the auld alliance, James had to contend with the unpopularity of his own domestic policy. His dependence upon the church had helped to give his bad relations with the nobility a religious slant. In the course of his reign a large number of his influential subjects had embraced Protestantism, and it was widely believed that James kept a blacklist of 350 nobles against whom he could institute proceedings for heresy if he chose, and that the blacklist was headed by the name of James' Hamilton cousin, the second Earl of Arran.

With the outbreak of war James' nobility refused to follow him in an invasion of England, and at Solway Moss on 25 November 1542 the Scottish army suffered a disgraceful defeat at the hands of a very much smaller English force. After little resistance the army scattered and many nobles were taken prisoner, seemingly eager to surrender rather than die in the service of an unpopular king and for the sake of an unpopular policy. On 14 December James himself died at Falkland, the victim apparently of a complete mental and physical breakdown. He left as his heir a baby girl, Mary, Queen of Scots, aged one week.

Each year of Mary's minority brought closer the ultimate victory of Protestantism in Scotland; yet the succession of events during the minority gave no impression that the victory was inevitable. The auld alliance was closest in the last year of its existence.

On the death of James V Mary of Guise did not become head of state as Margaret Tudor had done in 1513. Possibly Mary was too closely identified with the unpopular policy of James V. After a brief power struggle the regency fell to the man designated by precedent, the heir presumptive, James Hamilton, second Earl of Arran. Cardinal Beaton was imprisoned and Mary of Guise temporarily relegated to the position merely of Dowager Queen.

In July 1543 Arran negotiated with Henry VIII the Treaties of Greenwich, a peace treaty between Scotland and England and a treaty of marriage between the infant Queen of Scots and Henry's heir Prince Edward. It was further agreed that the queen should be sent to live at the English court. Arran was rewarded with a promise of the hand of Henry's daughter Elizabeth for his eldest son. Cardinal Beaton, however, secured his freedom in September. He quickly achieved an ascendancy over Arran, and in December caused the Treaties of Greenwich to be repudiated. His action led to the English invasions of 1544 and 1545, in which Henry showed his resentment by a devastation of the Borders and the Lothians, which the Scots named the 'Rough Wooing'.

The suffering caused by this devastation aroused a resurgence of anti-English feeling in southern Scotland which was as violent as it was short-lived. Henry VIII died in 1547, and the Earl of Hertford, who had led the invasions, became Duke of Somerset and regent for Edward VI. He continued Henry's policy by invading Scotland in 1547, when he won the Battle of Pinkie, which caused the Scots severe losses but achieved nothing politically. Oddly enough, even at the time of Pinkie the tide of anti-English feeling was receding, for the auld enemy seemed only half so inimical when Scotland and England had come to contain many Protestant co-religionists; and the danger that Scotland would become an English province in the reign of Edward VI was finally frustrated when Mary of Guise arranged that her daughter should be sent to the court of France in 1548.

From this point onwards anti-English feeling declined very rapidly, while anti-French feeling came to a head. This change of attitude followed the religious persecution organised by Cardinal

Beaton soon after he gained his freedom and his ascendancy over Arran. Throughout the reign of James V the church, which was in a supine condition, had been losing the respect of all classes with alarming rapidity. The poor quality of James V's ecclesiastical appointments and the financial interests which made it impossible for him to take any hand in reforming the church from within made the decline of the church's political influence in the future very certain. Cardinal Beaton was well aware of the threat of Protestantism; persecution of heretics was his answer, but it was an answer doomed to failure.

Cardinal Beaton was murdered at St Andrews in May 1546, but his death did not spell immediate defeat to the Catholic and pro-French party. After Pinkie the English advantage was not followed up, and Mary of Guise gained greatly in strength through the military support sent her from France after the departure of Mary, Queen of Scots in 1548. Mary strengthened the alliance between Scotland and France by a visit to France in 1550 which paved the way for her taking over the regency from Arran. Mary became regent in 1554, and Arran was compensated with the French duchy of Châtelhérault. When Mary, Queen of Scots reached the age of sixteen in 1558 she was married to the Dauphin Francis, eldest son of Henry II. The following year Henry II died, and Mary's husband became Francis II of France, and together with Mary joint sovereign of Scotland. Nonetheless the extension of French influence over Scotland was more apparent than real. It resulted entirely from the determination of Mary of Guise to conserve a Catholic inheritance for her daughter. The last year of the regency and the opening of the reign of Mary, Queen of Scots were to show the disillusionment with France which had followed Flodden brought to its logical conclusion.

CHAPTER 14

JOHN KNOX AND MARY, QUEEN OF SCOTS

Ian B. Cowan

THE personalities of John Knox and Mary, Queen of Scots are inextricably bound together in the folklore of history, and yet personal contact between them was confined to seven short years. During these years, Knox was always critical of the queen's policies but that criticism seldom gained political backing and the measure of this impotence can best be judged by the fact that in the combination of events following the murder of Riccio which led to the deposition of Mary, Knox was absent, first in Ayrshire, and then in England. Any part which Knox played in the downfall of Mary can thus be attributed only to the climate of opinion which Knox had created in Scotland before that event, and not to any personal participation in the overthrow of the queen.

On this score Knox himself would have expressed little doubt as he saw Mary as a queen whose sole concern was to restore Catholicism, and he could thus write: 'Sche plainlie purposed to wrak the religioun within this Realme to the Roman Antichrist she hath maid her promeise, and from him sche hath taken money to uphold his pompe.' On the other side stood the forces of Protestantism ably led by their self-appointed champion, John Knox, who in his *History of the Reformation in Scotland*, gave lasting credence to the idea that Mary lost her throne because she was a Catholic queen in a Protestant realm. On both points, however, this thesis may be questioned.

The extent to which the Scottish people had embraced Protestantism before Mary's return to Scotland on 19 August 1561 is debatable, but as a religious movement the Reformation had clearly limited support. The major fervency was to be found on the east coast in Angus and the Mearns, Fife and Lothian, while in the west, Kyle in Ayrshire was the centre of the reformed cause. Of the towns, Dundee in which the faithful 'exceeded all the rest in zeall and boldnes' led the way but Edinburgh was much less enthusiastic, and as late as 1565 it was reported on one occasion that as many attended the mass as the Protestant service.

The part which Knox played in the growth of that reformed faith was limited. Born at Haddington about 1514, he was ordained as a priest in 1536 and apparently having failed to secure a benefice, acted thereafter as a notary and tutor. Not until 1545 when he became a follower of George Wishart did Knox evince any interest in the new religious doctrines which had been evident in Scotland for almost two decades. Thereafter, although he committed himself to the reformed cause in April 1547 by joining the murderers of Cardinal Beaton in the castle of St Andrews and subsequently acting as their minister, this stage in his career was cut short when the castle fell to the French in whose galleys Knox was condemned to row until his release in early 1549. Only at this juncture, in an England which had become fully committed to Protestantism after the accession of Edward VI in 1547, did Knox become prominent. Knox's interest in this period of his career, however, was largely in the country of his adoption, although as preacher at Berwick with another congregation at Newcastle, his opinions undoubtedly began to reach a fairly wide circle of his countrymen, many of whom flocked to hear him preach. A contact was thus established which, although interrupted by Knox's flight to the continent when England returned to Catholicism upon the accession of Mary Tudor in 1553, was never again to be severed. Nevertheless, with the exception of a fleeting visit to Scotland in 1555–6 during the course of which he engaged the loyalty of the Scottish Protestant movement, but otherwise demonstrated its inherent weakness, Knox remained on the continent until the outbreak of the Scottish Reformation in 1559. During these years, principally spent at Geneva, Knox was as much concerned with the plight of Protestantism in England as in Scotland and most of his preaching was to exiled English congregations. In his writings both countries figure prominently. *The First blast of the Trumpet against the Monstrous Regiment of Women* was directed jointly against the rule of Mary Tudor in England and that of the queen regent, Mary of Guise, in Scotland. Admonitions and advice were sent to Protestants in both kingdoms, and in formulating a doctrine of rebellion contrary to Calvin's theory that 'one cannot resist magistrates without resisting God', Knox was not thinking of Scotland alone. In the event, however, the accession of Elizabeth in 1558 rendered such a revolution unnecessary in England, and Knox's final position was consequently reached in that year in an *Appelation to the Nobility and Estates of Scotland* in which the people's right to resist blasphemous laws to the death was clearly asserted. To preach revolution was one thing, however, to carry it out was another, and at the end of the day, the outbreak of hostilities in Scotland owed little or nothing to John Knox or his writings.

On the contrary it can be argued that the onset of the Scottish Reformation owed much more to Mary, Queen of Scots and the policies carried out in her name by her mother acting as queen regent. Mary had been born on 7/8 December 1542, and had become queen seven days later following the death of her father James V. From that moment she became a pawn in a power struggle between England and France for influence over her realm. First advantage went to the former, but following the renunciation of the Treaties of Greenwich and the subsequent 'Rough Wooing' which brought about the destruction of many religious houses, the ruinous condition of which has frequently been erroneously attributed to Knox and his fellow reformers, circumstances favoured the French. With Mary's departure for France in 1548, ostensibly for her own safety, the Franco-Scottish alliance seemed more secure than ever. In the event, the queen of Scots was to remain in France for thirteen years, and this period saw the shaping of Mary's personality at a court largely under the dominance of her mother's family of Guise. Nevertheless, although Mary's adverse characteristics have frequently been attributed by her opponents to this early upbringing, her life, certainly before marriage, seems to have been a stereotyped courtly existence in which the social graces were more important than diplomatic and political intrigue.

In Scotland, during her absence, the struggle between the governor, James, Earl of Arran, and the queen mother, Mary of Guise, continued unabated, the latter's cause being strengthened after 1548 as French ascendency in Scotland slowly increased. With the replacement of the governor by Mary of Guise as regent in 1554, that influence quickly became more overt. The new regent was a skilful politician in her own right and by various stratagems, including that of temporarily tolerating incipient Protestantism in order to assure herself of the support of the burghs in which that movement was strong, she gradually outmanoeuvred all her political and religious opponents. Nevertheless, in the last resort she relied heavily upon France. French troops garrisoned Scottish castles and French administrators advised the queen regent to a point to which Scotland could be regarded as a province of France. Matters came to a head in 1558 with the marriage of the Dauphin and Mary for not only was Francis given the crown matrimonial but also, in spite of promises that the kingdom should revert to the legal heirs if no child was born of the marriage, Mary signed three documents assigning her kingdom in this event to the King of France. It was those circumstances, coupled with the growing restlessness of the Scottish nobility who were losing all influence within their own kingdom, which principally brought the lords to take up arms against their queen in 1559.

This revolutionary outbreak was not entirely unpremeditated, however, for as early as 1557 a 'Godlie Band or Covenant' had been subscribed by a number of the Scots lords, who had also envisaged inviting Knox to return to Scotland. In the event, Knox was stopped at Dieppe, but the connection between the political motivation which was largely the mainspring of the revolution, and the religious vindication which Knox and his fellow Protestants could confer upon it, was already evident. When the hour of action finally approached, Knox was again invited to return in November 1558 and with his arrival at Leith on 2 May 1559, the revolutionaries who had earlier got off to a somewhat uncertain start were able to proceed with a new justification.

The commitment of the lords themselves to the purpose must always remain doubtful. Some were undoubtedly genuinely Protestant, but others may have been swayed in that direction by other factors. Not least among these were economic interests for lords and lairds alike, who had increasingly conspired to secularise the lands of the old church and who may have seen their final tenurial security in religious change which would sweep away the existing church and any claim which it might make upon its former lands and revenues. Other tangible advantages linking the political revolution with incipient Protestantism stemmed from the considerable accession of physical strength, especially from the burghs, which might be expected as a result of this identification. Knox himself, moreover, with his gift of preaching, which he most effectively demonstrated in St John's Kirk in Perth, could be utilised to engage the sympathies of the populace at large. If on occasion, the resultant enthusiasm brought about the destruction of religious buildings as at Scone, Stirling and Linlithgow, Knox appears to have accepted the inevitability of such action, although he himself was far from condoning it. Even with the support of 'the rascal multitude' and the advantages of combining religious and political forces, success was by no means assured. Without a measure of good fortune which included a political crisis in France which prevented reinforcements being sent to Scotland, the death of Mary of Guise and above all the decision of Elizabeth of England to intervene, the Scots lords would have been hard pressed to sustain their challenge to the authority of the crown.

Even when that victory had been achieved, difficulties remained. In the absence of Mary, any solution could only be tentative, and as a result the main settlement – the Treaty of Edinburgh (1560) was essentially a peace treaty between France and England whereby each country agreed to withdraw its forces and the French on their part recognised Elizabeth's title, an admission which became a barrier to any ratification of the treaty by Mary. In addition certain concessions were made to the Scots, including authority to call a parliament, but with the reservation that all religious questions were to be submitted to the 'intention and pleasure' of the king and queen. In the event the lords did not abide by these conditions and the 'Reformation Parliament', which somewhat irregularly included many lairds, accepted the Scots Confession of Faith, declared the mass illegal and abrogated any authority derived from Rome. Concessions stopped short at this point, however, and there was no statutory recognition of the Reformed Church as such.

Ostensibly this was to remain the measure of Knox's success for many years thereafter, and these concessions were permanently at risk as Mary consistently refused to ratify those statutes. Moreover, the ambitious programme of the reformers for the polity and endowment of their church, the *Great Book of Reformation*, usually styled the *First Book of Discipline*, was dismissed as a book of 'devout imaginations', and no effort was made to dismiss existing benefice holders. The secular interests which had contributed to the success of a Protestant Reformation thereafter conspired against it. Family connections, including that of the leader of the Lords of the Congregation, the Duke of Châtelhérault whose half-brother was archbishop of St Andrews, were more important than any loyalty to the Reformed Church, which in its hour of triumph had to compromise as best it could. In organisation a general assembly, mirroring in its composition the estates of the realm, had to deputise for the godly sovereign whom Knox for one would have welcomed as head of the church, while a mixture of superintendents, reformed bishops and commissioners of the assembly had to administer the church regionally instead of the godly bishops who should have replaced the existing incumbents. No decision of the *First Book of Discipline* has engendered more controversy than the expedient which would have placed the organisation of the church in the hands of superintendents, but contemporary evidence would appear to indicate that either the office was to be permanent, or regarded as temporary pending succession to the bishoprics. Knox himself does not appear to have objected to the office as such, and his later objections to bishops in place of superintendents, appears to have arisen from his doubts as to the suitability of the proposed holders of the dignity, rather than from any antipathy to the office itself, to the restoration of which he eventually agreed in 1572. Only at congregational level did the reformers' organisation plans meet with more immediate success, as albeit slowly, kirk sessions came into being. In endowment likewise compromise was the only solution, and the Reformed Church was forced to share with the crown, one third of the taxable wealth of benefices of the old church. If the Reformation was a conspicuous political success, clearly from a Protestant viewpoint, it left much to be desired.

Nevertheless, the magnitude of Knox's achievement should not be overlooked. He had successfully carried through a Protestant Reformation, although three years before this had appeared to be an unrealisable ideal. He had done so by attaching the religious aspirations of his followers to the political ambitions of the Scots lords who were prepared to accept Protestantism as part of their programme in return for the material and spiritual advantages which Knox and the Protestants were able to offer to them. If the reward conferred by the victorious nobles was less than just, the commitment to Protestantism had been honoured. In this respect Knox's manoeuvres were highly successful, and it is as a victorious political revolutionary that he should be remembered first and foremost. Moreover, if Knox's programme thereafter met less success than it deserved, the views of the *First Book of Discipline*, of which Knox was the principal compiler, long remained in the fields of education and social relief, the ideals which the church strove to realise. If, on the other hand, the views of Knox on church organisation were to be supplanted by those of Andrew Melville and his fellow Presbyterians, it was the ideals of Knox which were to shape the beliefs and attitude towards worship adopted by the church. In this respect the Scots Confession of Faith complemented by the sections of the *Book of Discipline* dealing with worship and belief constitutes a permanent memorial to Knox. At one fell swoop a new radical Calvinism, which would only accept usages and belief which were grounded in scripture, replaced the beliefs of many centuries. The seven sacraments were reduced to two – communion and baptism – which were only rightfully ministered when conjoined with public preaching. The private celebration of either sacrament was totally banned and communion was to be administered sitting around a table in the manner of the Last Supper. Kneeling to receive the communion elements which were to be administered in both kinds was to be abandoned, as to do so implied the real presence in the elements, and as transubstantiation had been condemned, to kneel before bread and wine was idolatry. The radical break with the past did not stop short at this point, church festivals, including Christmas and Easter, were declared 'utterlie to be abolischet' on the grounds that the days set apart for such remembrance had no assurance in scripture and the events which they commemorated were of such importance that they should be remembered throughout the whole Christian year and not only at one season. Even the concept of a valid ministry was reinterpreted and examination as to fitness and worthiness, followed by a call to preach, as Knox himself had been called at St Andrews in 1547, was all that was deemed necessary. The idea of an Apostolic succession was firmly rejected on the grounds that 'the mirakle is ceassed', and with this statement above all, Knox gave birth to a new Reformed Church, in which continuity of a sort is only discernible in the retention of certain administrative processes derived from the old church, and most notably in the figure of the 'godly bishop' or superintendent, who, bereft of any special spiritual powers, could be fittingly described as a 'pseudobishop'. In the creation of such a church, whose views were to be assailed, but never seriously threatened until more recent times, lay the abiding triumph of Knox and his fellow reformers.

This verdict, however, is necessarily given in retrospect. Without our advantage of hindsight, Knox could not be certain that victory in his terms had been won. Faced with an unsatisfactory financial settlement and denied full statutory recognition, Knox's constant fear was that of a successful counter-reformation. These fears were intensified when in December 1560, Francis II died and the realisation that Mary would return to Scotland had to be faced. Mary returned in August 1561 and thereafter for Knox the confrontation between the two churches was symbolised in the conflict between Mary and himself. At a personal level this confrontation was certainly more symbolic than real as the number of direct clashes between Mary and Knox were few, and while in the pages of his *History*, it is Knox who emerges triumphant from these interviews, the one-sided nature of the evidence must be borne in mind as must the fact that Mary, who was every inch of six feet tall, seldom showed herself to be lacking in personal courage. On the reverse side of the coin, moreover, Knox could show himself singularly unwilling to risk the wrath of his queen as is demonstrated by his absence from Edinburgh in the closing fifteen months of her reign. In the years before this, moreover, Knox had become politically isolated from most of his former allies, who, unlike himself, were prepared to compromise with their queen. Thus while Knox attacked the queen's mass from the pulpit the Protestant nobility decided to acquiesce in Mary's wishes in this respect. Isolation and political impotence heightened Knox's fears of a Catholic revival, but were these fears justified? Was Mary an ardent Catholic and did she at any point attempt to restore Catholicism in Scotland?

The key to Mary's attitude can be determined at the moment of her arrival as she made no attempt to join forces in the north-east with the pro-Catholic Earl of Huntly but instead landed at Leith and aligned herself with the party of Lord James Stewart and William Maitland of Lethington, both of whom were politically committed to the Protestant cause. Thereafter, while false promises continued to be made to the papacy, whom she assured she would be prepared to die rather than to abandon her religion, the last four years of her reign saw little indication or any attempt to aid her co-religionists beyond extending personal protection to some. Nevertheless, if Mary did not actively seek to promote Catholicism, the door was always open to such a change in so far as Mary refused to officially countenance the Reformed Church and the Treaty of Edinburgh and the religious actions of the Reformation Parliament failed to gain ratification. This failure, however, sprang from political considerations outwith the realm and internally Mary was to act on more than one occasion as though the statutes had the force of law. Thus while the act forbidding the saying of the mass remained unratified, a proclamation of the privy council with similar intent was frequently acted upon. Mary showed herself equally willing, moreover, to accept the idea that power previously exercised by the pope had passed to the crown, and this theory was acted upon in nominations to benefices and the confirmation of sales of church lands. If such actions in themselves do not fully reveal Mary's attitude to Catholicism in Scotland, this was demonstrated in a more positive fashion by the part which Mary played in the downfall of the principal Catholic noble in the realm, the Earl of Huntly, at the Battle of Corrichie in 1562. Principal responsibility for this action, which was occasioned by the need to curtail the activities of an all powerful noble, must lie with Mary and not with Lord James Stewart, who although he became Earl of Moray as a result of the affair, could not have successfully carried through such an expedition without the queen's approval.

In making this decision Mary demonstrated that political realities were more important than religious loyalties, and this self-same trait can be seen again and again in the queen's actions. This attitude is also seen in the fact that while she refused to recognise the Protestant Church she accepted in 1562 a measure of financial compromise by which the Reformed Church should be maintained from a general taxation of the benefices of the old church. By this arrangement two-thirds of their former revenues were left with the old incumbents, and the remaining one-third was to be collected by the government for allocation between itself and the reformed ministry. In this arrangement, practical financial considerations, particularly those of the crown itself seem to have been uppermost and other actions reveal a similar purpose. Mary's attitude towards her co-religionists was at best therefore fairly lukewarm, and as a result by 1565 communication between herself and the papacy had almost come to an end. In these circumstances, it is hardly surprising that Knox's rantings against Moray went largely unheeded, especially since Mary's policy of religious compromise was complemented by one of similar political designs in which, guided by Moray and Maitland, she ruled her Protestant kingdom with apparent skill.

Mary's reign until 1565 can therefore be described with some justification as a conspicuous success, but within two years total failure had ensued and the queen had been forced to abdicate. This change in fortune can be explained in varying ways, but clearly explanations couched in religious terms have little to commend them for although Mary on the eve of her marriage to Henry, Lord Darnley, shows herself more willing to aid Catholicism than at any time before, the condoning of a Catholic evensong in Edinburgh, coupled with other slight indications of a shift in policy, probably meant no more than a contemplation of a relaxation of the law against mass-mongering. Whatever Mary's motives, political reaction to her marriage made further concessions impossible, and as her personal position became more precarious, Mary revealed the extent to which her religious zeal was tempered by political reality when, faced with the complete collapse of her policies, she began in 1566 to show further favour to the Reformed Church whereby succession to lesser benefices was assured and a degree of statutory recognition achieved. Even Mary's personal devotion to Catholicism, hitherto irreproachable, was seriously weakened at this juncture and after her marriage to Bothwell according to the Protestant form of service, it is scarcely surprising that the pope declared it was not his intention to have any further dealings with Mary 'unless in times to come he shall see better sign of her life and religion than he has witnessed in the past'

Mary's fall from Catholic grace through her failure to promote Catholicism, or at least to maintain her personal faith, did not contribute to her fall from power. Indeed had she followed the course which so deeply distressed her Catholic friends at an earlier period in her career, her position as queen of Scots might have been assured. Other reasons must therefore be sought for the cause of Mary's downfall and while arguments based upon her femininity and defects of character cannot be entirely dismissed they have little to commend them. Mary was certainly not helpless as her actions before the Battle of Corrichie attest, as does similarly the resolution with which she acted against the opponents of her marriage to Darnley when in chasing them over the border, it was reported that 'the queen's courage increased man-like, so much, that she was ever with the foremost'. Mary's downfall therefore cannot be easily attributed to feminine frailty in moments of political stress. Likewise arguments based upon her sexuality and passionate nature tend to overlook the fact that neither of her Scottish marriages were simple cases of infatuation. Both had sound political advantages to commend them. As her husband Darnley's own claim to the English throne would strengthen her own, while as the bridegroom's mother, Lady Lennox, if not Darnley himself, was a staunch Catholic, such a match would be to the liking of other Catholic powers and the pope. Above all, however, Mary may have hoped, with Darnley as king, for an extension of the personal power which she had hitherto lacked. These advantages and the disadvantages of the match – the displeasure of Elizabeth, the wrath of the nobility and that of Knox and the church – all appear to have been seriously weighed before the final decision was taken, and even then there was no precipitate rush towards the marriage bed until political expediency dictated otherwise. If in her later marriage to James Hepburn, Earl of Bothwell, passion can be more readily discerned, it is also clear that political reliance upon the earl, which had increased as Mary realised that her husband was an ineffectual drunkard, became a matter of complete necessity, for which Mary was prepared to sacrifice her religious beliefs, following upon the murder of Darnley.

Neither passion nor religious fanaticism brought about the downfall of Mary. Politics alone was at the heart of the matter, and such considerations appear always to have been Mary's prime motivation. In the period immediately following upon her return to Scotland her policies appear to have been directed towards gaining recognition as Elizabeth's heir, although it is equally possible that the conviction expressed in 1558 that she was rightful Queen of England never quite deserted her. The refusal to ratify the Treaty of Edinburgh, which would have entailed recognising Elizabeth's title, points in this direction as does the search for a powerful continental suitor, who as her husband could help her implement her claims. Elizabeth's only weapon in this fray, the promise that if Mary married to please her, she would be made her heir, was clearly ineffectual if Mary could find a powerful husband who would help her implement her immediate claim. For three years the two queens and their ministers parried with one another on this issue with the final advantage eventually resting with Elizabeth, who when it became evident that Mary could not find a continental suitor, announced that she would not name her heir. Mary at this juncture faced the choice of a future devoid of political significance with increasing dependence upon the policies of Moray and Maitland, or of attempting to exert her personal influence to a far greater point than hitherto. The prerequisite for the latter course was marriage, but unfortunately Mary's choice, Darnley, was unpleasing to the nobility and the church. Nevertheless, her resolute actions after her marriage bear the hallmark of a queen enjoying real political power for the first time. For multifarious reasons this advantage proved transitory, and in order to retrieve a situation which Mary increasingly blamed on the ineffectiveness of her husband, new advisers were required.

Outwith the ranks of the nobility, David Riccio, the queen's French secretary, became a close confidant, so much so, that a hostile nobility and a jealous husband conspired in his murder before their pregnant queen on 9 March 1566. Mary's resolution in the circumstances was praiseworthy, and the guilty nobles followed in turn by Knox, who does not seem to have been implicated in the murder, but evidently feared the queen's wrath, left Edinburgh shortly after the event. The incident not only confirmed Mary in her loathing of her husband, but increased her sense of isolation. At this juncture Mary's principal desire appears to have been to rid herself of Darnley while her greatest need was a new and powerful ally. The latter condition was met by Bothwell, but whether he conspired to grant her other wish will always remain a mystery. If Bothwell remains the chief suspect in the actual slaying of Darnley, and he certainly appears to have been involved in the mining of Kirk o' Field if not in the actual strangulation of the fleeing Darnley, Mary's part in the affair also continues to be a matter of debate. However, this much remains clear: Mary made no secret of the fact that she wished to be rid of her husband, and it was she who delivered him into the hands of his enemies by bringing him from Glasgow to Edinburgh. Various reasons have been advanced for this, including the thesis that Mary was pregnant by Bothwell and wished to hide her moral shortcomings. It is much more likely, however, that political realities rather than morality governed Mary's actions at this juncture, and having prepared the scene, no further action was required on her part but to await the *dénouement*. With the deed accomplished, Mary, however, found herself no freer than before, and Bothwell, supposedly her husband's slayer, previously a useful asset, thereafter became politically indispensable. It was, however, this political alignment with Bothwell, and not her adulterous affair with the earl, which caused the nobility to take to arms. Lack of morality might in retrospect be sufficient grounds for deposing a queen, and hence the importance of the Casket Letters which were later produced to justify this point of view, but it required a political opposition to effect such a deposition. Mary's mistakes on this occasion were irretrievable, and defeat at Carberry on 15 June 1567 was followed a month later by enforced abdication in favour of her one-year-old son, James.

Ten days after her surrender to the victorious lords, Knox returned to Edinburgh to gloat over his fallen rival, and preach at the coronation of her son in the parish church of Stirling on 29 July 1567. Ironically, however, the factors surrounding Mary's eclipse also encompassed Knox, for following Mary's escape from Lochleven castle in 1568, subsequent defeat at Langside and flight to England, successive Scottish regents found it necessary to placate Mary's captor Elizabeth to whom Knox remained completely unacceptable.

Political impotence, coupled with ill-health, meant that while in the years before his death in 1572 his considerable reputation brought to him the veneration owing to an elder statesman of the kirk, few listened to his words of advice or admonition. Nevertheless, his place in the annals of history was assured and lest there be any doubt on that score he left behind him his *History of the Reformation of Religion within the Realm of Scotland*, not only a masterpiece of language and style and an important historical source, but also a superb autobiography which has largely contributed to posterity's view of Knox and the part which he played in the Reformation movement. If, however, the traditional view of Knox was somewhat shaped by the pen rather than by deed, his great rival Mary Stewart was not to be outdone in that respect. If few even of her more avid contemporary supporters wished to dwell upon the events of her reign in Scotland, her prolonged captivity and final execution in England allowed her to pose, and be presented as a champion of Catholicism. Her real aims and intentions, however, were probably consistent with her earlier ambitions, as even in captivity Elizabeth's throne appears to have been her principal objective. Her plotting at this stage of her career was as inept in England as it had been in Scotland, and she paid the price accordingly. At the end, however, she played to perfection the martyr's role for which she had already been cast by her champions, and thus achieved an immortality which her struggle with Knox alone could not have conferred upon her.

CHAPTER 15

JAMES VI AND
VANISHING FRONTIERS

Gordon Donaldson

O NE of the few historical facts which has almost universal currency is that James VI of Scotland became King of England, and even Scots who should know better too often call him 'James the First'. But the genealogical accident which took him to the English throne is not the most important fact about the sixth James. His accession to England saw the disappearance of the frontier at the historic border, but within Scotland itself he eliminated other frontiers – between political and ecclesiastical parties, between different ways of life and even different races – and welded his countrymen into a unified kingdom of which he was the unquestioned head.

The prospect of such achievements was remote indeed when he was crowned at the age of thirteen months. He had been raised to the throne by a mere faction among the nobles, and civil war against his mother's supporters went on for six years. The first regent, the Earl of Moray, never conciliated the Hamiltons, who favoured the deposed Mary, and it was by a Hamilton that he was murdered in 1570. His successor the Earl of Lennox, Darnley's father, was also murdered, in an affray arising from the war with the Marian Party in 1571. The third regent, the Earl of Mar, was no more able than his predecessors to restore tranquillity to the distracted country before he died after thirteen months in office – it is said of a broken heart because he loved peace and could not attain it. The fourth, the Earl of Morton, ruled until 1580, but even then the king was only fourteen and the great families returned happily to their custom of competing among themselves for the direction of affairs. The period since Flodden in 1513 had been one in which there were three minorities – of James V, of Mary and of James VI – so that in the space of more than seventy years there were no more than twenty-two years of rule by a monarch of mature age.

The old problems of curbing the nobility and extending law and order, which had exercised kings for generations, were intensified by new problems arising from the Reformation. Dissension between those who supported Protestantism and the English alliance and those who stood by Rome and the traditional alliance with France exacerbated ancient feuds. Active or militant Roman Catholicism was hardly significant, if only because of the dearth of priests, but there was much latent sympathy with Catholicism in certain areas, and no one could have predicted how much support a skilfully led Roman Catholic revival might have enjoyed. This problem was tied up with that of the king's mother, who was also his rival and who lived, though in captivity in England, through the first twenty years of James' reign.

There was another problem which arose from the Reformation. In Scotland the Protestant Church had been set up not on royal initiative but as the outcome of two revolutions – one in 1560 against the Queen Mother, Mary of Guise, and the second, in 1567, against Queen Mary herself. It is true that the Protestants professed their readiness to accept the rule of a 'godly prince' in the person of James, and a new generation might become reconciled to royal control over the church, but it was not going to be easy to shake off the tradition of ecclesiastical independence. The Reformed Church had developed its general assembly, comprising the same elements which formed a parliament – any nobles who cared to attend, lairds representing the shires and burgesses chosen by town councils, alongside a number of ministers. Thus parliament, as well as the king, had a rival, and the assembly was an admirable platform for any militant faction.

Such a faction arose in the shape of the Presbyterian movement. Initially the Reformed Church had had a quasi-episcopal constitution, with superintendents and other individual overseers, and in 1572 it was decided, with general approval, that the crown should appoint ministers to bishoprics; these bishops would sit in parliament, exercise the functions of superintendents and be subject to the general assembly in spiritual matters. This arrangement was challenged by Andrew Melville, who returned to Scotland in 1574, after five years at Geneva, to become principal first at Glasgow University and then at St Mary's College, St Andrews. A logical thinker with no notion of tact, diplomacy or expediency, Melville argued that, as all ministers were equal, power should not lie with bishops or superintendents but with committees or courts, especially presbyteries. This in itself meant that it would no longer be open to the crown to influence the church through bishops, but Melville went further in his application of the doctrine that church and state formed 'Two Kingdoms'. Laymen in the commonly accepted sense of the term were to be wholly excluded from ecclesiastical government: barons and burgesses were no longer to attend the general assembly unless they happened to be elders, and crown and parliament were to have no authority over the church. But Melville did not propose a reciprocal exclusion of ministers from power in the state, for God was the head of both kingdoms and the ministers could 'teach the magistrate how the civil jurisdiction should be exercised according to the Word'. One minister told the king, 'There is a judgment above yours, and that is God's, put in the hand of the ministry, for we shall judge the angels, saith the Apostle.' This meant the rule of a clerical oligarchy in the shape of the majority in the general assembly.

With so many disturbing elements in church and state, there were ample grounds for the growth of factions, founded partly on principles and partly, as ever, on personal and family feuds. The traditions of Queen Mary's party were inherited by what may be called broadly a conservative faction, sympathetic to proposals for Mary's restoration, favourable to Roman Catholicism or to episcopacy, and anxious for the alignment of Scotland with France or Spain. The existence of this group constantly aroused hopes among Roman Catholic agents that Scotland could be rallied to the papal cause as a base for a crusade against heretical England. On the other side was an ultra-Protestant faction, hostile to Mary and anyone else tainted with 'papistry' and eager for the alliance of Scotland with England against the Romanist powers of the continent. This faction gave some countenance to the Presbyterian ministers, who for their part used their pulpits for propaganda in favour of an English alliance and against Rome. This party was also hand-in-glove with the English puritan politicians who were always trying to divert Elizabeth's foreign policy into an anti-Catholic crusade.

Morton, the fourth regent, was a good friend to England and had no place in his government for former supporters of Mary. He was equally a good friend to episcopacy but, although he censured Melville, he took no action to prevent the growth of the Presbyterian party, and, although he questioned the legality of the general assembly, he did not suppress it. In 1578 the assembly adopted Melville's proposals and went on to condemn the office of bishop. This in itself was bound to lead to a clash with the state, for the place of bishops in ecclesiastical administration, as well as much else that Melville wanted to sweep away, was founded on statute law; the assembly could proclaim a programme, but only parliament could put it into effect. If Morton did nothing to check the Presbyterian threat, he did nothing, either, to prevent the growth of a faction opposed to him, and he neglected to ingratiate himself with the young king. James was being brought up in Stirling Castle, where the dominant figure in his education was George Buchanan, an elderly academic and a stern disciplinarian who thought it his duty to instil into his pupil a hatred of his mother as an adulteress and a murderess, to drill him in classical scholarship and to indoctrinate him with concepts of constitutional monarchy; Buchanan did much to shape and perhaps to warp James' personality, but the king, when he grew to manhood, was to reject many of his tutor's lessons.

After Morton's fall, in 1580, rival factions in turn seized power in a series of *coups d'état*. The king, now fourteen, gave his adolescent devotion to an accomplished cousin from France, Esmé Stewart, and created him Duke of Lennox. There is little reason to believe that Lennox had any real interest in either the revival of Roman Catholicism or the restoration of Mary, but he was regarded with wild optimism by Roman Catholic agents and with equal suspicion by the Presbyterians, whom he defied by making a fresh appointment to the archbishopric of Glasgow. A reaction came in 1582, when a party of ultra-Protestant lords, led by William Ruthven, Earl of Gowrie, seized the king's person in the Ruthven Raid and formed an administration which lasted for ten months. They tried to reach a firm understanding with Elizabeth and they allowed the

Presbyterians to develop their organisation, though still without statutory authority. When the king escaped from the Ruthven Raiders, Lennox was dead, but an administration was formed under James Stewart, created Earl of Arran, who brought back into office some former Marians and other conservatives who had been excluded under Morton. This government passed the 'Black Acts' which reaffirmed episcopal government and made it plain that supremacy over the church was to rest with the crown-in-parliament, and it drove Andrew Melville and many of his followers, as well as the lords who had taken part in the Ruthven Raid, into exile in England. At the end of 1585 the exiled lords returned from England in force and overthrew Arran.

By this time James was nineteen and his own views began to influence policy. In one of his earliest pronouncements he declared his intention to be a 'universal king', not the agent of a faction but able to choose his ministers at his pleasure. Not a strong party man by temperament, he aimed at a *via media* to which he could reconcile the majority – he hoped all – of his people. His material interests also prompted him to take this line. One objective was to succeed Elizabeth, and this inclined him to favour the Protestantism which was maintained in England. At the same time, he was aware of the strength of English Roman Catholicism, and there was a possibility that Spain might intervene either before or at Elizabeth's death and re-establish a Roman ascendancy. If, therefore, James maintained an equivocal policy he would commend himself to English Roman Catholics and perhaps even succeed to England under papal auspices. Besides, he had always a prudential regard for his own safety, and to show himself an intransigent Protestant might encourage the pope to authorise a fanatical Jesuit to assassinate him.

An attempt to maintain a balance between the rival Scottish parties was made after Arran's fall in 1585, for the government which was then formed was a kind of coalition, in which men who had been in office under Arran were retained alongside ultra-Protestants. At the head of it was John Maitland of Thirlestane, himself a former Marian and the brother of Mary's secretary, William Maitland of Lethington, but shrewd enough to see the importance of keeping on good terms with England and with the Presbyterians.

A league with England was concluded in 1586, accompanied by an English pension for James and an assurance that Elizabeth would not oppose his claims to the English throne unless he provoked her. Such strong inducements to good behaviour went far to ensure James' acquiescence in his mother's execution in 1587 and his neutrality when the Spanish Armada sailed in 1588. The league with England pleased the Presbyterians and ultra-Protestants and reduced their political force, for they were no longer likely to act as English agents, and it was safe to make concessions to them. In 1586 an attempt was made to combine Presbyterian and episcopalian elements in the church system, but when this proved unacceptable to the Presbyterians they were tacitly permitted to go ahead with the unofficial development of their organisation. Simultaneously, the bishops were deprived of the bulk of their properties, and the result was a temporary eclipse of episcopacy.

The political force of the contrary faction was reduced by Mary's execution, for their plotting could now have only the unpatriotic aim of assisting Spain to conquer Britain. The earls of Huntly, Errol and Crawford in the north-east and Lord Maxwell in the south-west were active enough in communicating with Philip of Spain, but they seem to have been uncertain of their objectives and had little support beyond the bounds of their own family and territorial influence. It seemed safe enough for the government to follow its policy of conciliation by refraining from strong measures against them. The difficulty was that leniency to the 'popish earls', as they were called, infuriated the Presbyterians and went a long way to nullify the concessions to them. On the other hand, acquiescence in the progress of Presbyterianism nullified the pretence that the king looked favourably on the cause of Rome.

It must have become evident that conciliation all round was as yet premature. To be a 'universal king', superior to faction, required force or money or diplomacy. As James had neither money nor men at his disposal, coercion was impossible, but he had an ample stock of tactical skill. There is no direct evidence of the trend of his thought, but the necessary inference is that he decided to lean on the Presbyterians until he had destroyed the political danger of the Roman Catholic faction. In 1592 an act of parliament officially authorised the Presbyterian system of church government. The measure did not amount to what Andrew Melville had asked, for it did not concede ecclesiastical independence, the office of bishop was not abolished and nothing was done for the endowment of the Reformed Church. James' amiability cost little in political, and nothing in financial, terms, but with the support of the ultra-Protestants he was now able to put pressure on the northern earls to abandon their intrigues with Spain, and Andrew Melville accompanied a royal army which marched against them. They showed that, while they would intrigue and bluster and even raise armed forces, they would not face the king in the field. They were forced to go abroad in 1595 and at last made a formal submission to both parliament and assembly in 1596.

This menace being removed, it was time to turn on the Presbyterians, and the king did this with a rapidity which makes the conclusion inescapable that his moves had been planned. Events played into his hands. The Presbyterians had been involved in politics since at least as far back as the Ruthven Raid, when they gave their blessing to that 'act of reformation' as they called it. More recently, they had taken up the cause of 'the bonnie Earl o' Moray' (son-in-law of the Earl of Moray who had earlier been the darling of the Protestants). Despite the moving ballad, which presents Moray as 'the queen's true love', his murder by the Earl of Huntly was the outcome only of a long-standing feud between two nobles who supported rival policies, but James had a personal preference for Huntly and refused to punish him as the Presbyterians demanded. Another troublesome peer whom the ministers favoured was Francis Stewart, Earl of Bothwell, nephew of Mary's Bothwell. Francis gained notoriety by his alleged resort to witchcraft to raise storms when the king sailed to Denmark in 1589 to bring home his bride and by repeatedly forcing his way into the royal presence with no other apparent aim than to demonstrate the king's lack of power. James was ready enough to believe in the seriousness of the witch cults which seem to have been common at the time, but in his timid and cautious soul he may also have had a reluctant admiration for Bothwell's dash and verve. However, Bothwell, besides being at feud with Maitland of Thirlestane, endeared himself to the ministers by leading the opposition to the king's leniency to Huntly and the other 'popish earls', and some Presbyterians acclaimed him as a 'a sanctified plague' who would make the king 'turn to God'. Ministers were not content with rebuking the king for his personal behaviour, but persisted in trying to interfere in both domestic and foreign policy and over-reached themselves. Andrew Melville addressed James as 'God's silly vassal' and one of his colleagues characterised all kings as 'devil's children'. A rather mysterious riot in Edinburgh at the end of 1596 was represented by the king as an illustration of the danger of clerical power, and he turned it to account to bring Edinburgh to grovelling submission and to secure for himself a voice in the selection of ministers for the leading towns.

From 1596 to 1597, when the political dangers from both Catholic and Presbyterian factions were effaced, the king passed from defence to attack. He used a remarkable range of devices to revive episcopacy. He could appoint a minister to the title of a bishopric; the general assembly could appoint a minister as visitor of a district and could decide that presbyteries and synods should have 'constant moderators' or permanent chairmen; parliament could restore to the bishops the bulk of their revenues. All these things were done, and when a minister who held the title and revenues of a bishopric acted as visitor of his diocese and was constant moderator of the synod he began to look very like a bishop. In 1610 the general assembly gave its approval to an episcopal constitution. This success was not achieved without a certain amount of characteristic trickery. The general assembly approved at first only of constant moderators of presbyteries, but the king, by the simple device of falsifying the minutes, made out that the approval extended to synods as well. Similarly, when parliament in 1612 ratified the restoration of episcopacy the assembly's minutes had again been falsified, for certain limitations on the powers of bishops were omitted.

James could not have proceeded so far without taming the general assembly. Melville's influence had depended on the support of the majority of the ministers who regularly attended the assembly, but as it always met in the south hardly any of the more conservative ministers from the north turned up. However, the act of 1592, which authorised the assembly, had given the king the power to name its place of meeting, and James began to name places like Montrose and Aberdeen, where the radicals would not swamp the house. He also exploited his power to fix the date of meeting. When he advanced the pre-arranged date, no one could object, and he then went on to defer it. In 1605, when some ministers insisted on constituting an assembly after the king had postponed it, they were successfully prosecuted. Then Andrew Melville and some other leading militants were summoned to London, ostensibly for a conference, and were not allowed to return to Scotland. For the remainder of the reign, while assemblies might be restive, they were never defiant. The king's power to legislate for the church had been acknowledged by parliament in 1606, but James, who remarked with characteristic shrewdness that 'prerogative is a secret which ryves [tears] in the stretching', preferred to work by constitutional means. Whereas episcopacy had been reaffirmed by parliament in 1584 and presbytery authorised by parliament in 1592, he dexterously arranged that in 1610 a general assembly (containing equitable representation from the whole country) passed the acts to restore episcopacy.

It was not only because of the king's severity towards the Presbyterian leaders that his changes in church government were accepted. The ministers were vocal, but they had little power in themselves. They might perhaps try to stir up the people, but the changes in church government made little difference to the everyday working of the church: kirk sessions continued to operate, and the bishops actually increased their numbers and effectiveness; and presbyteries still met to carry out their functions without much reference to the bishops. Consequently, there was little that the ordinary worshipper could disapprove of, if he noticed any change at all. It was perhaps more important that, as Scottish society was largely dominated by the nobles, if the king could appease them he could disregard ministers and people alike. Now, nobles who had acquired church property had no taste for the financial proposals of Melville, who claimed all ecclesiastical revenues for the Reformed Church and denounced the diversion of any of them to laymen as sacrilege. Besides, the Reformation had transferred to the crown the control of church property, and this made the nobles dependent on the king for the transformation of their rights in church lands into hereditary holdings and for grants of additional lands. Wise kings had always used patronage to gain support, and now the king had at his disposal patronage on an unparalleled scale.

While there is thus some truth in the statement that James bought the nobles with the lands of the monasteries, there were other elements in his dealings with them. His assertion of the divine right of his kingship was the necessary answer, framed by a king who was himself a theologian, to the claims of the Presbyterians that he was answerable to the ministers. James did not deny that he was God's vassal, and indeed rather gloried in the fact, but he believed in One Kingdom, comprising both church and state, of which he was the earthly head, without the need for ministers as intermediaries. Yet he was far too shrewd to obtrude his dignity in his day-to-day dealings with his subjects. Divine right meant that James had always a strong sense of his responsibilities, and he remarked sagely that 'the highest bench is slidderiest [most slippery] to sit upon'. Besides, while he dogmatised about divine right, he had an easy familiarity with nobles and commons alike which took the sting out of his dogmatising and gave him opportunities to use his undoubted gifts of cajolery. The Earl of Mar was 'Jockie o' the sclates' because, when he had shared James' schooling, he had shown a marked ability in arithmetic. The Earl of Haddington was 'Tam o' the Cowgate', from his place of residence in Edinburgh. Moreover, James had not studied both contemporary Scotland and Scottish history without learning that conciliation paid better dividends than severity. He preferred to avoid head-on collisions, and there were few executions or forfeitures.

Yet, while James conciliated the nobles, he did not depend much on them for the conduct of administration. He declared at one stage that he would not use great men to manage his affairs, but only 'such as he could correct and were hangable'. The 'hangable' men on whom he relied – and none of whom he ever hanged – were younger sons of noble houses or men of middle-class origin. Maitland of Thirlestane himself was the first chancellor in the century who was neither a prelate nor a peer, and on Maitland's fall James at once selected ministers who were to serve him well throughout the rest of his reign. His bishops, too, were middle-class administrators who served in the state as well as the church.

Frontiers between political factions, frontiers between parties in the church, were going down, and frontiers between feuding noble families followed them, according to the design of a king who had

a marked distaste for bloodshed and even for the sight of arms –
possibly, it has been suggested because of ante-natal experience,
when the daggers of Riccio's murderers flashed before his mother's
eyes three months before his birth. After the riot in Edinburgh in
December 1596 there was a period of unprecedented tranquillity,
lasting for forty years into the reign of James' son but appropriately
called 'King James' Peace'. In fact, while James' victory over the
Presbyterians is spectacular, the achievement which did most to
shape the future of Scotland was his success in instilling a new
respect for law and order. Many efforts were made to improve
criminal justice, but it was characteristic that James laid the
emphasis on the prevention of crime rather than its punishment,
and it was for this reason that he instituted justices of the peace.
They achieved relatively little, probably because the king was too
cautious to invest them with powers which would have infringed
the rights of the nobles' courts and perhaps more was done
through the unobtrusive but persistent efforts of the kirk sessions.
The sessions constantly held up certain standards of conduct and
they dealt on the spot with minor offences by word and deed
which, if unchecked, could easily have led to serious crimes. In the
towns the sessions worked closely with the town councils, and
James himself saw clearly the parallel between the work of the
sessions and the functions he proposed for his justices of the peace.
At a different level, it was significant of the growing maturity of the
Scottish state that James, after carrying out much-needed measures
of financial reorganisation, was able to introduce to Scotland
something like regular taxation. The reign also saw the institution
of the Register of Sasines, which provided a unique record of all
transactions in real estate. All in all, the king succeeded in making
Scotland what he called 'a weill governit commonweal'.

The Scottish parliament had never developed into an effective
check on a resolute king and had seldom been the scene of independent debates. James increased its representative character by
introducing shire commissioners to represent lesser landowners – a
measure which strengthened it against the general assembly – but
he also perfected machinery which enabled him to control its
proceedings and secure its acquiescence in his measures. His main
instrument in ruling Scotland, especially after he went to England,

was the privy council, to which he directed a stream of instructions and so governed Scotland 'through the post'. He boasted that he could rule Scotland by his pen, which others had not done by the sword.

While the government thus became more intensive, it also became more extensive, at the expense of ancient frontiers, geographical, racial and cultural. The problem of 'putting order on the, border' was one which had defeated James' predecessors. The lands on both sides of the border had constituted something of a land apart, with its own code of behaviour; the borderers were apt to regard Anglo-Scottish warfare as a kind of rough game in which no one should be seriously hurt, were disinclined to regard either Edinburgh or London and were able to find a refuge across the frontier when either government tried to take action. After 1603 the problem could be tackled as a joint Anglo-Scottish operation, and the Borders, now the 'Middle Shires' of James' enlarged kingdom, were disciplined by mounted police until they hardly knew themselves. In one year more than 140 of 'the nimblest and most powerful thieves in all the Borders' ended their days on the gallows.

As only the North Channel separated the western Highlands and islands from Ireland, the situation there had been not unlike that on the Borders. After 1603 the Scottish government could collaborate with the English administration in Ulster, and James was then able to reduce the west Highlands to obedience. He put an end to the policy of raising up feudal magnates at the expense of clan chiefs, and relied instead on royal officials, including bishops, and on the clan chiefs themselves, whom he made responsible for the good behaviour of their followers. The Reformed Church was extended to the west, to bring not only the gospel but also the kirk session discipline. James was responsible, too, for the settlement of Protestant Englishmen and Lowland Scots in Ulster, in order to drive a wedge between two areas of Celtic Catholicism. The design was well-conceived, but this, James' sole experiment in creating rather than abolishing a frontier, has been a source of trouble ever since.

In Orkney and Shetland, where the earls wielded almost sovereign power, the problem was not one of too little government but – so at least the natives thought – too much government, and government by the old Norse laws, which gave the earls peculiar opportunities to demonstrate the truth of the old saying that 'justice is mighty profitable'. Once again a bishop was called in as a royal agent; Earl Patrick Stewart spent the last years of his life in prison and the Norse laws were abolished in 1611.

James' concept of One Kingdom, initially the answer to the challenge of the Reformed Church, was coming to have a wider meaning. It was fatal to the feudal, baronial or clan characteristics of Scottish society and to any deviation from the king's laws. As the various frontiers went down, it became increasingly true that there was indeed one kingdom in Scotland.

One aspect of the work of a busy and paternal government was a flow of well-intentioned economic legislation, mainly designed to restrain the export of raw materials and thereby encourage manufactures, the introduction of skilled foreigners to teach their crafts and the issue of patents for the 'projects' of various inventors. Some new industries did take root, and there is a good deal of evidence of expanding commerce, notably the export of coal and salt. However, probably less was done to bring about commercial expansion by legislation than by the new conditions of order and security. Farmers, likewise, could now sow their seed with some confidence that no human agency would prevent them from reaping their harvest, and agriculture benefited also from the widespread substitution of proprietorship for tenancies. There is ample evidence of the increasing wealth of the merchant classes and the farmers alike.

Economic improvements, added to peace and stability, were conducive to intellectual and cultural activities. Among the king's subjects were John Napier of Merchiston, the inventor of logarithms, and Timothy Pont, Scotland's first cartographer. Two universities were founded – Edinburgh in 1582 and Marischal College, Aberdeen, in 1593 – bringing Scotland's total to five. Although neither owed anything to royal initiative, a scholarly king delighted to patronise universities and he decreed that Edinburgh University should be known as 'The Academy of King James'. The number of parish schools had been increasing, and an act of the privy council in 1616 was the first measure for the maintenance of a school in every parish.

Architecture was finding new outlets. Hitherto Scottish residences, with the exception of two or three royal palaces, had been essentially fortified places, castles or tower-houses, with little adornment. Now that feuds and disturbances were falling out of fashion, defence was less necessary and, although some were reluctant to abandon their towers, if only because 'the world may change again', the utilitarian tower-house gave way to what was more like a castellated mansion. Purely domestic buildings, without pretence at fortification, also appeared, conspicuously in the palace built at Kirkwall about 1600 by the king's cousin, Earl Patrick Stewart. Another cousin, the troublesome Earl of Bothwell, inserted into the courtyard of Crichton Castle a domestic range with an Italianate façade unique in Scotland. The king's own building, at Edinburgh Castle and Linlithgow Palace, represents a Jacobean style, some of whose features were imitated by his subjects in their own houses. Scottish architecture was notably enriched by a style quite different from the Jacobean houses of England; there was some debt to Danish models, but also considerable independence.

If architecture thus had a vernacular character, in language and literature the trend was towards assimilation to England. The Scots never had a printed Bible in their own tongue, but depended on English versions, and the Reformed Church was an instrument in habituating them to standard English, with the result that Scots practically disappeared as a literary vehicle even before the union of the crowns. The king was himself a poet of some competence and even in the 1580s he was assembling other versifiers around him. The tradition of a courtly group of poets was continued later in the reign by William Drummond of Hawthornden and Sir William Alexander. Jacobean poetry was closely associated with the cultivation of music, in which the king also took an interest. Former monks and priests brought the musical skill of the old church into the service of the new; English musicians provided the music of the court; the song-schools in the burghs were maintained, and schoolboys and undergraduates had opportunities to learn vocal and instrumental music.

It is in this reign that we first find an appreciable number of portraits of Scotsmen, though the artists were often foreigners. The main outlet of painting was the mural decoration and painted ceilings of which so many specimens survive and which suggest that Scottish houses were internally a riot of colour. The detail of the work was not always of the highest quality, but the general intention to introduce gaiety and brightness is unmistakable. The subjects, occasionally scriptural, were often secular and sometimes obscene, and indicate an outlook far removed from a dismal puritanical austerity. Many churches were adorned with sepulchral monuments showing a very high standard of craftsmanship in a Renaissance style, following a fashion common in both England and Denmark.

James' accession to the English throne brought him enlarged prestige as well as immunity from the *coups d'état* which had punctuated his earlier years. But there were disadvantages. Removed from everyday contact with subjects who could presume on their familiarity to criticise him, he was surrounded instead by obsequious prelates and flattering courtiers. His ablest achievements belong to the days of his adversity before 1596, when he had to meet challenge after challenge; in the days of his prosperity he was less willing to attend to business with his old shrewdness and he lost his sureness of touch. It was remarked that the Scottish kings were like the horses of Mar, which 'in youth are good but in their old age bad'. Perhaps it was James' misfortune that he lived to be almost fifty-nine, which made him older than all the sovereigns of his house except the first two and the last.

Not content with his changes in church government, James began, from 1612 onwards, to move towards changes in worship. There was much support for improvements, and a process of revision initiated by a general assembly at Aberdeen in 1616 produced three drafts of a new service-book. But, whereas the first and second represented Scottish tradition, the third was more like a version of the English Prayer Book. Moreover, the king brought forward five other proposals: the observance of the main holy days of the Christian year; kneeling at communion; private communion; private baptism; and confirmation by bishops. Changes in worship, unlike the revival of episcopacy, affected what the ordinary worshipper saw in his church Sunday by Sunday. Although grudging approval was given to the Five Articles by a general assembly at Perth in 1618, opposition was so intense, especially to kneeling at communion, that the king, who had not lost all his common sense, saw that he must go no further. No new service-book was issued and in 1621, when parliament (again through the support of representatives from the north) approved the Five Articles, it seems that James gave an undertaking that if they were approved he would propose no more innovations. Not only did he keep his word, but his bishops were sensible enough not to press the Articles on clergy or people.

Economic prosperity no doubt helped to make people content with James' government and added to his subjects' respect for him. It was not mere flattery when one of his servants referred to 'this dilectable time of peace under your Majesty's happy reign and most excellent government'. There might be occasional grumbling, over his ecclesiastical innovations and over his taxation, but the days were to come when men would look back with regret to the 'great wisdom' of 'blessed King James'.

CHAPTER 16

MONTROSE AND ARGYLL

Edward J. Cowan

IN the seamless web of history the destinies of individuals are sometimes strangely intertwined. One such strand was woven into the complex fabric of the Covenanting era in the complementary careers of James Graham, fifth Earl of Montrose, and Archibald Campbell, eighth Earl of Argyll. Both were Covenanters and both 'the Great Marquis' to their respective admirers who, exaggerating differences between them more apparent than real, transformed both into symbols which they themselves would only partially have recognised.

Born in 1612, five years Argyll's junior, James Graham was handsome, talented and militarily gifted. He shared with Archibald Campbell a taste for mathematics, history and golf. Both were medallists in archery at St Andrews University. Montrose spent his youth on his Perthshire and Angus estates. He made frequent visits to the home of his brother-in-law, Colquhoun of Luss on Loch Lomondside, where he acquired some Gaelic and the traditional Colquhoun dislike of clan Campbell. After an excursion to the continent in the 1630s he was presented at court but due to the venomous tongue of the Marquis of Hamilton, who personally supervised the mismanagement of Scottish affairs during the following decade, he was coldly received by Charles I. His day would come. In youth the ingenuous Montrose was believed to have 'taken upon him the part of the hero too much and lived as in a romance'. He carried his romanticism to the gallows, but in his career there is an elegiac quality reminiscent of his own poetry.

In contrast the biography of Argyll can be characterised as pedestrian prose. Possessed of a well-known obliquity of vision, 'gley'd eyed Archibald' appears cast by nature in the role of villain. Charged with shiftiness, cowardice, unreliability and a vacillating opportunism, qualities in themselves seldom incompatible with political success, his *métier* lay in intrigue rather than military endeavour. Yet there is ample testimony to his personal charm, conversational accomplishment and his 'large and understanding heart'. He was also MacCalein Mor, chief of the most powerful Highland clan, which had risen on the ruins of the lordship of the Isles. As the instrument of crown policy the Campbells had smoked out many a 'byke of lawless limmers', including MacDonalds, Mac-Leans and MacGregors, whose territories they promptly engrossed. Clan affairs preoccupied Argyll at Inveraray until his appointment to the privy council in 1628. His orbit remained emphatically Highland. His austere Presbyterianism led to a clash with the epis-copal authorities in the 1630s. He was also an early supporter of the most profound and literarily gifted of the Covenanting theorists, Samuel Rutherford.

The careers of both men have been distorted by successive his-torians bent on finding their own political or religious bias reflected in the age. Argyll described himself as 'a distracted man, a distracted subject of a distracted time wherein I lived'. Both he and Montrose were bewildered human beings struggling against a wave of complex forces which would eventually engulf them. Both were martyrs to the faithlessness of Charles Stewart, dying for ideals greater than themselves. Argyll, a man of his time, was undoubtedly devious. Although at his trial, for example, he strenuously denied having ordered the burning of Forther Castle in Angus, a surviving letter not only proves the contrary but contains the rider, 'you need not to let know that you have directions from me to fire it'. Montrose, also a prisoner of his age, sacked Aberdeen in 1644 and was power-less to prevent massacres of the Campbells at Inveraray and Inverlochy, had he been so inclined. Yet he was on the whole more consistent, less a politician, more a man of principle. As staunch Calvinists both subscribed to what has been called 'the thesis of progressive comprehension', namely that previous agreements or bargains (saving a covenant with God) could be made redundant by subsequent revelation. And when the wave finally broke on the rocks both died convinced of their own salvation.

The 'small cloud in the north' was expanded into a storm which engulfed England, Ireland and Scotland in civil war, largely through the folly of Charles I. The union of 1603 constituted a severe psychological blow to the Scots. With the removal of the court the nobility lacked a political focus, the burgesses detected a detrimental effect on Scottish trade. In controlling the privy council and the Lords of the Articles James had drawn the teeth of parliament; Charles seemed bent on silencing it forever. His Act of Revocation of 1625 attempted to solve the three-fold problem of crown finance, ecclesiastical endowment and the collection of church revenues by compelling the surrender of church lands in lay hands. Although unsuccessful this act, coupled with a proposal to abolish heritable jurisdictions, both panicked and antagonised the nobility and landowners. Arbitrary and increased taxation lent fuel to the flame.

An identification in the minds of some Scots of church and nation rendered the kirk the powder keg of the impending holocaust. Many laymen involved themselves in church courts (such as kirk sessions) as a means of alleviating political frustration. In the Lowlands a steady erosion of the kin-ties created a proportional reliance upon the paternalism of the church. Charles' obsession with liturgical revision, of foreign inspiration and smacking of popery, was anathema to the Scots. His tendency to advance churchmen (including bishops) in civil affairs, culminating in the appointment of Archbishop Spottiswoode as chancellor in 1635, caused great alarm. Many held the assertion of parliamentary sovereignty to be the obvious counter-weight to royal prerogative but parliament was muzzled and supplication rejected. Charles' arbitrary imposition of a new code of canons in 1636 reinforced such a view.

The Scots considered that much was innovatory, popish and heretical in the Prayer Book of 1637, described by Montrose as 'the brood of the bowels of the whore of Babel'. Its public reading in St Giles was the signal for revolt. Edinburgh swarmed with petitioners demanding its withdrawal; rioting and mobbing were daily occurrences. Montrose was elected as a representative of the nobility to a committee of petitioners known as the 'Tables', which provided a forum for opposition and functioned as a substitute parliament. As a privy councillor it was Argyll's duty to attempt to control the situation. Not for a year did he align himself with Montrose.

In February 1638 Alexander Henderson, minister of Leuchars,

and the lawyer Johnston of Wariston drew up the National Covenant. One of the first to subscribe it was Montrose, so infected by the excitement of the times that he was prophetically told he would never be at rest until 'lifted up above the rest in three fathoms of rope'. Such delirium was widespread. The kirks were packed, pews occupied for hours on end; the intellectual fodder of the revolution was provided by the pulpit and thousands came to feed.

The Covenant exploited the widespread fear of popery and the advance of Antichrist. It listed all statutes in favour of the reformed religion, so conferring a novel status on Scottish parliamentary legislation and signifying the constitutional struggle to come. Just as 'banding' was the traditional means of ensuring protection and maintenance, the Covenant was conceived as a bond for the maintenance of religion. It also owed a great deal to the concept of federal theology which preoccupied a number of the followers of Andrew Melville. There was also an Apocalyptic element. The Scots shared the widely held seventeenth-century belief that the Second Coming as prophesied in the Book of Revelation was imminent. In the minds of some, Scotland's divine and historic role was to prepare the world for this event. The need for preparation, however, precluded a total obsession with other-worldliness. The legislation of the Covenanters is pervaded with a desire to reform society as a whole. Not only private morality but the improvement of industry, trade, agriculture, as well as poor relief and educational reforms are encompassed within their vision. The commitment in the Covenant to defend both religion and king would cause the rift between Argyll and Montrose. The former did not consider the interests of church and king to be always compatible; Montrose did. In 1638 the main strength of the Covenant was that it was all things to all men. It was both the focus of Scottish nationhood and the symbol of revolution. Those who took up arms to defend it appealed to patriotism and the fear that Stewart despotism would reduce Scotland to the status of a province.

Royal sanction was obtained for the first meeting of a general assembly for twenty years. When Hamilton attempted to dissolve the Glasgow assembly of November 1638 on the grounds that it was unconstitutional, Argyll spoke against him. According to Wariston, his declaration for the Covenant at this point 'incouraged and strengthened the cause mor nor if he had doone it befor'. The thwarted Hamilton distinguished Argyll as 'the dangerousest man in the state'. The assembly proceeded with the annulment of canons and liturgy and the deposition of the bishops. To his dying day Montrose would reject the bishops. With Argyll he played a leading role in suppressing internal opposition to the Covenant and in achieving the capitulation of the king. Their disagreement arose over a subsequent course of action.

The problem of the legality of resistance had taxed the ingenuity of commentators for centuries. Medieval theorists believed that kingship was divinely sanctioned but that God might engineer the removal of the tyrannical monarch. Montrose was at one with John of Salisbury, who first formulated resistance theory in the twelfth century, in asserting that 'patience in the subject is the best remedy against the effect of a Prince's power too far extended'. The means of obtaining moderate government was 'to endeavour the security of religion and just liberty', both safeguarded by law and parliament. 'And if Parliaments be frequent and rightly constituted, what favourite counselour or statesman dare misinforme or mislead the king?' The essentially medieval notion that the king must be rescued from bad counsel justified the subscription of the Covenant. Having secured the religious demands and regular parliaments, Montrose feared the further diminution of royal prerogative. The tyranny of subjects was 'the most fierce, insatiable and insupportable tyranny in the world'.

Argyll also basically believed in a balanced constitution but he held that 'nothing is impossible or unfeasible for an enslaved people to do against tyrants'. He was more keenly aware of the split between king and kirk presaged by Andrew Melville's 'Two Kingdoms' theory. The Presbyterian concept of parity in religion could easily be extended to the secular sphere. 'Popular furies would never have end, if not awed by their superiors', wrote Argyll, 'the people will soon learn their own strength and from thence infer that the popular power excels that of the noblesse.' He believed that the historical role of the Scottish nobility was to serve the king and defend the people, 'every one ... his Majesty's shadow our care should ever be to carry ourselves to his people, as we desire his Majesty should appear to them and so make up to him a treasure of their love'. As one well grounded in the works of George Buchanan, who had refined resistance theory to justify the deposition of Mary, Queen of Scots, he could envisage the possibility of supplanting the king altogether. Such an awareness was no doubt heightened by his position as clan chief. He well knew that the 'misthryving' of the chief could result in his rejection, as he found to his cost in later years.

One of the most perceptive of contemporary historians, Gordon of Ruthven, remarks that the King of Scots 'is kinge of men . . . not intituled efter the countrie as other kinges, but efter the natione', a useful fiction for king and subjects alike. Charles alienated the strong Scottish attachment to monarchy, which, as Argyll observed, favoured the regulation of monarchy rather than its destruction. Montrose and Argyll disagreed as to the extent of such regulation.

Charles' visit to Scotland in 1641 was long remembered by the Scots as the year in which the sovereignty of parliament was asserted at the expense of royal prerogative. He was forced to ratify the legislation of the truly revolutionary session of 1640 which met in defiance of prorogation. A spate of legislation included compulsory subscription of the Covenant, the abolition of the Committee of Articles and a Triennial act ensuring a parliament every three years. In 1641 he was further compelled to allow that henceforward virtually all civil appointments be made with the advice of parliament. He experienced 'tyranny of subjects' with a vengeance.

Montrose challenged the legality of the 1640 parliament. Neither the sinister reply that 'to do the less was more lawful than to do the greater', nor suggestions that a dictatorship and a canton north of the Forth be established for a nameless, if obvious, candidate, assuaged his growing uneasiness. His 'Cumbernauld Bond' subscribed by eighteen similarly alarmed individuals expressed anxiety at 'the particular and indirect practicking of a few'. He countermanded Argyll's discovery of the bond with allegations that 'King Campbell' was plotting Charles' deposition. While Argyll may well have nurtured such ambitions, that he would have voiced them in any but the most general terms is inconceivable. He certainly could not allow such assertions to pass unchallenged and Montrose was imprisoned while the testimony of witnesses was examined. Most gave vague statements but the evidence of one John Stewart occasioned a stream of oaths from MacCalein Mor. 'Many wondered thereat', but he was acquitted of treasonable intent.

From prison Montrose begged an audience with the king to impart information of the greatest importance, but before this could be granted, Argyll fled Edinburgh due to a plot on his life. The 'Incident' is an obscure affair with some basis in reality. Some of Montrose's sympathisers discussed the kidnapping of Hamilton and Argyll; the intended victims just possibly publicised the plot to increase their political capital. They returned unscathed in greater favour than ever. Argyll was given a marquisate. Shortly thereafter Montrose, who was incapable of influencing Charles against his favoured subject, was released largely through Argyll's good offices. News of calamitous events elsewhere in his dominions necessitated Charles' departure from Scotland; the Catholics had risen in Ireland.

Montrose's worst fears were realised in the Scottish commitment to the Solemn League and Covenant of 1643. Military support for the English Parliamentarians constituted armed rebellion. He rightly believed that English Independents were cynically using the idea of an international Presbyterian crusade for political ends. The ideal of a Presbyterian establishment in England, Ireland and Scotland 'according to the example of the best reformed churches', a phrase narrowly interpreted by the blinkered Scots, would remain a pious aspiration. During the negotiations on the second Covenant Charles frantically attempted to win over Argyll, who characteristically withheld support for either side until the last possible moment. He was finally swayed by the king's acceptance of a cessation of fighting in Ireland, where the Roman Catholics, widely credited with large scale massacres of Protestants, were to retain such possessions as they had won.

Catholicism was what Argyll feared most. Irish Franciscans claimed several thousand converts in the Hebrides in the 1620s. In 1626 Iain Muideartach, chief of Clanranald, informed the pope of his willingness to lead a crusade to restore Scotland to Catholicism. Gaelic-speaking Scots and a majority of Irish chieftains, 'from whose stock first we sprang', would co-operate. Many of the clans mentioned had ancient scores to settle with the Campbells. Even before Argyll declared for the Covenant, Charles and Hamilton discussed the exploitation of this antipathy. In 1639 the king com-missioned Donald Gorm of Sleat and the Earl of Antrim, an Irish MacDonald, as his lieutenants in the Highlands. Shortly thereafter Donald along with MacLeods, MacLeans and Clanranald himself planned the logistics of a descent on Argyll territory. The charge that Argyll used the Covenant to further his own interest is there-fore correct, but he had no choice. The anti-Campbell coalition, so important in the seventeenth and eighteenth centuries, was the brainchild of Charles I. In explaining their attachment to the Stewart cause the conservatism of the clans was matched by a desire to recover territory held by the Campbells. Thus an army held itself in readiness, waiting for a leader; and in return for cessation the Irish Catholics promised Charles military assistance. Antrim finally sent some 1,500 men to Scotland under the command of the leg-endary Alasdair MacDonald, young Colkitto. The Catholic crusade was being waged on Argyll's own doorstep.

Argyll, recognising Montrose's military ability, twice tried to woo him to his cause. Montrose refused, went to Oxford, where he convinced Charles of his loyalty, and on 1 February 1644 he was commissioned as lieutenant-general in Scotland with a marquisate to follow. So began the Glorious Year and the greatest adventure of Montrose's life.

Disguised as a groom, he penetrated the Covenanting lines and joined up with Colkitto in Athol. The two men complemented one another beautifully. Montrose had the gift of inspiring his followers to achieve the impossible; characterised by the MacVurich shenachie as 'active, intellectual and courageous', he overcame the rivalries of the clans by sheer force of personality. Colkitto was a proven warrior, a tower of strength who understood the warfare of the hills. In his one surviving letter to Argyll, Montrose enjoined him to submit to Charles, 'ready to embrace his penitent children . . . although provoked with unspeakable injuries'. The alternative was reduction by force. 'I rest your friend if you please . . .' Friendship was impossible. Argyll replied by mustering an army to pursue the elusive Graham.

At Tibbermore (1 September 1644) the cry of 'Jesus and no quar-ter' did not avail the Covenanting army. Montrose scored his first dazzling victory. Hard pressed by Argyll he then marched north where he sacked Aberdeen. Then began one of the wild marches for which Montrose is famous, a frantic manoeuvering for position on the draught-board of the Highlands, through Strathavon, Tomintoul, Rothiemurchus, Abernethy, Badenoch, Deeside and Strathbogie. At Fyvie he was almost caught napping, believing Argyll to be far to the south, but Montrose eluded his incompetent adversary.

Montrose's dilemma was that he could frolic in the Highlands till Judgement Day so far as the Lowlanders were concerned. Whenever he crossed the Highland line the clans deserted. With winter advancing Colkitto advocated a descent on the lion's den. Montrose tended to agree with the Campbells that it was 'a far cry to Loch Awe' and even farther in winter, but his doubts were overcome. His army marched along Loch Tayside through Crianlarich to Glen Orchy and the fabled Loch Awe. Argyll hastened to Inveraray, confident of picking off the starving and frozen royalists at leisure. Once home he learned the incredible. Montrose was advancing down Glen Shirra. Loch Fyne offered an escape route. He took it, leaving several hundred clansmen to die and the riches of Argyll to the marauders. This enterprise 'did shaike the grandour of Mac-Calein with such terrible and shivering fitts, as that great oake did bow lyke a reid before the wind'.

Argyll realised his stock was low and, supplied with reinforcements, he insisted on personally pursuing the invader as befitted the clan chief. Having retreated through Appin, Loch Levenside and Mamore to the Great Glen, Montrose looked to be trapped between Mackenzie of Seaforth ahead and Argyll behind. Ingenuity, fortitude and desperation took him up the Tarff and down Glen Roy in the harshest of winter conditions among the highest mountains in Britain. At Inverlochy on 2 February, he took an incredulous Argyll completely by surprise. He had been robbed of command by a fall from his horse and could only observe the onslaught from afar. The bitter lament of a Campbell widow condemned a chief who took to the loch and left his kindred to their fate. A jubilant Montrose informed Charles that he would soon 'have reduced this country to your Majesty's obedience and conquered from Dan to Bersheeba'.

Further honours were gained at Auldearn and Alford and in August 1645 he won another victory at Kilsyth, an anguished Argyll escaping by water for a third time. Intoxicated royalists like the poet Drummond of Hawthornden considered 'the Golden Age is returned . . . the many-headed monster near quelled'. To others the Graham's achievements were 'above what can be attributed to mankind'. Scotland appeared to belong to Montrose.

Yet the optimism was premature. At his triumphal entry to Glasgow his Highlanders were already melting away like the proverbial snow off a dyke. Colkitto departed to let more Campbell blood. He transformed his ancestral Kintyre into a smoking ruin and even after the Covenanting army had butchered his clansmen at Dunaverty in 1647 Argyll was still directing relief operations. Colkitto met a violent death in Ireland some months later. Montrose's military success owed much to Colkitto and the Highland terrain; he was ill-suited to Lowland warfare. In attempting to break through to England and the king he was surprised by David Leslie and his experienced cavalry. At Philiphaugh (13 September 1645) the Glorious Year ended in a bloodbath. Montrose would have chosen death on the battlefield but, persuaded to flee, he returned north to spend an abortive year attempting to reorganise resistance. Meanwhile Charles had surrendered to the Scottish army; he commanded Montrose to disband his troops. September 1646 found the marquis aboard a sloop bound for continental exile.

Although Argyll continued to correspond with Charles he no longer believed that any agreement was possible. He rejected the Engagement, an undertaking made by Hamilton to assist the king in return for a Presbyterian establishment, on the lines favoured by Montrose. On the defeat of the Engagers at Preston in 1648 he immediately contacted Oliver Cromwell, who visited Edinburgh. Cromwell was much impressed by Argyll's political dexterity in purging parliament of the Engager majority but in spite of their mutual respect the brief alliance was an unnatural one.

Against his better judgement Argyll was forced to rely increasingly on 'the airie opinion of the clergie'. On his later admission he was beginning to lose his grip: 'my thoughts became distracted and myself encountered so many difficulties in the way, that all remedies applied had the quite contrary operation'. The parliament of 1649 set about the creation of the new Zion during Scotland's brief and unhappy experiment in theocracy. Royalists were excluded from office; lay patronage was abolished; death was decreed for blasphemy, idolatry, parent cursing, incest and witchcraft; the codification of Scots law was discussed. But Argyll was disgusted by the outrageous demands of the ministers. He attempted to exploit widespread revulsion at the execution of Charles on 30 January 1649 by reaching some accommodation with his heir.

The exiled Montrose was the darling of Europe. If he fretted at the inactivity of the court in exile, the king's execution gave him a fatalistic firmness of purpose. For two days he retired from the world to emerge encased in black armour, determined to sing Charles' 'obsequies with trumpet sounds' and write his 'epitaph in blood and wounds'. Argyll's envoys arrived at the Hague to trade Charles II a throne for his signature of the covenants. Although Montrose still adhered to the 1638 covenant he realised Charles was no Covenanter and his innate honesty compelled him to advise against signing; he would attempt restoration by conquest. The young king, however, continued to negotiate with the Scots even as he sent Montrose to his death. A tragic charade was beginning: Montrose would die for a deceitful king; Argyll would welcome a covenanted king he knew to be insincere; Charles II would sign anything for a hollow title.

The marquis' last campaign was quickly over. Landing in Orkney he added some thousand Orcadians to half as many Danish and German mercenaries. They crossed the Pentland Firth to be cut to pieces by the army of the Estates at Carbisdale on the River Oykell on 25 April 1650. Montrose, again persuaded against a warrior's death, spent two days in the wilderness of Sutherland only to be captured by MacLeod of Assynt and surrendered to the victors.

Since he had already been condemned as a traitor in 1644, no trial was required after the long ride to Scotland's Jerusalem. He was met in the Canongate by the local justice officers and, bound to a seat in the hangman's cart, the procession trundled uphill to the Tolbooth. Argyll once observed that 'whatever honour we have at the crime, we immediately forget and pity the criminal when he comes to suffer'. So with James Graham. The Edinburgh mob, primed to stone the traitor, was reduced to tears at his passing. As the cart passed Moray House the eyes of Montrose and Argyll met briefly before the latter 'creipit in at the windows'. If Argyll read his own destiny in that gaze it is not recorded. At that very moment a

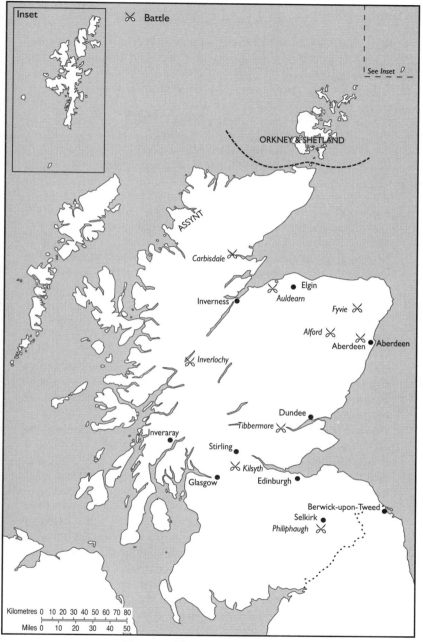

Figure 18 The Montrose campaigns

letter from Charles was en route to Edinburgh disowning Montrose. When his own time came he could expect cold comfort from the 'merrie monarch'.

In prison Montrose penned his farewell to the world:

> Let them bestow on ev'ry Airth a Limb;
> Open all my Veins, that I may swim
> To Thee my Saviour, in that Crimson Lake;
> Then place my pur-boiled Head upon a Stake;
> Scatter my Ashes, throw them in the Air:
> Lord (since Thou know'st where all these Atoms are)
> I'm hopeful, once Thou'lt recollect my Dust,
> And confident Thou'lt raise me with the Just.

On 21 May 1650 he walked down the High Street to the Mercat Cross and a thirty-foot gallows, dressed in all his finery 'more like a bridegroom than a criminal'. On the scaffold he made a short speech denying he had sinned against man and owning his king and his God. He paid the executioner, ascended the ladder, cried God's mercy 'on this afflicted land' and was pushed off. Argyll had been up all night while his wife gave birth to a daughter 'whois birthday', he wrote, 'is remarkable in the tragick end of James Grahame . . . He got sum resolution . . . how to go out of this world but nothing at all how to enter into ane other'. His sober report is remarkable not so much for its lack of charity as its total absence of vindictiveness towards a man who had consistently opposed him for the past ten years and who had totally destroyed his credit as a military leader. He was to learn that life can be more vexatious than death and in the following years he must sometimes have envied Montrose his fate.

Two months later Charles was in Scotland playing the role of the covenanted king in a bitter farce. His experiences in his ancestral kingdom fostered a lifelong detestation of the covenants, Presbyterianism and Scotsmen. He was not only lectured incessantly by worthy divines but was also forced to renounce his parents. King Campbell was dead but Argyll the king-maker effectively rendered Charles impotent. He gambled on the Scottish affection for monarchy and his own control of the king to counteract widening divisions in the Covenanting ranks. His plans were foiled when Cromwell defeated the Scots in 'the brunt or essential agony of the battle of Dunbar'. David Leslie had effectively out-generalled Cromwell who was retreating to England, but the ministers and the Estates attempted to transform Leslie's troops into a 'Gideon's Army' by purging undesirable elements. When the depleted Scots advanced down the rain-soaked slopes of the Lammermuirs near Dunbar on 3 September the strong right arm of the Lord was shattered and Scotland went to pieces. The Whigamores of the south-west attributed defeat to Charles' insincerity. Some joined 'God-intoxicated' Oliver who occupied the south of Scotland; others fought him. Within six months of Montrose's execution his supporters were the uneasy allies of MacCalein, grouped around the king. In a final throw of the die Argyll himself set the crown on the king's head. A marriage between Charles and a Campbell was briefly considered and rejected. Argyll now went down the wind. He dismissed Charles' proposed invasion of England as folly and retired to Inveraray. Defeat at Worcester proved him right and placed Scotland at Cromwell's feet.

Totally devoid of political strength his attempts to manoeuvre for position were universally condemned as 'juglings and dissembling devices'. The Cromwellians considered him to be 'the last person any way considerable that standeth out', but in August 1652, threatened with an invasion of Argyll, he undertook to live peaceably under the English government though he continued to pray for his 'distress'd prince'.

Montrose had jestingly warned that his ghost would haunt Scotland and Montrose Redivivus did stalk the Highlands. In 1653 the Earl of Glencairn led an abortive rising. Argyll's son, Lorne, supported the royalists. He was a complex man whose idea of fun was 'a hundred good stories over a four hour drink' and who, in true Campbell fashion, was constantly at loggerheads with his father. While their unhappy relationship was well publicised, the recalcitrant offspring was a useful device which almost saved Argyll at the Restoration. The Campbells simply resorted to the age-old ploy for the preservation of estates, placing father on one side, son on the other. Lorne's intercession for his father's life in 1661 was unsuccessful but the estates did remain intact.

The commander-in-chief of the English administration was George Monk, the first man to succeed in containing the Highlands, partly by the intelligent establishment of garrisons at Inverness, Inverlochy and Perth, partly through enlightened and conciliatory policies. He it was who in the end engineered the restoration of Charles II and who betrayed his sometime ally, Argyll. One of Argyll's last public acts was his opposition to the Act of Union of 1657, on the grounds that it neither safeguarded religion nor Scots law, nor was taxation proportional to that of England. The man who had once envisaged, 'all of one language, in one island, all under one king, one in religion, yea one in Covenant', demanded a union on equal terms or not at all.

In 1660 Argyll hastened south to greet Charles, was refused an audience and shipped back to Scotland to stand trial for treason. While he was imprisoned in Edinburgh castle the flag was flown at half mast, not on behalf of its illustrious captive, but to mark the burial with full honours of the reassembled remains of the Marquis of Montrose. He occupied his time compiling a little volume *Instructions to a son*, which shows he was in no doubt of the outcome of his trial. 'Infinitely unhappy are they who survive their credit and reputation', he wrote. 'There is no better defence against the injuries of fortune and vexation of life than death.' Much of the case centred on a topic dear to Argyll's heart – how answerable was a man for actions performed in his public capacity as a member of government? The able defence of George Mackenzie (the 'Bluidy Advocate' of Covenanting mythology) suggested minimal personal responsibility. To his intense relief and delight he was acquitted of any part in the execution of Charles I. The prosecution made little headway until Monk furnished the court with correspondence proving the defendant's complicity with the Cromwellians, which was, as Argyll said, 'the epidemical fault of the whole nation'. On the scaffold he counselled his audience to adhere to God and the covenants in the 'sinning and suffering time to come'. Then (27 May 1661) the guillotine known as the 'Maiden' devoured her victim. His head was placed on a spike on the Edinburgh Tolbooth, recently vacated by that of Montrose.

The beliefs of an age are often the key, as they are frequently a barrier, to the understanding of it. Both Montrose and Argyll died convinced of their own righteousness. If the former saw himself as an Old Testament general fighting for a Davidic king, Argyll could remark, 'We are not born for ourselves . . . Moses the man of God chose rather to suffer affliction with the people of God than to enjoy the pleasures of sin for a season.' They chose different roads to salvation albeit one such route was straighter than the other. In the final analysis both subscribed to the sentiment of Montrose's famous verse:

> He either fears his Fate too much,
> Or his Deserts are small,
> That puts it not unto the Touch,
> To win or lose it all.

If both lost in the short term, the verdict of history places both among the victors, in the annals of Scotland the nation.

CHAPTER 17

RESTORATION AND REVOLUTION

Rosalind Mitchison

T HE central fact of this period is that both restoration and revolution were made in England. They were not decisions made by
Scots nor were they made with a view to Scottish needs or wishes.
If they were acquiesced in by most of the 'political nation' in
Scotland this was because of a recognition of superior English
military and economic strength, and in each event a significant
section of Scottish society did not acquiesce. The opposition elements
thus gave rise to two movements, the Covenanters, predominantly
of the south-west, in the restoration period and the Jacobites,
predominantly of the north, after 1689. Both these movements
have received one-sided historiographical treatment: the earlier
movement has been regarded as religious and the later as political.
We will understand both better if we accept that the religious and
political impulses of the two were in related proportions. They
were both movements against the established political structure
and its ecclesiastical policy. In the Covenanting movement politics
seem to be the foundation impulse: the Covenanters would not
accept as godly any government not chosen by themselves, and were
prepared to wage war on the ungodly. In the Jacobite movement
the two motives were more evenly mixed. Jacobitism drew from
a confused mixture of loyalism, Catholicism, distaste for any but
episcopal government and hatred of the house of Argyll.

English dominance was, at least in 1660, masked by the fact that
England could not in practice run Scotland. With the disappearance
of the military dictatorship of the Protectorate went the capacity
to do so, in troops, in money and in the political stability necessary
for a sustained policy of interference. Scotland therefore had to
work out her solution within the framework of the general political

settlement. This structure imposed a certain element of political stability on the country, but left open a wide area for development. The response to this was, on the whole, remarkable in achievement; it was shown in politics, law, the arts and intellectual life, and even in the temporary middle way of a working relationship between episcopal and Presbyterian church government. In some aspects the current of activity was shared with England, and may even have been derived from there, but on the whole it is still true to look on Scottish culture in this period as self-sustained, when Scottish government was not.

The Restoration did not simply mean the return of Charles II, but also of his machinery of government: the privy council and parliament, the social sector that controlled these (the nobility), the courts and a church at least nominally episcopal. For none of these elements was restoration a simple return to the past. Once the restored parliament had got into its stride it passed the Act Rescissory, annulling all legislation since 1633, but in fact the clock could not be put back so simply. Crown, nobility and church had all changed during the interregnum. It took everyone some time to appreciate the depth of this change.

The prospect for Scottish development did not look particularly bright in the early 1660s. 'Restoration' always includes a *revanche* element, anxious to pay off old scores. As always after revolution and war there was little to pay them with. To the poverty of Scotland from economic backwardness had been added the poverty from over-taxation and English occupation and the further depression of economic life by a decade of government in English economic interests. If England after 1660 no longer directly regulated Scotland's trade, English jealousy and rivalry circumscribed it. There were direct English restrictions on the import of Scottish commodities, coal and salt, both valuable exports. More seriously there were indirect influences from the continuing rivalry between England and the Netherlands for trade supremacy and the wars into which this dragged the British crown.

The future looked bad also because of the hold of the Covenant (by which was now meant the Solemn League and Covenant) over people's minds. Fanaticism was not easily got out of the system in spite of the political failure and religious division that it had caused. 'Covenant theology' had originally evolved as a method of preaching morality within the framework of predestination, but with the national covenants this had given way to a concept of a binding legal settlement, dictating political and religious policy and impervious to political facts. The insistence of the 'remonstrant' minority that it was the true kirk had torn in two both church and state. The split had been perpetuated for government ends under the Protectorate and now gave rise to unrest in Lowland Scotland, particularly in Galloway and in Fife. The south-western section of this movement was the first significant political activity in Scotland which did not rely on leadership from the nobility, and its existence is a powerful reminder of the change produced in the position of the nobility by their enforced submission, first to the kirk and second to the English in the 1650s. The nobility could not be fully restored in authority, and in the government's brusque attempt to do what it could in the direction of such restoration lay the origin of the large body of unbeneficed Presbyterian clergy. The restoration of patronage, and the explicit acknowledgement of episcopacy that accompanied it, forced out over 250 ministers in 1662, and these formed a nucleus of propaganda and resistance throughout this period. The schism was kept alive by the strong professional identity of the clergy. Society did not yet accept the idea of religious or social dissent, so a movement of this kind could not hope to be passive. It was, in fact, a continual source of violence in a country which could not afford, and did not know how to administer, any system of regular policing.

So in the 1660s both poverty and division cast a gloom over the outlook. There were, however, some gains from the last thirty years which gave ground for optimism. To begin with there had been a distinct, if hesitant, step in the direction of the secularisation of politics and society everywhere outside the embattled areas of Covenanting strength. The king himself had cut down the share of ecclesiastics in government, and was determined that neither they nor religious motives should openly dictate policy. Episcopacy was restored because it was convenient as an instrument for governing the church and for controlling parliament and because it helped to keep the two kingdoms together, but it was not emphasised or given any sacramental function. Ministers ordained by presbyters were not required to seek reordination. Though the kirk still controlled a great part of life, religion and the rival claims of church and state to authority had a less total hold on people's minds. The awakening intellectual interests of the country are evidence of this.

Another sign of improvement is that from 1660 to 1690 the food supply and population of the country seem to have achieved a better balance than had been there before. Though the years 1659–60 appear to have been ones of food shortage and the harvest of 1674 fell badly short of need, the period as a whole was one of adequate supply. Whether this was the result of a larger area under cultivation and better transport, or whether it was also the result of a population reduced by emigration and death in earlier decades, we cannot say at present, and probably never shall be able to say. All we can say is that for most of this period most areas of the country produced enough food to feed their inhabitants, and at times there was even some for export.

A further advantage was that by the 1660s in much of Lowland Scotland schooling had come into existence. The Act of 1633 requiring parishes to provide a school and schoolmaster had been widely implemented. General education, demanded by the *First Book of Discipline*, had been made a nationally accepted aim, and was well on the way to be an established fact. The response made by the East Lothian parish of Yester to the rigours of invasion, battle, plunder and conquest in 1650–1 was a small-scale image of this. As soon as life had become sufficiently normal after the battle of Dunbar for the kirk session to meet again, it applied all available funds to the schooling of poor children. By 1660 the bulk of Lowland parishes had a school, and had had it long enough to have a good supply of literate adults, a fact which had considerable influence on the problem of government in both church and state. A literate public was familiar with the doctrine of Calvin and could be schooled by the catechism. It was familiar with biblical imagery and biblical passions. Sermons were expositions of doctrine to a populace well trained in argument. In some ways this made the country more governable. Arguments of law and logic could be understood and used. The kirk session provided a local court in which men of no great social standing could exercise responsibility in business and government. But literacy also laid the country open to the propaganda of militant dissent. Much of the rhetoric of this section has all the crudities and distortions of the self-educated orator. Intemperate literature, polemical sermons, the use of the Bible as a textual lottery, all brought irrational and unforeseeable risks of rebellion.

Education was an achievement of the kirk. It was the ministers who had pressed for it, and who persuaded the landowners to support it. Landowners and peasantry paid for the schooling of the children, but it was the kirk which controlled and inspected it. This victory was a sign of the long-established professionalism of the ministry, a body with its own discipline, way of life and sense of responsibility. The ministry had become a partly hereditary group. Sons of ministers went into the same profession: daughters married into it. It had spiritual as well as executive prestige. The profession had also personal links with the lesser landowning families, and the unified structure of Scottish education was beginning to bring forward a small peasant entry to the profession. The existence of this separate, self-conscious class of ministers was to provide one of the challenges of the period. How far was the restored government going to be able to incorporate them in its structure and hold their allegiance?

This professional class should be regarded as including all those in orders. The main mistake of the restoration was the decision to force out over a quarter of these men over the issue of patronage. There was no lack of alternative recruits: the kirk could still be supplied with qualified ministers. But these would work under difficulties while the 'outed' ministers, even if of moderate opinions, remained at hand, to act as a focus for opposition in the parishes. And it was characteristic of the time that very few 'outed' ministers were moderates. They were men who had come to office during the accomplishment of the revolution in the period of ecclesiastical domination, when pulpits were the mouthpieces of political programmes. They had shared the conviction that God had placed the guidance of Scotland in the hands of their order; through them he had intended great things for the world. The language of the Old Testament, in which so much religious and political argument had been conducted, was not such as to advance the ideas of moderation if they had been acceptable on other grounds. The 'outed' formed a nucleus of opposition, for most of the time with physical impunity, and in many cases they made a network of an illegal alternative church. This church could be conducted by secret meetings, but when it felt strong enough preferred 'field preaching', which meant massive meetings in the open, at which attenders, as was usual in the seventeenth century, were armed. These meetings were dangerous in themselves, and still more dangerous in their effect on those outwith their body. Extremist organisations possessed of uncompromising argument have often exercised an attraction over the public in general when that public has been prepared to admit part only of the claims of the arguments. We had numerous opportunities of appreciating this kind of influence in the twentieth century in which the base of the argument has been the overriding claims of nationalism rather than those of God. The pull of the Irish Republican Army on sentiment in Ireland and of illegal Zionist organisations in the 1930s and 1940s in Palestine are instances of the power of one over-simplified line of thought and propaganda on a public not prepared to disagree totally with the fundamental premise. In states lacking a well-organised system of legal opposition, all the grievances of sections of the community (and clumsy governments inevitably provide such grievances) add to the pull of sympathy for the outlawed organisation. Seventeenth-century Britain had yet to learn to accept the idea that there might be something wholesome in organised opposition. Neither the supporters nor the opponents of government yet allowed for the rights of the other. In Scottish politics (in particular) there was almost no mechanism in the 1660s for expression of patriotic dissent in politics. There was some mechanism in ecclesiastical matters because of the real attempt of this period to weld together the strengths of the Presbyterian system with the political convenience of episcopacy.

It would be over-complimentary to see the new structure of bishops in presbytery as an attempt to get the best of both systems of church government. It seems rather to have been an inevitable compromise. There were again bishops ruling a church in which the Presbyterian church courts were well established and with a large amount of Presbyterian opinion. Since the split between remonstrant and resolutioner clergy made it impossible to hold a general assembly that both would accept, the highest court of the

Presbyterian system had to be dispensed with. But for short periods the vigour of a Presbyterian system can spring from the parish and presbytery level, and these functioned as before. Only at the synodal level, not an important one in either Presbyterian theory or practice, was it necessary for the two systems of church order to interact. The church structure was thus not so much a compromise as a partition. Compromise, however, spread over the area least suitable for it, the actual conduct of church services, in which minor liturgical vestiges were submerged in apparently spontaneous exhortatory prayer and vast sermons. The contemporary habit of referring to church services as 'sermons' shows how small the element of worship had become. All this 'compromise' was simply hand-to-mouth expediency. It was certainly better than religious persecution, but it left frustrated those who wanted an orderly liturgy and seemly services as well as those who thought the existence of bishops and lay patronage sinful. It was based on the principle of letting sleeping dogs lie. But, as British governments discovered in the twentieth century, sleeping dogs have a way of waking up. Presbyterian sympathies survived, and, with constant agitation from outside the church and occasional misgovernment within it, lost nothing in strength, while episcopal sentiment had little to hold to except the support of government.

Probably more influential for good in this period than the uneasy church settlement was the fact that the nobility had been tamed. No longer would they be able to 'band' and put pressure on the government. Tolerance of private feuding and organised violence, at least in the Lowlands, was no longer necessary to government. Disputes had more and more to be settled by law, and this meant that the law had to develop, in content, in authority and in the professionalism of those who served it. Paradoxically not all the developments in the use of courts to settle disputes can be regarded as in the interests of stability and peace. In particular the way in which the Earl of Argyll used his own court to build up an empire in the west over lands peopled by other clans, by Macleans, Stewarts, Camerons and Macdonalds, left a problem in political resentment on which most of Highland Jacobitism in the eighteenth century was to be based. But in general the use of courts, particularly those of the crown, was an improvement on the use or threat of force. By removing the shadow of violence from overmighty neighbours it made possible the independence of lesser landowners, and so eventually, the unification of nobles and lairds in a landed interest and its contribution to the economic achievement and the culture, visual and verbal, of the eighteenth century.

Even in this period the signs of this development begin. The craggy, cramped tower-houses of the early seventeenth century are superseded by the classical adaptations of Sir William Bruce. Landed society, or at least a part of it, was prepared to appreciate good silver, elegant gardens, local history and science. It was beginning to turn to the idea of economic development, but there were sharp limitations in the concepts that it was as yet able to handle in this field. Wealth, it was dimly felt, might, and ought to, accrue mysteriously from some outside agency, from colonial trade or from a new industry brought in like an exotic plant from elsewhere. The need to integrate any new development to society and to the economy as a whole was not seen, nor was the basic need of improved management within the existing sectors. We have a picture of the limitations of the vision of the landed class in the *Glamis Book of Record*, where we see the young Earl of Kinghorn restore the houses and estate of the family from the effects of his father's political mistakes. It is all done by care and rearrangement. If debts cannot be paid off then at least they can be placed in the hands of friends. At no point does the idea of increasing revenue by better economic exploitation come into the earl's mind. The political and economic disasters of his father had taught him to cut his coat according to his cloth but not to question whether the size of cloth was immutably fixed.

Improvement, at least of agriculture, lay far in the future. Meanwhile there were tastes and interests to be encouraged that would not only be one of the main springs of improvement but would further limit the share of life engulfed by religion. There was a long overdue relaxation in the limits of markets and the control of trade by established burghs, marked in particular by the Act of 1672 which made a severe dent in burghal privilege. This was a response of government to the demands of new or expanding activities, and indicates that economic interests were increasingly being regarded as a proper sphere of politics. There were more things for men to think about than the relations of church and state, and the 1680s appear to have been a period of relative, if limited prosperity. The Scottish privy council made a real effort to establish minor industries. The aim was to manufacture in Scotland the consumer needs of the upper classes: glass, paper, good quality woollen cloth for instance. None of these were notable successes but recent research has shown that some industries survived more hardily than we used to think. Appropriately enough one of the more enduring of these, paper, owed its existence not only to the indirect influence of increasing law and order but to the direct needs of the instruments of this progress, the lawyers' production of *paperasserie*.

Still, the developments of this period were very limited. Their significance stands as aims, not as achievements. The country moved away from famine and disorder, and slightly away from poverty and fanaticism. Progress was limited by the inadequacy of the instruments of government as well as by rigidities of mind and the influence of polemic. For much of the time one has the impression of a country at war. Immediately after the Restoration there were still the effects of the heavy burden of taxation and occupation, and the need to pay for the demolition of the English fortresses. It soon became clear that the church settlement was to leave out a considerable minority who would attend conventicle but not church. These could not easily be persuaded or forced back into the fold, especially when there was a large body of clergy outside it. In some south-western presbyteries the entire body of ministers was 'outed'. Their charges were obviously unattractive since they subjected the occupiers to the risk of verbal and physical violence, so the occupiers, though of suitable ecclesiastical and political flavour, were not men likely to succeed in wooing back the recalcitrant. In the south-west the gulf in political and religious opinion between the nobility, often Catholic, and their tenantry meant that though nobles could oppress their tenants they could not lead them. In the mid-1660s came the Dutch War, with increased taxation, and the futile rebellion by conventiclers that led to the scrambling fight at Rullion Green. The government showed that it had weapons and techniques suitable to the task of holding down a hostile population: execution, imprisonment and occasionally torture, as well as fines and the quartering of troops. It was using them in a haphazard way, the result of amateurishness combined with a basic lack of conviction. At best such techniques can only limit a hostile body: they are unlikely to convert it.

Things improved after Rullion Green with the government of Lauderdale and his attempt to meet dissent halfway. Compromise with those 'outed' who would make any sort of terms was the order of the day. There was some success in this, but the hard core of Covenanting resistance was untouched, and the compromise itself involved asserting state powers over the church which caused much misgiving. The Act of Supremacy (1669), in which the assertion was made, was crudely worded, but indirectly it showed the big social change of the Restoration period, the shift in the balance of power, both in politics and in social structure, away from the clergy. Lauderdale's rule, which carried on through the 1670s, stood for compromise and lay culture as well as for personal profit. In fact one of its problems was the increased coherence of lay groupings. One of these was landed society, both nobility and gentry, which in these years developed the capacity to oppose the policy of the crown in parliament. Another was the lawyers, who were in fact a section of landed society. This is the period of the first organisation and lucid exposition of Scots law, culminating in 1681 with Stair's *Institutes*. The 1670s also saw the drawing together of the Faculty of Advocates into a professional group with their own loyalty and ethos. Pressures were building up for the adaptation of monarchical government to a system with a more active role for debate and opposition.

The 1680s would probably have been a difficult time for an old-fashioned type of government in Scotland, even if the Covenanting issue had been solved. But it was far from solution. The illegal conventicles became large-scale armed gatherings. Lauderdale's effective rule ended in 1679 with the murder by Covenanters of Archbishop Sharp, the main connecting link of government in church and state, and the disorderly rebellion in the west that was crushed at Bothwell Brig. Again English politics dominated Scottish, for the attempt at moderation and conciliation was abandoned in 1683 with the unravelling of the elaborate structure of plots against the king's person in both countries. The close connection between politics and religion in Scotland meant that investigation of treason was also repression of religious extremism. This repression bred still more intemperate resistance. Covenanting leaders declared war on those who accepted the existing government; the government responded by shooting out of hand those who would not renounce this policy. In fact neither side, in this so-called 'killing time', killed very many of its opponents, but it was a time of fear on all sides. Murders by Covenanters and executions by troops were both arbitrary uses of force and created general fear.

The noticeable feature of the 1680s is that both sides were gradually deserted by opinion. The overt display of state control over the church included a Test Act which could not be accepted by any who hoped for any change in the church, whether Presbyterian or episcopal in sentiment. The internal divisions of the Covenanters and their resort to brutality in 1679 also shook off supporters. In the 1680s it became impossible for sincere supporters of a Presbyterian order to approve of them. It would be unrealistic not to allow some element of success to the more active and intelligent repression carried out by Claverhouse in the south-west from 1682. By forcing apparent conformity at the risk of fines he moved the issue from martyrdom to inconvenience. But the main element in reducing support for the Covenanters came from the clear indications that their movement was more concerned with politics than with prayer. The famous series of documents voicing covenant policy, from the *Sanquhar Declaration* to the *Apologetical Declaration*, show this.

The most interesting and revealing of these documents is the *Queensferry Paper*. It is a medley of Whiggery in Scottish terms, that is the claim of the saints to choose a godly ruler, and in English terms, where the talk is of civil rights and of the end of government as the maintenance of all men in their rights and liberties. The ideas soon to be developed and published by Locke go hand in hand with the law given by God to Israel. The foreign elements of Whiggery are soon abandoned, but even so the argument moves inexorably from religion to politics. The Covenanters are committed to overthrowing the 'kingdom of darkness' in favour of the 'kingdom of Christ', and it is clear that these kingdoms are conceived as in this world. So the existing monarchy, all monarchy, is denounced. The Covenanters, as the true kirk, now set up their laws and government for Scotland.

This can be seen as the last manifestation of the movement for a second reformation in the 1630s and 1640s. Its conservatism can be seen in the statement that the Covenanters cannot be accused of separation 'for if there be a Separation, it must be where the Change is, and that is not in us'. But the policies of the 'good old days', to which it looked back, had already led to disaster and conquest. Among those who had had sympathy for the Covenanting ideal the *Queensferry Paper* may have brought home the realisation that this ideal would involve a return to chaos in both church and state. For the threat to church order was as direct as that to the state. The paper denounced as 'carnal' any form of majority rule by the Presbyterian system. Those who believed in the divine right of presbytery could no longer support the Covenanters.

At the same time the succession of James VII in 1685 put a strain on those who saw the monarchy as a support of the episcopal church. James was an open Catholic, whose policy of leniency to his own church was accompanied by leniency also to those outside the episcopal church. This left the established church without its main support, the government and law. The pressure the king brought to bear on all aspects of government in support of this policy was a reminder that the crown had still a repertoire of weapons inherited from days when unlaw and disorder had had to be countered by drastic action if they were to be countered at all. The use of such weapons in an era of relative stability brought into Scottish politics the idea of imposing limitations on the powers of government. Scottish opposition was coming to assume some of the ideas of English Whiggery, and in so doing was to bring the two countries closer together.

So the 1680s see the country turning to more secular politics, and beginning to think that political problems must be answered in terms of law, powers and administration, rather than in those of covenants with God. The movement in this direction was half-hearted. The episcopal church was not prepared to repudiate the king, even though he was a Catholic, and the episcopal church had the willing or grudging support of many, probably of the greater part of the country. The unease that the trend to secular politics produced may be the reason why the only overt sign against James' government, the Argyll rebellion, gained no support. The Scots were prepared to put up with James. But they were also prepared to accept the ready-made revolution against him from England. They would do more than just accept, and would use the occasion to put through parliament a verbose but important attack on the weapons of the crown, the *Claim of Right* (1689). They went on to establish openly the reality of parliamentary opposition that had been growing as a practice since Lauderdale's day and to make it effective by destroying the old Committee of the Articles, the crown's mechanism for control of parliament. The revolutionary settlement was to be ruthlessly Presbyterian, against the new King William's wishes, with over two-thirds of the existing clergy 'outed' in their turn. Since the only clergy uncontaminated by submission to bishops was the remnant of those thrown out in 1662 it was logical that this self-appointed true kirk should insist on the rectification of the point on which they had been forced out and have lay patronage abolished. As, in fact, the ecclesiastical part of the new settlement was far more intolerant than the secular, it is not surprising to find that the opposition to the whole settlement, Jacobitism, was founded at least as much in religion as in politics. Secularisation was still incomplete, but it had come some way.

The revolution also signifies the acceptance of a change in the topic of government. The economic prosperity of the country had become a preoccupation of government, and private economic advantage had become normal and accepted aims for the upper class. The rising professional group of lawyers, laymen, would soon rival in influence the established group of the clergy. The country stood on the brink of a period of active experiment in lay government by privy council and parliament in uneasy harness together. The state had attempted even to set bounds to the actions of the clergy. In particular it attempted to moderate the vengeful policy of the Presbyterian ministers. It was unsuccessful in this. The clergy were not prepared to observe the bounds set by the state. Wisely the government turned a blind eye to this resistance, and continued to assert that it was the effective ruler. In the long run it would be.

Though the Scottish revolution followed the English it did not do so peacefully, and the actual fighting of the revolution epitomised the changed nature of Scottish politics. In the summer of 1689 took place the Battle of Killiecrankie and the siege of Dunkeld. The

Highland clans that fought for James VII against his nephew William did so for secular reasons, from resentment at the Campbell domination that the revolution settlement would make permanent. On hearing the news of the Jacobite victory at Killiecrankie the privy council prepared to retreat to England. It recognised that England now set the stage of Scotland's politics by being ready to attempt reconquest of Scotland with English aid from beyond the border. It was saved from this step by the defence of Dunkeld. Dunkeld, and therefore Scotland, was held for the revolution by a 'regiment' of Covenanters, later to be known as the Cameronians. This 'regiment' was in origin a band of men engaged in 'rabbling' the episcopal clergy, forcing them from their parishes after the revolution by threat of force. The apotheosis of this band into a regiment looked for a time like official reliance on fanaticism, but in a short while it became apparent that the 'regimental' aura had superseded the religious. Its habit of praying with sentries posted was a reminder that it was formed to enlist religion in the defence of the state. Behind this shield of force the politicians of Scotland were to carry on the process of secularisation and learn the arts of political adjustment and the acceptance of reality in the 1690s, until English dominance, already the key to the new political system, became so overt that it had to be openly faced in the issue of Union.

CHAPTER 18

UNION OF THE
PARLIAMENTS

T. C. Smout

SCOTLAND in the period from 1690 to 1707 was a land of troubles that ran wide and deep beyond the games of politicians and the posturings of kirkmen. In many ways the ordinary person in the street and the fields had other things to think about than saving the shreds of national parliamentary independence.

In the first place the 1690s was a decade of agricultural depression and famine: it began with low grain prices, but the years 1695, 1696, 1698 and 1699 were all associated with extremely high prices and widespread crop failure, exacerbated at the end by a severe winter and cattle murrain. By 1700 it was all over. Farmers then began to renew their complaints of gluts of food on the market and low prices because no one would take it. This oscillation between extreme scarcity and high price in bad years and superfluity and very low price in good years provided the worst possible kind of economic environment for agricultural change. English visitors who came to Scotland from their own more advanced farming scenes were depressed by the wild landscapes devoid of enclosure, the weedy crops and thin animals, but what was the point of change if in one year you could not raise anything to sell and in another year scarcely sell anything you raised? The first tracts on improving husbandry were written in this period before the Union, but there were few able to profit from reading them.

We shall never know how many Scots died of hunger and associated diseases – especially 'famine-fever', typhus, which everywhere stalked in the tracks of dearth. Many stories were handed on for generations afterwards: about men dropping dead with grass or raw flesh in their mouths; about sons vainly trying to carry their father's corpse to be buried and falling from hunger by the way;

about respectable tenants forced to beg bread for their children from pitiless neighbours who themselves succumbed later to the wrath of God. In some of the villages of the north-east graves are said to have been made just above high-water for those who died of hunger after trying to stay alive on the shellfish beds: certainly in Dalkeith the kirk session ordered a lime pit to be dug for the bodies of those vagrants from the Borders who were trying to reach Edinburgh on the chance of finding food and who perished within sight of their destination. Edinburgh herself, with rare generosity, opened a kind of refugee camp in the Greyfriars kirkyard and distributed poor relief to the hungry irrespective of their parishes of origin. It was more usual to do as Stirling did, to list the town's own poor and relieve their need while refusing succour to the incoming stranger. There seems little doubt that the towns experienced much less hardship and disruption from the famine than the countryside, possible because they had efficient markets and the ability to import corn: the parish registers of Dumfries, for instance, show scarcely a quiver of exceptional mortality through the later 1690s, but places like Spott in East Lothian and Kingsbarns in Fife, small rural parishes in very fertile counties, evidently suffered badly.

We tend to be very shocked by it all, in retrospect: contemporaries were not unmoved, but they did not see it in quite our light. There had been famines before, perhaps worse than this, certainly in the first half of the century and in the late sixteenth century. They were tragic, but they were the will of God, visitations on a sinful people – you could regard them as punishment for not having instituted a properly covenanted church and king, as the Cameronian dissenters in the south-west did; or you could regard them as just deserts for the national pastimes of levity, fornication and Sabbath-breaking, as the Church of Scotland did; or you could regard them as 'King William's Ill Years', retribution for expelling the anointed James VII, as the Jacobites did. And although the period 1695–1700 did cause a severe jolt to the rural economy, it could in no way be said to have ruined it: by the early 1700s the position was back to normal, vacant holdings being absorbed again into cultivation and the old inefficient ways of husbandry being resumed because there seemed to be no alternative. People had managed before to get over such times: no doubt they would have to manage again. Everyone who lived off the land was poor – landlord, tenant, cottar, crofter – in comparison to their English equivalents, but they had no reason to expect to become any poorer.

In the towns, however, the period 1690–1707 saw in some respects a deepening economic crisis. Partly this was the effect of war against France, which was waged at King William's behest from 1688 to 1697, and began again in 1701 to last until after the Union. War brought French privateers into the Firth of Forth and the Firth of Clyde; the Jacobites who had captured the Bass in 1692 made it a base for their activities and almost severed the supply line of the corn trade from the north-east coast to Leith. Scotland had no navy and could do little to defend herself until she commissioned a couple of frigates at the very end of the period: the Royal Navy under English command did little except use war as a pretext for stopping Scottish ships in the Clyde from sailing to the English colonies in America in contravention of the Navigation Acts. All this was ruinous to merchants: the Convention of Royal Burghs spoke of the 'great and unsupportable loss' and said that if privateers were not controlled 'the tread of the royall borrowes will be entirily destroyed and all merchants discouraged'. It was special pleading, but at times such a verdict did not look far wrong.

Furthermore a war against France was a war with Scotland's best trading partner (apart probably from England herself), and it entailed the loss of the valuable import trade in wine, brandy and salt on which there were high profit margins to be earned; it also cut off the chance of exporting herring, salmon, coal, wool and cloth, which in earlier years had earned substantial sums by sales in France. Nor, unhappily, was there much chance of compensating for such losses by expanding trade to other markets. England took Scottish cattle and linen and some coal and corn, but placed tariffs and marketing restrictions upon them which seemed to restrict the possibilities of growth. Holland was beginning to reduce her intake of Scottish woollen cloth and coals, apparently because they could not compete for cost and quality on the Dutch market with alternative supplies; the same was true of salt and cloth (though not of fish or wool) in the Baltic. Altogether there were most ominous signs of the contraction of external markets to the Scottish merchant, and it was clear that even the return of peace would not put everything automatically right in the cities, but what could restore prosperity was not at once easy to see.

Town and country alike were, in these years, affected by the restoration of the church to a Presbyterian polity. Admittedly there was no question of a return to the extreme forms of general assembly control which had characterised the heady days of the 1640s, and in wide areas north of the Tay it proved impossible even to remove episcopalian ministers from their manses and their kirks before the Union. But the restored assembly showed much enthusiasm for puritan forms of control, being no whit less anxious than the church under the bishops to punish fornication by the kirk stool, even more sabbatarian, and earnest in calling for fasts of repentance to avert the wrath of God. The kirk instituted an examination of the schools and universities to make them more Godly and more efficient. One effect of the new regime was the withdrawal of favour from those who had done much to illuminate the reign of Charles II and James VII – Sir Robert Sibbald the naturalist and topographer, Archibald Pitcairne the physician and Sir William Bruce the architect – though all continued to work during the 1690s, and perhaps Bruce's finest mansion– the core of the present Hopetoun House – was built between 1699 and 1702. The saddest symbol of the intellectual climate of these years was a Unitarian student at Edinburgh, Thomas Aikenhead, executed for the blasphemy of denying the divinity of Christ on the testimony of one witness, and with the collusion and approval of the Edinburgh ministers. He has surely an even better claim to be regarded as a religious martyr than the rebellious and fire-eating Convenanters who had perished at the scaffold in the Grassmarket under the previous rulers. Scotland did not in the late seventeenth century welcome free discussion. We do well to recognise the deeply authoritarian and closed traditions of her society; we are certainly not dealing with a democracy which believed in maximising the opportunities for freedom and individual choice.

After the revolution of 1690 the country was ruled under its new constitution with a certain increase in ostensible independence. The head of the state was King William: no one of course tampered with the Union of the Crowns. His representative in Scotland was the Commissioner, personally appointed, and assisted by a nominated privy council, but the Lords of the Articles, the old steering committee of parliament, had gone, and parliament now could claim a degree of independence from the crown which none of its predecessors had enjoyed. There is not very much sign that around 1690 it felt much need to cherish this independence. There was a great deal of talk at the time of the revolution of merging with the parliament of England in a union of the type that came later; the king wanted it, the representatives to the Scottish convention wanted it (according to one account they were unanimous in their wish); even Andrew Fletcher of Saltoun, later to be the leading opponent of such a settlement, said, 'we can never come to any true settlement but by uniting with England in Parliaments and Trade'. The main reason why it did not come about then was that the English did not want it at all. What had they to gain by sharing power with the rascally Scot? Yet the Scottish representatives were never again so anxious for union, or so uncritical of the distant monarch from whom the power flowed.

Two incidents in the 1690s in particular shook confidence in the king – Glencoe and Darien. The Massacre of Glencoe in 1692 was a nasty outgrowth of the problem of pacifying the Highlands which had bedevilled the government since the rising under Dundee in 1689. The Master of Stair, who held state office as secretary, determined to make an example of those who were still in rebellion against the crown. MacIan, the head of the Macdonalds of Glencoe, made his submission to the government, but it was rejected on a technicality, and King William signed and countersigned orders 'to extirpate' the clan. They were in fact put to the sword by the treacherous attack of a detachment of soldiers whom the Macdonalds had been entertaining peacefully in the glen for a fortnight; and although many escaped the chief himself and some thirty-seven of his men perished. The incident had nothing to do with the ancient Campbell–Macdonald feud, even though the soldiers happened to belong to Argyll's regiment. Indeed, had it been merely an incident between 'barbarous' clans no one would have minded very much; the scandal was that the secretary and the crown should have been in collusion to attack a peaceful and unarmed band of men who believed themselves to have received the royal pardon. The reputation of William never recovered from this blow.

The second incident, the events that led to the failure of the Scottish colony at Darien, were more complicated and prolonged. The idea of creating a national plantation and a monopoly company to run it must be seen in the contexts, on the one hand, of envy of the imperial power of England, Holland and France and, on the other, of the depression in Scotland's traditional foreign markets in Europe. The idea can be traced back to a discussion in privy council as early as 1681. In 1693 forty-eight merchants and others of commercial experience and standing signed a bond calling attention to the 'great advantages that may redound to this nation by promoting a trade to the coast of Africa, America and other foreign parts', and in 1695 the king agreed to an Act which the Scottish parliament had promoted setting up a Company of Scotland with a monopoly of trade to distant continents and with the right to make colonies and raise capital.

The moving spirits at this stage were almost certainly a group of London Scots who hoped, with English merchants' backing, to burst open the monopoly of the English East India Company, currently under pressure in the capital itself; maybe they hoped under the Scottish flag to move into Far East trade and to supply England as semi-legalised interlopers, much as the Ostend and Scandinavian East India Companies did in the eighteenth century. Certainly they hoped to raise half the capital in the south. Unfortunately they hopelessly miscalculated the power of the established East India interest in the Westminster parliament: news of the moves in Scotland led eventually to the proscription of the Company of Scotland in England – its directors were threatened with impeachment and the attempt to get subscriptions was declared illegal. Nor was this all: English consuls abroad, especially at Hamburg, were successfully able to dissuade foreigners from investing, and the king unequivocally came down on the side of London, dismissing Lord Tweeddale as his Commissioner for his inability to keep the Edinburgh parliament under control. Not for half a century had there been such a division of interest and bitter conflict between the two kingdoms in the union, and it was self-evident in Scotland that the monarch had no real interest in the north except to keep it as the leashed running-dog of the wealthier southern kingdom, on which his power as a monarch able to rule in state and to wage war on France ultimately rested.

Nevertheless the Scots pressed on with their scheme for a Company, raising what money they could within Scotland by popular subscription, and considering schemes on which they could base its trade. It was here that they made their fatal error. Persuaded by the visionary dreams of William Paterson, a London Scot of undeniable imagination and personal magnetism, deluded also by Lionel Wafer, a pirate surgeon who claimed to corroborate by his practical experience of the area the hopes of Paterson, the directors opted for settling at Darien on the Isthmus of Panama from whence they hoped to establish a great trading emporium with an opening to the Caribbean on one side and ultimately to the Pacific on the other. Two expeditions were sent out, the first in 1698, the second in 1699: the resources behind them were inadequate, the provisioning of the ships was bad, the standard of command at sea and on land deplorable (with a few exceptions). The colony was overwhelmed in the end by incompetence, disease and Spanish hostility. Everything was exacerbated by William's orders that no English colony was to give succour to the Scots, understandable enough since they were trying to settle in territory over which the Spanish claimed sovereignty at a time when William was trying to keep Spain out of a military alliance against France. Failure was inevitable from the moment the Scots, lacking resources, set their hearts on the swamps of the Isthmus of Panama, but the king's hostility gave them an opportunity to blame outside causes. At least one of the later efforts of the Company of Scotland to redeem its fortune by individual voyages to Africa and the Far East was successful, but not on the scale necessary to salvage its losses.

When the ultimate failure of the Darien scheme became known in Scotland in 1700 the mood of the country turned extremely bitter, very Anglophobic and very much against the king; there was talk of calling a Convention of Estates at Perth to defy the government, recalling the atmosphere of 1641. Nevertheless the Union of Crowns survived because the Scots were divided so deeply between the Jacobites and the rest, between Presbyterian and episcopalian, between one political faction of grandees in parliament and another. Obviously, though, no one at this moment in Scotland was going to express a preference for a closer union with England, even as an economic panacea. There was no sense at all in which, as is sometimes suggested, the Scots 'had' to go into a fuller union because after the failure at Darien they 'had' to have access to imperial markets. On the contrary they were preparing to settle down in 1701 and 1702 to what one contemporary observer called a 'kind of glade poverty'. Darien led not to union, but to national disillusion and stalemate.

It was the death of William III and the accession of Queen Anne without heirs in 1702 which created the opportunity for a new political initiative: for the Union of Crowns to continue it would be necessary for both parliaments to agree on one person to whom the crown should pass after the death of Anne. In its prevailing mood it was unlikely any recently elected Scottish parliament would knuckle under and meekly follow an English lead; the queen, impressed by her predecessor's advice in his latter days to solve the Scottish problem by amalgamating the two parliaments, appointed Scottish and English commissioners to negotiate to this end – after desultory conversations, in which the English showed less interest even than the Scots, these were broken off. The queen then had no alternative but to call for new elections in Scotland and to meet the problem head on. The New Parliament, to be the last to meet in Edinburgh up to the present time, assembled in May 1703; the queen appointed the Duke of Queensberry as her commissioner and hoped for the best.

The consequences for the crown were a complete disaster. It was not perhaps the case that the members of the New Parliament were soaked in 'nationalist fervour in revolt against English domination and selfishness', but they were certainly much less under the control of the commissioner and the Westminster government than the last parliaments of William III had been; the latter had given the crown trouble, but in the end they knew which side their bread was buttered and for reasons of self-interest did not press their opposition too far. The New Parliament was divided into three main factions – a 'Court' party, normally obedient to the commissioner, with about 100 adherents; a Jacobite or 'Cavalier' party of about seventy; and a 'nationalist' group, the 'Country' party, of about sixty. In addition there were about a score of members who were known as the 'Revolution men', supporting the principles of the 1690 settlement in favour of a Hanoverian successor and broadly supporting the 'Court' party but not of it. The composition of the government tried to integrate as many of these factions as possible, and it had Cavaliers among the officers of state to the chagrin of the 'Revolution men', but nothing could disguise the fact that the Court party had no automatic majority and that there was therefore always the possibility of toppling Queensberry or of altering the coalition by embarrassing him. This has to be borne in mind to understand what followed.

The parliament in the course of 1703 presented for the royal assent two bills which greatly alarmed the queen and England. One became in 1704 the Act of Security and Succession, which declared that Scotland would not follow England into the Hanoverian succession except on conditions securing the crown, parliaments, religion, liberty and trade 'from English or any foreign influence'. The other became the Act anent Peace and War, which reserved to the Scottish parliament the right to make treaties, alliances, peace and war; hitherto Scottish foreign policy had been the monopoly of the crown, and therefore by the early eighteenth century practically the monopoly of the English cabinet. The motives for the passage of these bills were complicated: some hoped by doing so to defeat Queensberry or exclude a rival faction from office; some were swayed by the oratory of Andrew Fletcher of Saltoun, the most persuasive nationalist in the Country party, who was seeking to limit the power of the crown and the English government and to enlarge thereby the power of the Scottish parliament. There is not much evidence, however, of a concerted plan to abandon the Union of Crowns – rather of an atmosphere of dissatisfaction about how the existing constitution was working and a wish to embarrass an unpopular and vulnerable Commissioner.

The English government, however, was in no mood to examine the subtleties of northern party politics. It was at this point in 1704 that England became convinced the Scots were out to challenge royal authority, and that English safety was threatened by the danger in Scottish secession. A runaway Scotland, they thought, would quickly turn Jacobite and make common cause with France; things would return to the old menacing situation of the late Middle Ages when England could never venture an army abroad without a risk of attack from over the Tweed. Consequently they bent all their energies to the task of bringing Scotland into an Incorporating

Union. The very arrangement which they had so contemptuously avoided considering on many previous occasions, and as recently as 1690 and 1702, became now their first priority.

In pursuit of their aim the English used four weapons: veiled military threats, economic sanctions, bribery and negotiation. The sanctions were largely embodied in the Alien Act of March 1705 which stated that unless Scotland either appointed new commissioners for a union of parliaments, or adopted the Hanoverian succession by Christmas, Scottish estates in England would be confiscated and (more seriously) Scottish exports of linen, cattle and coal to England would be prohibited. Imports of wool from England, already illegal in theory, would now be effectively stopped. It cut right at the heart of Scottish trade, for with Scotland's flagging fortunes in European commerce her exports of cattle and linen to England and her export of raw wool (much of it originating in England) to the continent constituted the greater part of her ability to earn foreign exchange. The Act was later rescinded, but the other threats remained, and pretexts were evidently found for preventing the movement of Scottish cattle over the border until after the Union.

Bribery was an alternative means of bringing pressure to bear; its nature, extent and effectiveness are matters widely disputed among historians. As it was done secretly it is naturally hard to substantiate in detail, but it can be shown that the Duke of Argyll (who became commissioner in 1705 in succession to the Marquis of Tweeddale, who had in turn succeeded the Duke of Queensberry when he fell in 1704) was bribed by the promise of military promotion, an English peerage for himself and a Scottish peerage for his brother before he would come down on the side of Incorporating Union. Similarly the Treasurer-Depute, the Earl of Glasgow, appears to have had £20,000 to dispose of from English funds for crossing the palms of the queen's friends in Scotland: if some of it went to paying arrears of salaries it was made fairly plain the recipients would go hungry unless they toed the line.

Had threats and bribery alone been sufficient, however, it would hardly have been necessary for the English to enter into such detailed negotiations as they did, still less for England to make a series of concessions which made the Union eventually much less of an incorporating job than it is usually assumed to be. The course of events in Scotland from 1704 until May 1707 was as follows. Tweeddale succeeded Queensberry in May 1704 when the latter at last proved unable to hold his motley majority together, but Tweeddale, who emerged with some thirty supporters from the Country Party to form the New Party or *Squadron Volante*, was dedicated to a reform of the existing Union in the direction of federalism rather than incorporation, and was really crushed by the Alien Act as he could not follow the wish of the queen to press for incorporation. He also proved too weak even to save from summary execution the crew of an English East Indiaman, the *Worcester*, under Captain Green, who were arrested in Scotland on a fabricated charge of piracy against one of the Company of Scotland's ships. The execution of these miserable scapegoats at the instance of a Scottish lynch mob on the sands of Leith in April 1705 marked the peak of anti-English feeling in the wake of the Alien Act, whose threats had not impressed the population at large whatever they might have done to politicians thinking quietly at home. Tweeddale fell and was replaced by Argyll, who led the government until June and then handed office again to Queensberry. The complex manoeuvrings of the next few months left few parliamentary reputations for honesty and consistency intact; the Duke of Hamilton, leader of the Country Party but a man with extensive estates in England, shocked his followers by proposing on 1 September that nominations for appointing commissioners for union should be left to the queen. This had the effect of allowing the government to set up a body in which all favoured incorporation except one, the Jacobite Lockart of Carnwarth. They began to deliberate with their English counterparts in April 1706; on the 4 November, the first article of Union was put to the Scottish parliament and accepted by 115 votes to 83. The whole treaty was ratified on 16 January 1707 by 110 votes to 67; it came into force on 1 May 1707 and the parliamentary independence of Scotland came to an end.

The terms of the Union, however, show how far it was necessary for England to make concessions to the Scots which in the long run proved a bone in the throat of real incorporation. There was to be free trade and the open admission of the Scots to the English market and to English colonial privileges, which, it was argued by both English and Scottish propagandists, was a great advantage but not really accepted as enough by the royal burghs who represented the major part of the formal 'trading interest' and most consistently of all opposed union, but they were bought off by a promise of an Equivalent Fund to boost Scottish development and an undertaking that their particular privileges would stay intact even after the treaty. The church was exempted by special legislation from any threat of amalgamation with the Church of England. The existing law of Scotland was similarly defended, which kept the professions of the lawyers intact. As for the landed classes, the continuation of particular economic privileges granted before the Union was one sop, the granting of forty-five seats in the English Commons and sixteen seats in the English Lords was another. They also had every expectation that the Scottish privy council would be kept in being after the Union as a theatre for their talents and ambitions, but it was in fact abolished within a year.

The Scottish establishment, therefore, by no means came badly out of the Union. In voting for it they were aware that all bourgeois career patterns were effectively protected from English encroachment, that the gentry and nobility had a political sphere reserved for them, and that economic arguments (which were often stressed in the course of the final debates) favoured entry. They must also have been aware that the alternatives included the danger of English attack and conquest if independence was declared, of civil war between Jacobites and others in the case of a disputed succession, and of the very illusory, shadowy nature of the parliamentary liberty they were called upon to surrender. Even the New Party came round in the course of 1705 and 1706 to supporting Incorporating Union; maybe it was, as one historian has said, 'duped by a promise of handling that part of the Equivalent which related to the losses of the Company of Scotland and also undue representation in the sixteen peers', but one of its members explained in a private letter why men of his sympathies would in the end vote for parliamentary union – 'Trade with most, Hanover with some, ease and security with others, together with a general aversion to civil discords, intolerable poverty and . . . constant oppressions.' It seems a catalogue of good reasons and, from their point of view, a fair summary of the national interest.

Who was not asked? The common people of Scotland were neither represented in the Scottish parliament nor listened to by it, though anti-union petitions and the mobbing and rioting against the pro-union members which went on before the final voting greatly alarmed the government and encouraged its opponents. Sir John Clerk of Penicuik was to write later that 'the articles were confirmed in the Parliament of Scotland contrary to the inclinations of at least three-fourths of the Kingdom'; the Jacobites set about making immediate preparations for a rising. When the Union was passed, however, people took it with the greatest calmness. A Jacobite plot of 1708 never got off the ground; the rebellion of 1715 had no popular support in the Lowlands, and very little else suggested passions on the subject.

In the end one is forced to the conclusion that the Union of Parliaments did not at the time seem of overriding importance to very many Scots. Real independence in the sense of control over foreign policy had gone in 1603. For many years the gentlemen in Parliament House in Edinburgh had seemed to be little better than puppets dancing to the tune of the London government, and nothing since 1703 had encouraged people to regard them very differently. The church mattered more than parliament to most people, and that was to go on; so were the law, the colleges, the schools and the town councils. Economic control of most things still rested in the north. There were estates to manage, farms to farm, goods to sell and ships to sail; London was a long way off and the role of government interference in everyday life was extremely small by modern standards. Most Scots would, quite rightly, have laughed at the idea that the Scottish nation came to an end in 1707. There was more to life and nationality than an assembly of members of parliament, and it was another century at least, perhaps two, before the erosion of what was distinctively Scottish about the Scots reached such a level as to justify serious doubts about national survival: it was the end of an auld sang, perhaps, but it was not yet the end of an auld people.

FURTHER READING

General

Dickinson, W. Croft. *New history of Scotland* vol. I. *Scotland from earliest times to 1603*. Nelson, 1961.

Grant, I. F. *The social and economic development of Scotland before 1603*. Oliver & Boyd, 1930.

Mackenzie, W. C. *The Highlands and Isles of Scotland*. Moray Press, 1937.

McQueen, J. and Scott, T. (eds) *The Oxford Book of Scottish Verse*. Oxford University Press, 1966.

Mitchison, R. *A history of Scotland*. Methuen, 1970.

Rait, R. S. *The parliaments of Scotland*. Maclehose & Johnstone, 1924.

Smout, T. C. *A history of the Scottish people 1560–1830*. Collins, 1969.

Wittig, K. *The Scottish tradition in literature*. Oliver & Boyd, 1958.

Recent publications

Houston, R. A. and Knox, W. W. J. (eds) *The New Penguin History of Scotland from the Earliest Times to the Present Day*. Penguin, 2001.

Lynch, M. (ed.) *The Oxford Companion to Scottish History*. Oxford University Press, 2001.

Lynch, M. *Scotland, a New History*, 2nd edn. Century, 1992.

Menzies, G. (ed.) *In Search of Scotland*. Polygon, 2001.

Whyte, I. D. *Scotland before the Industrial Revolution: an Economic and Social History c. 1050–c. 1750*. Longman, 1995.

Various authors, *The New History of Scotland*. First published Edward Arnold, 1980s; reissued Edinburgh University Press, 1990s.

Various authors, *Historic Scotland series*. Batsford, 1990s.

Chapter 1

Burn, A. R. *Agricola and Roman Britain*. English Universities Press, 1953.

Macdonald, Sir G. *The Roman wall in Scotland*, 2nd edn. Oxford University Press, 1934.

Richmond, Sir I. *Roman and native in North Britain*. Nelson, 1958.

Robertson, A. S. *The Antonine wall*. Glasgow Archaeological Society, 1970. (Rev. edn. T. & A. Constable, 1968.)

Tacitus. *The Agricola and the Germania*. Trans. H. Mattingley and S. A. Handford. Penguin, 1970.

Recent publications

Breeze, D. J. *Roman Scotland: frontier country*. Batsford, 2000.
Hanson, W. and Maxwell, G. S. *Agricola and the conquest of the north*. Batsford, 1991.
Keppie, L. *Scotland's Roman remains*. John Donald, 1998.
Maxwell, G. S. *The Romans in Scotland*. Mercat Press, 1989.

Chapters 2, 3, 4 and 5

Adomnan. *Life of Columba*. A. O. and M. O. Anderson (eds). Nelson, 1961.
Anderson, A. O. (ed.) *Early sources of Scottish history*, vol. I. Oliver & Boyd, 1922.
Aneirin. *The Gododdin: the oldest Scottish poem*. K. H. Jackson (ed.). Edinburgh University Press, 1969.
Bede. *Ecclesiastical history of the English people*. B. Colgrave and R. A. B. Mynors (eds). Oxford University Press, 1970.
Chadwick, H. M. *Early Scotland*. Cambridge University Press, 1949.
Cruden, S. H. *The early Christian and Pictish monuments of Scotland*, 2nd edn. HMSO, 1964.
Dillon, M. and Chadwick, N. K. *The Celtic realms*. Weidenfeld & Nicolson, 1967.
Hanson, R. P. C. and Barley, M. W. *Christianity in Britain, 300–700*. Leicester University Press, 1968.
Henderson, I. *The Picts*. Thames & Hudson, 1967.
Macquarie, A. 'The Kings of Strathclyde, c.400–1018', in A. Grant and K. J. Stringer, *Medieval Scotland: crown, lordship and community: essays presented to G. W. S. Barrow*, Edinburgh, 1993.
MacQueen, J. *St Nynia: a study of literature and linguistic evidence*. Oliver & Boyd, 1961.
Pythian-Adams, C. *Land of the Cumbrians: a study in British provincial origins*, AD 400–1120. Aldershot, 1996.
Thomas, C. *The early Christian archaeology of North Britain*. Oxford University Press, 1971.
Wainwright, F. T. (ed.) *The problem of the Picts*. Nelson, 1955.
Watson, W. J. *History of the Celtic place-names of Scotland*. Blackwood, 1926.

Recent publications

Bannerman, J. *Studies in the history of Dalriada*. Scottish Academic Press, 1974.
Campbell, E. *Saints and sea-kings: the first kingdom of the Scots*. Canongate, 1999.

Carver, M. *Surviving in symbols: a visit to the Pictish nation.* Canongate, 1999.

Duncan, A. A. M. *The kingship of the Scots, 842–1292: succession and independence.* Edinburgh University Press, 2002.

Foster, S. *Picts, Gaels and Scots.* Batsford, 1996.

Hudson, B. *Kings of Celtic Scotland.* Greenwood, 1994.

Lowe, C. *Angels, fools and tyrants: Britons and Anglo-Saxons in southern Scotland.* Canongate, 1999.

Smyth, A. *Warlords and holy men.* Edinburgh University Press, 1984.

Chapter 6

Brogger, A. W. *Ancient emigrants.* Oxford University Press, 1929.

Hamilton, J. R. C. *Excavations at Jarlshof, Shetland.* HMSO, 1956.

Shetelig, H. *Viking antiquities in Great Britain and Ireland,* vols I and II. Aschehoug (Oslo), 1940.

Wainwright, F. T. (ed.) *The northern isles.* Nelson, 1962.

Recent publications

Crawford, B. *Scandinavian Scotland.* Leicester University Press, 1987.

Graham-Campbell, J. and Batey, C. E. *Vikings in Scotland.* Edinburgh University Press, 1998.

Owen, O. *The sea road: a Viking voyage through Scotland.* Canongate, 1999.

Ritchie, A. *Viking Scotland.* Batsford, 1992.

Chapters 7 and 8

Barrow, G. W. S. *Feudal Britain.* Edward Arnold, 1956.

Barrow, G. W. S. *Robert Bruce and the community of the realm of Scotland.* Eyre & Spottiswoode, 1965.

Dickinson, W. C. *Scotland from the earliest times to 1603.* Nelson, 1961.

Dickinson, W. C. (ed.) *Early records of the burgh of Aberdeen.* Constable, 1957.

Powicke, Sir M. *The thirteenth century, 1216–1307,* 2nd edn. Oxford University Press, 1962.

Renn, D. F. *Norman castles in Britain.* J. Baker, 1968.

Ritchie, R. L. G. *The Normans in Scotland.* Edinburgh University Press, 1954.

Recent publications

Barrell, A. D. M. *Medieval Scotland.* Cambridge University Press, 2000.

Barrow, G. W. S. *The Anglo-Norman era in Scottish history.* Oxford University Press, 1980.

Barrow, G. W. S. *Kingship and unity: Scotland, 1000–1306.* Edinburgh University Press, 1989.

Campbell, M. *Alexander III King of Scots.* Colonsay, 1999.

Kapelle, W. E. *The Norman conquest of the north: the region and its transformation, 1000–1135.* Chapel Hill, 1979.

Chapters 9, 10, 11 and 12

Balfour-Melville, E. W. M. *James I, King of Scots.* Methuen, 1936.

Barbour, J. *The Bruce.* Trans. and ed. by A. A. H. Douglas. Maclellan, 1964.

Barron, E. M. *The Scottish war of independence.* J. Nisbit, 1934.

Barrow, G. W. S. *Robert Bruce and the community of the realm of Scotland.* Eyre and Spottiswoode, 1965.

Douglas, G. *Selections.* D. F. C. Coldwell (ed.). Oxford University Press, 1964.

Dunbar, W. *Poems.* W. M. Mackenzie (ed.). Faber, 1970.

Dunlop, A. I. *The life and times of James Kennedy, Bishop of St Andrews.* Oliver & Boyd, 1950.

Dunlop, A. I. *Scots abroad in the fifteenth century.* Historical Association Pamphlet no. 124, 1942.

Fergusson, J. *William Wallace, Guardian of Scotland.* Eneas Mackay, 1938.

Gillies, W. *An introduction to Scottish Gaelic literature.* Southside, 1973.

Mackenzie, W. M. *The Scottish burghs.* Oliver & Boyd, 1949.

Mackenzie, W. M. *The medieval castle in Scotland.* Methuen, 1927.

Mackie, R. L. *King James IV of Scotland.* Oliver & Boyd, 1958.

MacQueen, J. *Robert Henryson: a study of the major narrative poems.* Oxford University Press, 1967.

Nicholson, R. *Scotland: the later Middle Ages.* Oliver & Boyd, 1966.

Scott, T. *Dunbar.* Oliver & Boyd, 1966.

Recent publications

Boardman, S. *The early Stewart kings: Robert II and Robert III, 1371–1406.* Tuckwell Press, 1996.

Barrell, A. D. M. *Medieval Scotland.* Cambridge, 2000.

Brown, J. (ed.) *Scottish society in the fifteenth century.* Edward Arnold, 1977.

Brown, M. *James I.* Tuckwell Press, 1994.

Fawcett, R. *Scottish architecture from the accession of the Stewarts to the Reformation, 1371–1560.* Edinburgh University Press, 1994.

Fisher, A. *William Wallace.* Donald, 1986.

Grant, A. *Independence and nationhood: Scotland, 1306–1469.* Edinburgh University Press, 1991.

McDonald, R. A. *The kingdom of the Isles: Scotland's western seaboard, c.1100–c.1336.* Tuckwell Press, 1997.

McNamee, C. *The wars of the Bruces: Scotland, England and Ireland, 1306–1328.* Tuckwell Press, 1997.

Watson, F. *Under the hammer: Edward I and Scotland, 1286–1306.* Tuckwell Press, 1998.

Chapters 13, 14 and 15

Bingham, C. James V, *King of Scots*. Collins, 1971.

Brown, P. Hume. *John Knox: a biography*. 2 vols. A & C Black, 1895.

Cowan, I. B. *The enigma of Mary Stewart*. Gollancz, 1971.

Donaldson, G. *Scotland: James V to James VII*. Oliver & Boyd, 1965.

Donaldson, G. *The first trial of Mary Queen of Scots*. Batsford, 1969.

Fraser, A. *Mary Queen of Scots*. Weidenfeld & Nicolson, 1969.

Knox, J. *History of the Reformation in Scotland*. 2 vols. W. C. Dickinson (ed.) Nelson, 1949.

Lee, M. *John Maitland of Thirlestane*. Princeton University Press, 1959.

Lythe, S. G. E. *The economy of Scotland in its European setting, 1550–1625*. Oliver & Boyd, 1960.

McEwen, J. S. *The faith of John Knox*. Lutterworth Press, 1961.

Mathieson, W. L. *Politics and religion: study in Scottish history from reformation to revolution*. 2 vols. Maclehose & Johnstone, 1902.

Ridley, J. G. *John Knox*. Oxford University Press, 1968.

Willson, D. H. *James VI and I*. (Bedford History) Cape, 1956.

Recent publications

Cowan, I. B. *The Scottish reformation: church and society in the sixteenth century*. Weidenfeld & Nicolson, 1982.

Donaldson, G. *All the queen's men: power and politics in Mary Stewart's Scotland*. Batsford, 1983.

Goodare, J. and Lynch, M. (eds) *The reign of James VI*. Tuckwell Press, 2000.

Larner, C. *Enemies of God: the witch hunt in Scotland*. Chatto & Windus, 1981.

Macdougall, N. *James IV*. John Donald, 1989; Tuckwell Press, 1997.

Merriman, M. H. *The rough wooings: Mary Queen of Scots, 1542–1551*. Tuckwell Press, 2000.

Chapters 16, 17 and 18

Buchan, J. *Montrose*. Nelson, 1928; Hodder, 1949.

Campbell, W. *The triumph of Presbyterianism*. St Andrews Press, 1958.

Dickinson, W. C. *et al. A source book of Scottish history vol. III: 1567–1707*. Nelson, 1961.

Donaldson, G. *Scotland: James V to James VII*. Oliver & Boyd, 1965.

Ferguson, W. *Scotland: 1689 to the present*. Oliver & Boyd, 1968.

Foster, W. R. *Bishop and presbytery*. SPCK, 1958.

Henderson, G. D. *Religious life in seventeenth-century Scotland*. Cambridge University Press, 1937.

Holmes, G. *Britain after the Glorious Revolution 1689–1714*. Macmillan, 1969.

Mackinnon, J. *The union of England and Scotland: a study of international history.* Longman, 1896.

Mathieson, W. L. *Politics and religion: study in Scottish history from reformation to revolution.* 2 vols. Maclehose & Johnstone, 1902.

Pryde, G. S. *The treaty of union of Scotland and England 1707.* Nelson, 1950.

Smout, T. C. *Scottish trade on the eve of the union.* Oliver & Boyd, 1963.

Wedgwood, C. V. *The Great Rebellion vol. 1. The king's peace.* Collins, 1955.

Wedgwood, C. V. *The Great Rebellion vol. 2. The king's war 1641–1647.* Collins, 1958.

Willcock, J. *The great marquess: life and times of Archibald, 8th Earl and 1st (and only) Marquess of Argyll, 1607–1661.* Oliphant, 1902.

Recent publications

Brown, K. *Noble society in Scotland: wealth, family and culture from reformation to revolution.* Edinburgh University Press, 2000.

Campbell, T. *Standing witnesses: a guide to the Scottish covenanters and their memorials with a historical introduction.* Saltire Society, 1996.

Cowan, E. J. *Montrose for covenant and king.* Canongate, 1995.

Ferguson, W. *Scotland's relations with England: a survey to 1707.* Saltire Society, 1994.

Henderson, L. and Cowan, E. J. *Scottish fairy belief: a history.* Tuckwell Press, 2001.

Macinnis, A. *Clanship, commerce and the house of Stuart, 1603–1788.* Tuckwell Press, 1996.

Mitchison, R. *Lordship to patronage: Scotland, 1603–1745.* Edinburgh University Press, 1990.

Whatley, C. A. *Bought and sold for English gold? Explaining the union of 1707.* Tuckwell Press, 2001.

Whyte, I. *Agriculture and society in seventeenth-century Scotland.* John Donald, 1979.

Young, J. R. *The Scottish parliament 1639–1661: a political and constitutional analysis.* John Donald, 1996.

INDEX